THE UPPER COUNTRY

Regional Perspectives on Early America
JACK P. GREENE AND J. R. POLE, ADVISORS

The Upper Country

FRENCH ENTERPRISE IN THE COLONIAL GREAT LAKES

Claiborne A. Skinner

THE JOHNS HOPKINS UNIVERSITY PRESS
BALTIMORE

© 2008 The Johns Hopkins University Press
All rights reserved. Published 2008
Printed in the United States of America on acid-free paper
9 8 7 6 5 4 3 2 1

The Johns Hopkins University Press
2715 North Charles Street
Baltimore, Maryland 21218-4363
www.press.jhu.edu

LIBRARY OF CONGRESS CATALOGING-IN-PUBLICATION DATA
Skinner, Claiborne A.
The Upper Country : French enterprise in the colonial Great Lakes / Claiborne A. Skinner.
p. cm. — (Regional perspectives on early America)
Includes bibliographical references and index.
ISBN-13: 978-0-8018-8837-3 (hardcover : alk. paper)
ISBN-13: 978-0-8018-8838-0 (pbk. : alk. paper)
ISBN-10: 0-8018-8837-9 (hardcover : alk. paper)
ISBN-10: 0-8018-8838-7 (pbk. : alk. paper)
1. Canada—History—To 1763 (New France). 2. United States—History—French and Indian War, 1755–1763—Causes. 3. French—Great Lakes Region (North America)—History. I. Title.
F1030.S529 2008
971.01—dc22   2007040154

A catalog record for this book is available from the British Library.

Special discounts are available for bulk purchases of this book. For more information, please contact Special Sales at 410-516-6936 or specialsales@press.jhu.edu.

The Johns Hopkins University Press uses environmentally friendly book materials, including recycled text paper that is composed of at least 30 percent postconsumer waste, whenever possible. All of our book papers are acid-free, and our jackets and covers are printed on paper with recycled content.

For Denys Delage

Contents

Preface   ix

Glossary   xiii

PROLOGUE   The Fur Trade and New France to 1676   1

ONE   Frontenac and La Salle, 1673–1682   25

TWO   The Great Turtle and the Rock, 1683–1687   46

THREE   War in the Wilderness, 1687–1701   66

FOUR   The Foxes, 1701–1736   89

FIVE   Illinois and the Chickasaw Wars, 1700–1740   112

SIX   A Country More Worthy of His Majesty's Attention, 1736–1754   136

SEVEN   "A Few Acres of Snow," 1740–1754   157

Notes   175

Bibliographic Essay   187

Index   195

Preface

In December 2004, Dr. Robert J. Brugger of the Johns Hopkins University Press approached me to write an undergraduate survey of the French regime in the Great Lakes. Given the length requested and his admonition to "keep it simple," I had to decide carefully what exactly I wanted students to learn: Why, finally, do this region and its history matter? The recent 250th anniversary of the French and Indian War has produced a renewed interest in the Seven Years War and its role in the creation of the American Republic. Fred Anderson's magisterial *Crucible of War: The Seven Years War and the Fate of Empire in British North America, 1754–1766* has gone so far as to declare it "the most important event to occur in eighteenth-century North America."[1] In his account, our War of Independence directly resulted from the aftermath of this immense upheaval. This important point, in turn, raises an equally important question: If the French and Indian War triggered the American Revolution, what then triggered the French and Indian War? This book is an attempt to answer that question.

Between 1689 and 1763, England, France, and Spain fought five wars in the Americas from Panama to Hudson's Bay and from the Atlantic to the Great Plains. In the climactic final conflict, however, the flash point was the Great Lakes Basin, a region the French called *Le Pays d'en haut:* the "upper country." Claimed by the French in 1671 for its wealth of furs, the upper country became a target for English commercial expansion by

1680. Over the next twenty years, the two rivals and their Indian allies fought an increasingly bloody war for it. France won this first round, crushing England's ally the Iroquois Confederacy and stalemating English attempts to conquer Canada. Now, however, the French confronted an ironic problem: their Indian alliances had been built against an external threat and without the Iroquois, the coalition had no reason to exist. Over the next half century the French found themselves hard-pressed to hold the region against a succession of rebellions, internal wars, and external intrigues. When English traders again began to push west into Ohio in the 1750s, they did not encounter the cohesive French-Indian empire of the seventeenth century, but a region wracked by internal conflict. Thus, to the French, these interlopers seemed a mortal threat. Their ultimate response, a heavy-handed, bellicose policy in Ohio and western Pennsylvania, would ignite the French and Indian War and all that came after.

American students have little awareness of this nearly 75-year struggle. My own education in the early Middle West began 25 years ago studying Canadian history. A region we often relegate to an historical backwater is to their scholars the crucible of modern Canada. Marquette, La Salle, Frontenac, Du Luth, Cadillac, colorful but largely irrelevant characters for us, were critical figures in an imperial conflict which would ultimately lead to British conquest and an historical legacy very much alive and troublesome today. For the Canadians, the American Revolution was essentially a postscript. Despite the recent interest in the events of 1755–1763, the French Middle West remains a subject few Americans learn much about. It is, however, an emphatically *American* story and critical to an understanding of how we came to be who we are.

This book is not, for the most part, a work of original research, but rather a synthesis of some 250 years of scholarship. Due to the publication format, it has only limited citation and so a word about sources is in order. The book is organized essentially in two acts: the prologue and first three chapters chronicle the rise of the French regime in the Great Lakes to 1701 and the last four treat its trials and the fateful clash in Ohio. The interpretation presented in the first half is drawn from the work of William Eccles, whose revisionist point of view and piquant style drew me into the subject in the first place. I am also indebted to the work of Stephen Saunders Webb for introducing me to the complex linkages between the English colonies, Canada, and the Great Lakes country. Gilles Havard's studies of the Great Lakes and the Great Peace of 1701 were a considerable help in laying out the Indian world the French encountered and the diplomacy of the late seventeenth century. Finally, I would like to acknowledge my debt to the eighteenth-century Jesuit historian Pierre F. X. Charlevoix. Writing often only a few years after the fact, his accounts of battles, conspiracies, heroics, and folly have an urgency and humanity that has contributed a great deal to the detail and narrative tone of this book. Chapters four through seven draw on the work of Dale Miquelon. His discussions of the Great Lakes country in the first decades of the eighteenth century, the diplomatic context in which its story took place, and his analysis of the changing role of Canada in French foreign policy all form essential parts of the account offered here. Francis Jennings gave me an understanding of the shifting balance of power among the Indian nations in this second period. The last chapter again draws on Eccles, particularly in the Canadian resistance to the imperial role assigned it by France.

The book, to a great extent, focuses on Wisconsin, Illinois, Michigan, and Indiana. For Wisconsin, I have relied on Louise Phelps Kellogg, R. David Edmunds, and Joseph Peyser. For Illinois and Indiana, I am indebted to Clarence Alvord, Carl Ekberg, Natalie Belting, Gilles Havard, and Charles Balesi. For the too-often neglected Anglo-French struggle along the southern margins of the region, I owe much to the work of Verner Crane, William Stitt Robinson, Michel Girault, and again Father Charlevoix. Titles for these authors and the rest of the sources used in this narrative are included in the concluding bibliographic essay.

What I have tried to contribute to the literature is a relatively concise record of *what* happened, *where,* and my best understanding of *why,* linking the traditional story of colonial America east of the Appalachians with the Middle West. Events in the Middle Colonies, New England, and the Carolinas had important repercussions beyond the mountains and vice versa. I have also sought to provide a sense of scale: how many people were involved, Indians, traders, and soldiers, set against the rising tide of

English colonization to the east. These numbers form a critical part in understanding the Anglo-French struggle for the region. Finally, I have expended a good deal of time and effort working with primary sources, less to prove new insights, than to find materials which would bring to life the world of the Great Lakes three centuries ago: its peoples, its waterways, the forts and villages which sprang up along them, and the military conflicts which convulsed the region and helped set the stage for the final confrontation in Ohio. Wherever possible, I have tried to inhabit the narrative with individuals, some famous, some less so, but all with a role to play in the larger drama.

I would like to acknowledge here a number of people for their help in the long process which resulted in this book: Leo Schelbert and A. G. Roeber for supporting my initial wanderings in the colonial Middle West nearly a quarter century ago; the late William J. Eccles, who exhaustively critiqued and encouraged an early ancestor of the manuscript and who passed away in 1998; my colleagues in the History/Social Science Department of the Illinois Mathematics and Science Academy for their ideas and support; my students Nami Jarret, Barbara Myers, Stephanie Hasselbacher, Bina Kapadia, Virginia Ryan, Ben Gurga, Amanda Wozniak, and all the others who gave lavishly of their limited free time in bringing Fort Saint Louis des Illinois to life; my wife and colleague Jean Kadel for her commonsense criticism and help in building the curriculum this story came out of; and my copy editor Michael Baker, who cheerfully hammered a great mass of stuff into what you see here.

Finally, I need to make a special acknowledgment. Over the last quarter century, a rich, often contentious literature has emerged regarding the cultural context of this story, particularly the nature of the French and Indian relationship. I lacked the space to include this debate here and so I posit that expediency has always taken precedence over culture and that "people have friends, nations have interests." Indian societies were no different. Here I have tended to rely on the scholarship and advice of Denys Delâge of Laval University. The gentlest of souls, he nevertheless retains a starkly Hobbesian understanding of how people behave. His expertise, support, and friendship have been indispensable in the preparation of this book.

Glossary

THE VOLUME CONTAINS French currency, weights, measures, and terms unfamiliar to most readers. Rather than explain them in passing, they are presented here.

CURRENCY

livre tournois: Also called the French pound; subdivided into 12 sous (or sols), each of 20 deniers
franc: 1 livre
écu: 6 livres

In late seventeenth-century New France, a carpenter might earn 300 livres in a year, a blacksmith 360, and a day laborer 180.

WEIGHTS AND MEASURES

arpent: 5/6 acre
league: 2 3/4 miles
livre: 3/4 pound
minot: Approximately 1 bushel
pot: Approximately 1 quart liquid measure

TERMS

coureur de bois: Early fur trader/smuggler
habitant: A Canadian commoner

poteaux en terre: Vertical log walls with the posts set in the ground
seigneurie: Estate or land grant
voyageur: Canoe man in the employ of a licensed trader or merchant

THE UPPER COUNTRY

PROLOGUE

The Fur Trade and New France to 1676

IN 1666, A JESUIT MISSIONARY set to paper an Ojibwa story of the culture hero Michabous, guardian of the Earth and its creatures:

> They believe that [Lake Superior] is a pond made by beavers, and that its dam was double, the first being at the place called by us the Sault, and the second five leagues below. Angered by the damming of the river the manitou Michabous came up the Saint Mary's, smashed the dams, and chased the beaver from the lake. In view of so mighty an enemy, the beavers changed their location, and withdrew to another lake, whence they afterward, by means of rivers flowing from it, arrived at the North Sea, whence they intended to swim to France; but finding the water bitter, they lost heart, and spread throughout the rivers and lakes of this entire country. And that is why there are no beavers in France and the French come to get them here.[1]

In the seventeenth and eighteenth centuries, strangers came to the Great Lakes. First French then English, they would make the region the cockpit of a great contest which would shape the history of a continent. It was a confusing time and the Indians sought to explain it in the context of the world they knew, one which would not last much longer.

In 1497 Giovanni Caboto, sailing for Henry VII of England, discovered the island of Newfoundland. He found little of consequence, but reported an extraordinary number of codfish off-shore. The news spread quickly and by 1550 cod accounted for 60 percent of all the fish consumed in Europe. By 1578 nearly 400 ships, Spanish, Basque, French, Portuguese, and English, worked the Gulf of Saint Lawrence. The drying stations of this exploding industry quickly attracted local Indians eager to trade. They wanted, in particular, cloth and iron goods. Late Stone Age people, they had little to offer in return, but there was one thing: beaver.

Europeans had used beaver fur for hatters' felt since the Middle Ages. Rising population and loss of habitat, however, had nearly wiped out the creature in the west. Russia had assumed the role of Europe's major supplier and could charge what the market would bear. In the late sixteenth century, demand rose as men's hats grew in size and grandeur. The underhairs of the beaver's coat have a rough surface which helped mat the felt into a particularly strong, waterproof material. Given the structural demands of the new fashion, beaver became the premier material for the gentleman's chapeau. Canada offered a new source which broke the Russian monopoly. In 1581 and 1582, a Breton ship turned a nice profit trading around the Gulf of Saint Lawrence for furs exclusively. In 1583 three fur-trading vessels set out from Saint Malo. Two ascended the Saint Lawrence River as far as Montreal and another coasted south from Nova Scotia to Maine. The following year, five traders set out from Saint Malo, and ten the next. By 1600, it was reported that the French were taking as much as 30,000 crowns in beaver and otter from the Saint Lawrence alone.

By the end of the sixteenth century, however, the English threatened to take over the fishery and growing competition among French fur traders had begun to cripple profits. In 1598, King Henri IV sought to establish a settlement which could protect French interests, regulate trade, and preserve order. The Canadian winter and scurvy wrecked early attempts at colonization, but in 1608 the French navigator Samuel de Champlain established a post on the lower Saint Lawrence which would take permanent hold. "I arrived there on the 3rd of July, when I searched for a place suitable for our settlement; but I could find none more convenient or better suited than the point of Quebec." By September, Champlain's post had taken shape: "I had the work of our quarters continued, which was composed of three buildings of two stories. Each one was three fathoms long, and two and a half wide, with a fine cellar six feet deep. . . . There were also ditches, fifteen feet wide and six deep. On the other side of the ditches I constructed several spurs, which enclosed a part of the dwelling, at the points where we placed our cannon."[2]

Having secured a base, Champlain set out to reconnoiter the river. By 1609, European goods had circulated among the Indians for nearly three-quarters of a century. Iron goods and fabrics the coastal peoples had obtained were, in turn, traded upriver to the Great Lakes. By 1525, European goods had appeared as far west as Lake Ontario, by 1580, Lake Huron, and by 1590 iron tools were replacing flint and stone implements in upstate New York. Access to the Saint Lawrence had become a matter of some importance and Champlain found himself in the midst of a war. Exploring near Montreal Island, he encountered a party of Huron, Algonquin, and Montagnais on their way to fight the Iroquois who controlled the south shore of Lake Ontario and the upper Saint Lawrence. Eager to form a commercial alliance, he accepted an invitation to join the expedition. The two sides met on Lake Champlain. As the battle began, the explorer "marched some twenty paces in advance of the rest, until I was within about thirty paces of the enemy. When I saw them making a move to fire at us, I rested my musket against my cheek, and aimed directly at one of the three [Iroquois] chiefs."[3] Having double-charged his matchlock, Champlain hit two with his first shot. One of his companions finished the third. Stunned, the rest of the Iroquois turned and fled. With this skirmish, Champlain had cemented an alliance with the Huron and begun what would prove nearly a century of warfare with the Iroquois.

Over the next six years, Champlain accompanied Indian parties as far west as the Georgian Bay, exploring the country and strengthening his ties to the Huron. He finally returned to Quebec in July 1616 and made no further journeys into the interior. In his middle forties, with a bad knee, he was no longer the man he had been a decade earlier. Moreover, the management of his trading post gave him more than enough to do. Henri IV had died by an assassin's hand in 1610 and support for the colony waxed and waned for the next half century. Rival traders sought to break Champlain's monopoly and he made repeated trips back to France to obtain funding and defend his title to the country.

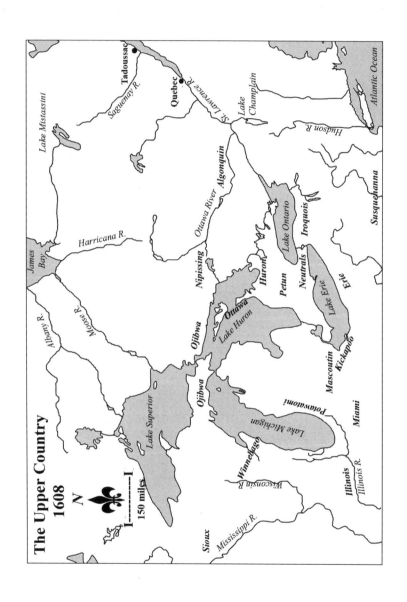

In 1629 the English captured Quebec and Champlain could not return until 1633. He spent the remainder of his life rebuilding the settlement and establishing posts upriver, dying at Quebec in 1635.

The "Sweet Seas," as Champlain called the Great Lakes, were home to perhaps 200,000–250,000 people in 1600.[4] They had arrived about 9000 BC, following the retreating glaciers. Originally hunter-gatherers, many had become farmers by around 500 AD as maize spread north from Mexico. Beans seemed to have arrived in the thirteenth century. Agriculture became common up to 45 degrees north latitude, roughly the north shores of Lakes Huron and Michigan. North of this, however, the frosts came too early. Thus the world the French encountered was a mixture of old and new. Northern Indians hunted and fished as they had for millennia. To the south, the inhabitants relied principally on farming.[5]

The Great Lakes peoples spoke three basic languages, divided into a host of dialects: Iroquoian, Algonkian, and Siouxan. The Iroquoian-speakers—the Iroquois and Huron Confederacies, the Susquehannock, and the Erie—accounted for between 60,000 and 110,000 people. The Algonkians—the Illiniwek Confederacy, the Ottawa, Potawatomi, Ojibwa, and a dozen smaller nations—comprised some 100,000 people. The Siouxan-speakers—the Sioux and Winnebago—had perhaps 40,000. The bulk of the population, as much as 80 percent, lived south of the 45-degree boundary. These farmers lived in large relatively permanent towns and population density could be considerable. Huronia, present-day Simcoe County, Ontario, had probably 25,000–30,000 people. North of the farming boundary, population densities tended to drop sharply. The Ojibwa and Cree who lived around Lake Superior and farther north had about one person for every two square miles.[6]

This northern country was a region of dense forests, lakes, and rivers. To avoid the trackless woods and the clouds of biting insects which infested them, people used the water as highways: first with rafts and then dugout canoes. These worked well enough on the rivers south of the Great Lakes, but were too low-sided for open water and too heavy to be carried around the rapids and waterfalls characteristic of the northern rivers. At some point, however, the Indians developed a new craft both lighter and more versatile than the dugout: the birchbark canoe, which could be carried, or portaged, around obstacles, and had a higher freeboard, which permitted the Indians to cautiously ply the lakes as well. The birchbark canoe allowed hunters to travel greater distances in search of game and fostered a long-distance trade in luxury commodities like copper, shells, mica, and tobacco. The range of the birch forests necessary for the construction of canoes roughly corresponded to the northern edge of the corn-growing region and this interface produced several nations of trader-farmers, the Huron and Ottawa in particular.

Given all of this, the French fur trade evolved into a system quite different from that of our Rocky Mountain Men. To begin, New France had no trappers. Until the invention of the spring trap around 1800, catching beaver was a daunting proposition. In spring, the Indians used deadfall traps, nets, and occasionally dogs. Since winter pelts brought the best price, the hunting took place in the cold months: "During the winter they capture them in nets and under the ice. They cut an opening in the ice near the beaver's house and put into the hole a net with some wood which serves as bait. The poor animal, searching for something else to eat, gets caught in a net made of good, strong, double cord; it must be hauled out quickly before it cuts the net to bits. Once it is taken from the water, through the hole in the ice, they kill it with a big club." Hardier souls used a more direct approach: "The other way of taking them under the ice is more noble. Not all of the Indians use this method, only the most skillful. With their hatchets they break apart the cabin or house of the beaver, which is indeed most wonderfully made."[7] As the beavers attempted to escape, the hunters would spear them and often had to leap into the freezing water to recover the creature. For all of his work, a good hunter might take fifty or sixty pelts between October and May.

Understandably, the French left the hunting to the Indians. Equally important, one could not simply trap the most valuable grade of pelt: *castor gras,* or greasy beaver. Indians used these, worn fur side in, for winter clothing. By spring, their robes had become saturated with body oil and grease from the cooking fires. The movements of the wearer had, moreover, loosened the outer guard hairs of the pelt, laying bare the underfur beneath. This fat-saturated fur soon became the most sought-after material for the hatter's trade. Here again, it lay in the interests of the French to buy fur rather than hunt for themselves. For their part, the Indians thought this fascination with the beaver comic. The Jesuit Father Paul Le Jeune tells of a common Indian joke: "The beaver knows how to make all things to perfection: It makes kettles, hatchets, swords, knives, bread; in short, it makes everything."[8]

The French system also arose from simple necessity. Champlain had arrived at Quebec in 1608 with 28 men. In 1620, he had 60 and a decade later 117. By 1640, the number had risen to only 240. The organization of the trade reflected the fact that the French simply lacked the manpower to do anything else. In practice, the real work fell to the Hurons. Each year, 200–250 Hurons would make the 1,400-mile round-trip from Georgian Bay to the Saint Lawrence to exchange pelts for fabrics, metal goods, and jewelry. Others would paddle to Sault Sainte Marie to exchange these and tobacco for furs, which they would then reship east. By the 1620s, Champlain had perhaps a dozen missionaries and interpreters in Huronia itself. The number would eventually reach twenty or thirty priests, interpreters, servants, and soldiers, but up to 1649 the trade remained Huron.[9]

This commerce predated the Europeans. Huronia lay near the northern maize boundary. Its inhabitants had corn and could also obtain tobacco, important in religious ritual, as an appetite suppressant, and for its narcotic properties, from their southern neighbors the Petuns. On the other hand, intensively cultivated with a population of perhaps 25,000 people, Huronia had few furs. However, close by lay birch forests for canoes. So it is no surprise that the Huron became traders, exchanging corn and tobacco with northern peoples for pelts. Lake Superior, moreover, had raw copper so pure that it could be worked cold into items of jewelry, which the Huron reexported south and east.

Up to this point, Huron commerce can be discussed in European terms. The *ends* of trade, however, differed sharply. Indians did not think of profit as a Dutchman might. Exchange obtained useful products, but the surplus did not become wealth in the European sense. At the beginning of the seventeenth century, the Frenchman Marc Lescarbot observed that "all savages do live in common.... If it happen, then, that our savages have venison or other food, all the company have part of it. They have

The Fur Trade and New France 7

this mutual charity, which hath been taken from us since that mine and thine have come into the world."¹⁰ Lescarbot had no illusions that he had stumbled upon the Garden of Eden. Rather, he perceived shrewdly that there was something else at stake here: "There is no man that giveth, intending to lose. If a great personage giveth to a mean man, that is for to draw some service from him. Even that which is given to the poor is to receive the hundredfold according to the promise of the gospel."¹¹ A successful trader earned prestige, but largely by giving his profits away as gifts. The Huron used trade much as individuals did. It gave them a kind of suzerainty over their neighbors the Petuns, Neutrals, and Tobacco People and allowed them to forge alliances among other nations.

The arrival of the French did not really change the system. The Huron benefited from access to European goods and the demand these enjoyed among their customers, but there was really nothing like a commercial revolution in the Lakes. On the other hand, the prestige of the alliance gave the Huron leverage with their neighbors. In 1634, they asked the interpreter Jean Nicolet to negotiate with the powerful Winnebago nation. He had a reputation for such things, having arranged an Iroquois-Algonquin treaty a decade earlier. Arriving in Green Bay, he planted two sticks in the ground and hung presents from them to announce his good intentions. Four or five thousand people quickly gathered from neighboring nations to see their first European. He did not disappoint: "He wore a grand robe of Chinese damask, all strewn with flowers and birds of many colors. No sooner did they perceive him than the women and children fled, at the sight of a man who carried thunder in both hands—for thus they called the two pistols he held."¹² The negotiations prospered and Nicolet returned with the desired treaty.

In this early period, the French had a powerful hold over the Indian imagination. In the 1830s, the Sauk chief Black Hawk related how his great-grandfather Na-Na-Ma-Kee had met his first Frenchman. The Great Spirit told him that he would meet a "white man who would be to him his father" four years hence and he fasted and dreamed for the next three in preparation.¹³ Na-Na-Ma-Kee and his two brothers traveled five days to the east, where they encountered a tent in which sat the son of the King of France. The Prince, too, had been instructed by the

Great Spirit to journey west to meet the Indians, who would be "his children." The King had laughed, but he crossed the Atlantic and journeyed to the place where he met Na-Na-Ma-Kee. From this encounter, said Black Hawk, the Sauk became part of the French alliance and his great-grandfather a chief. The alliance provided the Huron with considerable benefits, but at a price: war with the Iroquois. Prior to the arrival of the Europeans, warfare had been endemic among the Great Lakes peoples, but relatively small in scope and short in duration. The newcomers now raised the stakes.

By tradition the Iroquois Confederacy, the Mohawk, Oneida, Onondaga, Cayuga, and Seneca nations, began around 1570. Perennially at war, they had put aside their differences through the teachings of a Huron shaman Deganawida and the Onondaga chief Hiawatha. Over the next forty years, the united Iroquois drove the Algonquin from the upper Saint Lawrence. The vanquished appealed to the Huron and Montagnais, and the two sides were locked in warfare when the French arrived at Quebec in 1608. Champlain's alliance with the northern Indians gave them the upper hand for a time. In 1614, however, Dutch traders built a post, Fort Orange, on the Hudson River. Supplied with iron goods and later muskets, the Iroquois now struck back. By 1632, they had recovered the upper Saint Lawrence and, by 1637, had conquered the lower Ottawa Valley. Between 1645 and 1649, an epidemic struck Huronia, killing nearly half the population, and the Iroquois mounted a series of attacks which drove them from Georgian Bay. In 1651, the Five Nations pushed the Neutrals out of Ontario as well. By 1655, they had defeated the Susquehannocks and the next year the Erie nation fell. In the aftermath of this, most of the nations of the eastern Great Lakes and the Ohio River Valley fled west into Illinois, Wisconsin, Missouri, and Arkansas.

Iroquoian power had now reached its zenith. The Confederacy nominally controlled vast territories in Ontario and the Middle West. Adopted captives, moreover, had made up population losses from war and epidemics. With perhaps 25,000 people, it stood as the largest Indian power east of the Mississippi. For the French, these successes had been a disaster. In 1653, a Jesuit reported: "Before the devastation of the Hurons, a hundred canoes used to come to trade, all laden with Beaver-skins; the

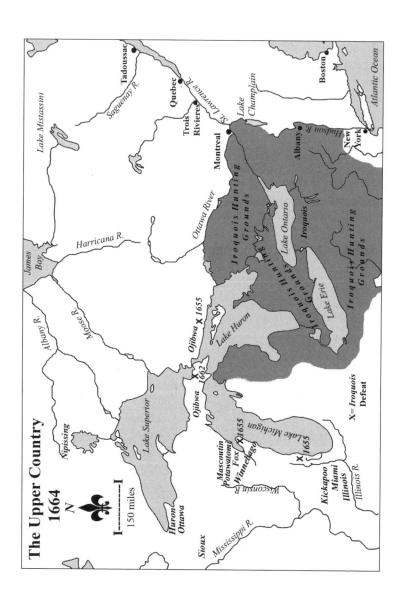

Algonquins brought them from all directions; and each year we had two or three hundred thousand livres' worth." The Five Nations had changed all of that, he reported; "the Huron fleets no longer come down to trade; the Algonquins are depopulated; and the more distant Nations are withdrawing still farther. . . . For a year, the warehouse of Montreal has not bought a single Beaver-skin from the Savages."[14] With their Indian trade in tatters, the colony faced ruin.

Iroquois power, however, was more apparent than real. Rather than submit, its opponents had, for the most part, fled, and remained defiant. Iroquois policy also sought to isolate the French from their fur suppliers and force them to trade exclusively with the Five Nations. This the French refused to do. Half a century of war had, thus, accomplished very little. Moreover, the tide had actually begun to turn. Each Iroquois success drew the Five Nations deeper into the interior and by the early 1650s war parties had to march as much as 600–700 miles to attack their enemies. Traveling on foot rather than by canoe, they had to obtain their provisions along the way. If the hunting failed, an expedition could quickly come to grief. Equally serious, if for any reason it had to retreat, it was vulnerable. Both problems now began to cripple the Iroquois. The first great failure came in 1655. A war party sent to Wisconsin to finish the Huron ran out of food and was defeated on Green Bay. The Illiniwek and Ojibwa then wiped out the survivors on their way home. In 1662, the Ojibwa destroyed another force sent to Lake Superior to avenge this defeat. Failing in the west, the Iroquois attacked the French settlements directly. The Canadians petitioned for aid and in 1663 Louis XIV royalized the colony and sent the 1,250-man Regiment de Carignan-Salières to Quebec two years later. In 1666, it mounted an expedition which forced the Mohawk to sue for peace.

The Canadians' plea for assistance arrived in Paris at a critical juncture. In the sixty years since the founding of Quebec, the world had changed a great deal. England had resolved a half century of political and religious conflict, restoring Charles Stuart as its king. France had weathered storms as well. Beginning with the murder of Henri IV in 1610, protracted religious upheavals, foreign wars, and aristocratic rebellion had wracked the country. These ended in 1661, when Louis XIV assumed personal control of his realm. With their newfound peace, the two princes began to look outward toward the Atlantic. Other events fed this confidence. Spain's "Golden Age" had finally run its course. The Thirty Years War (1618–1648) had inflicted a mortal wound and Spain now entered a decline which would last the next three centuries. The war had crippled Austria too. Checked in its bid to reunite the Holy Roman Empire under Habsburg authority, it would never again threaten Europe. The rest of Germany would languish, a polyglot nonentity, for another century. Holland remained the commercial powerhouse of Europe but, with an ambitious France to the south and a resurgent England to the northwest, the Dutch found themselves badly outflanked. In 1652–54, Oliver Cromwell's fleet stunned them in the first Anglo-Dutch war. Over the next quarter century, England would co-opt much of Holland's commerce. All in all, England and France found themselves in positions of relative power previously unknown. Now the question became: What should they do with it?

For Canada, the future seemed bright in 1667. It was a royal colony of the greatest prince in Christendom, and who knew what might be accomplished? In this euphoria, the Jesuit Father François Le Mercier observed: "We have seen Canada transformed. . . . it is no longer that forbidding and frost-bound land which was painted in such unfavorable colors, but a veritable new France."[15] He was, perhaps, guilty of overstatement. Lack of funds, the harsh climate, and war had all discouraged settlement. In 1663, New France possessed but three towns worth the name: Quebec, Trois Rivières, and Montreal, with a scattering of farms along the Saint Lawrence between them and a population of only 3,215. The English to the south by contrast had perhaps 60,000 colonists and, with the resurgent Stuarts at the helm, these might become a problem. Equally important, the fur trade excepted, New France had no staple export.

Responsibility for this unpromising state of affairs fell to Louis's finance minister Jean-Baptiste Colbert. He saw New France as a source of raw materials and a market for French manufactures. Furs would remain important, but only as a part of a much grander plan. In the early 1660s, Holland controlled some 80 percent of Europe's seaborne commerce. Colbert wanted a merchant fleet to challenge this virtual monopoly and a navy to crush it if competition and protection failed. Holland, however, dominated the Baltic Sea and the lumber, masts, and naval stores of Russia and Scandinavia. Canada's vast forests would provide the materials for his challenge. Additionally, the colony would export foodstuffs to France's Caribbean islands. Finally, the voyages required to move all of these goods would employ thousands of French sailors who could then be impressed in time of war.

A grand plan, but Colbert knew all too well the difficulties facing him. Rocks, shoals, and fog made the Saint Lawrence between Quebec and the Gulf extremely dangerous for shipping. Contrary winds often halted vessels for weeks in the narrow channel. The headland which marked the beginning of the river came to be known as Cap Tourmente (Cape Torment) for the often agonizing delays. Even more serious, ice blocked access to the channel five or six months a year and September gales reduced this further. It seemed unlikely that such a port could sustain a large-scale colonial enterprise. The plan would also require immense amounts of labor, which Colbert was loath to send. In a letter, the minister declared, "It would not be prudent to depopulate [Louis's] Kingdom which he should do to people Canada." Further, he questioned what precisely the new colonists would eat. "If his Majesty removed thither a greater number of men than what the land, now cleared, would feed 'tis certain that if they did not all perish at once they would at least suffer great privations." These would, in turn, become more of a burden than an asset to the colony. The proper course, he concluded, "is to cause justice to reign there, to establish a good police, to preserve the inhabitants in safety, to procure them peace, repose, and plenty, and to discipline them against all sorts of enemies; . . . being well attended to, the country will get filled up insensibly, and in the course of time may become very considerable."[16]

Colbert had more on his mind than mere expense, however. In the face of English naval power, investing in an American enterprise risked the King's prestige. Given this, he observed, "It would be better to restrict yourselves to an extent of land which the colony could protect by itself, than to claim too vast an amount, part of which one might perhaps be obliged one day to abandon."[17] It was not to be. While Colbert had envisioned a small, orderly agricultural colony, New France would quickly prove something different entirely. The removal of the threat to their homes freed the Canadians to dream dreams, and gave them the confidence to do so. Demographics played a role as well. In 1663, the population stood at around 3,000. By 1666, this had risen to 4,244, and the peculiar makeup of the total made for an explosive mix: the various monopoly companies which originally supported the colony had customarily hired only male indentures. This had resulted in roughly seven men for each woman of marriageable age. If one wished to marry, most men had one of two options: find an Indian wife or go home. Probably half of them chose the latter. Marriage involved more than romance or biology, as a farm took a great deal of labor: too much for one man without a wife and children. The Regiment de Carignan-Salières added to this problem. After the peace of 1667 Louis, to save himself the cost of shipping his soldiers home, offered them the choice of returning or remaining in the colony. Some 400 elected to stay as colonists and another 100 went into garrison. This disproportionately male society, tough, inured to hardship, and not overly fond of husbandry, would recast New France from a subsistence farming society into a confident, turbulent, aggressive, and spectacularly expansionist enterprise.

Just at this moment, the Canadians discovered an unlikely ally. To further his plans, Colbert dispatched Jean Talon to the colony to oversee Canada's development. A born promoter, he urged exploiting all of its resources at once: lumbering, fishing, farming, ship-building, and cattle-raising. He also advocated massive immigration, especially of women. Colbert, however, leery of investing so much in so dubious a project, feared sending out so many potential soldiers and laborers. Immigration remained limited and the population grew from 3,215 in 1663 to only 7,605 a decade later. Despite this, Talon persevered. While loyal to Colbert, he thought he saw something his master did not. Geography had imposed its own logic on the colony:

> Canada is of such a vast extent that I know not its limits on the North, they are at so great a distance from us; and on the south there is nothing to prevent his Majesty's name and arms from being carried as far as Florida, New Sweden, New Netherlands, New England; and that

through the first of these access can be even had to Mexico. All this country is watered diversely by the Saint Lawrence, and the beautiful rivers which flow into it laterally, that communicate with the diverse Indian nations rich in furs, especially the more northern of them. The southern nations may also be reached by way of Lake Ontario.... If these southern nations do not abound in peltries as do those of the north, they may have more precious commodities.[18]

The Saint Lawrence offered a highway to the fur country, returning traders reported evidence of rich mines, and there were rumors of a great river which might flow to the Pacific. To ignore the interior seemed absurd and even dangerous. England had seized New Netherlands in 1664, but her control of the region was tenuous. However, in 1670 Charles II, raised in France and privately Catholic, signed the secret Treaty of Dover with Louis XIV, agreeing to support his ambitions in the Netherlands in exchange for an annuity and a hazy promise to restore Catholicism in England. Thus, the Third Anglo-Dutch War coincided with a French invasion of the Netherlands. Holland sought aid from Spain, but French and English buccaneers had run amok in the West Indies and tied up such help as it might have provided. The Dutch had had to make a bitter decision: England threatened their trade, but France threatened their very existence. Therefore, Holland's survival depended on an accommodation with Charles II to break up the Anglo-French coalition. In one of the sorrier episodes of European history, the English had finally throttled the Dutch, and New York would remain theirs. Holland had never challenged New France directly, but now England might. The Saint Lawrence Basin thus represented both an opportunity and a threat. Whoever seized it controlled the heart of the continent. Whoever did not would find themselves with powerful enemies on their western flank.

Colbert's concerns notwithstanding, Talon sent men west to reconnoiter the country and claim it for France: "I have dispatched persons of resolution, who promise to penetrate further than has been done.... These adventurers are to keep journals in all instances, and . . . in all cases they are to take possession, display the King's arms and draw up procés verbaux to serve as titles."[19] In 1666, Adrien Jolliet made a voyage to Lake Superior with seven other traders. The next year, Nicholas Perrot went trading in Wisconsin and worked to bring its Indians into an alliance. In 1668, Talon recruited Jolliet and Jean Peré to look for mines along the shores of Lake Superior. The following year, the Sulpicians Dollier Casson and Galineé explored Lakes Ontario and Erie. In 1671, Talon sent Father Charles Albanel to Hudson's Bay to claim the country and the Sieur de Saint Lusson to Sault Sainte Marie on a similar errand. Finally, in 1672, he dispatched Adrien Jolliet's brother Louis and the Jesuit Jacques Marquette to look for the fabled western river which would lead to the Pacific.

Talon's explorations added an immense territory to France's New World claims, but there was a problem. He had drawn his agents, for the most part, from either the missionaries or Canadians who had gone west in their service. Men of good character with ties to the church and the governor's palace, the *intendant* could rely upon them. However, a new sort of trader had begun to appear. The demobilization of the Carignan troops had released some 400 French regulars into the colony as settlers. Thieves, brawlers, and murderers, some resumed their old ways. Drunkenness became more common. Between 1667 and 1670, the authorities hung one man and condemned another to the galleys for counterfeiting, indicted two others for kidnap and rape, and publicly flogged another for assaulting a child. These sorts of goings on began to drift over into the fur trade as well. The governor bundled one officer out of the colony for, among other things, selling brandy to the Indians and suspected several others of doing the same. Despite the hazards, it would appear that many of the ex-soldiers went into the fur trade. It had the sort of risk and adventure which had drawn them to soldiering and also offered a living without the sort of work they considered work: husbandry, trades, and the like. Montreal became the center of the trade. The fur traders turned what had begun as essentially a religious community into a brawling, bustling commercial center: all in all, a volatile addition to the colony's makeup.

Despite Talon's enthusiasm for expansion, Colbert remained unimpressed. Rather than having the French go west to trade, he preferred the Indians bring their pelts down to the Saint Lawrence, and he established commercial fairs at Montreal for the purpose. It was, it seemed, too late for that. More and more Canadians set out for the backcountry each year despite dire threats of service in the King's galleys or worse. These illegal traders became known as *coureurs de bois*, "bush runners," and by 1672, they had become a force to be reckoned with. In a letter to Colbert, the governor requested troops both as further protection against the Iroquois and as a check to the coureurs, "who will finally become, if care not be taken, like the Banditti of Naples or the Bucaneers of Santo Domingo—their number augmenting every day . . . despite all of the ordinances that have been made. . . . Their insolence as I am informed, extends even to the formation of leagues, and to the distribution of notices of rendezvous; threatening to build forts and repair towards [New York] and [Albany], boasting that they will be received and have protection there."[20] None of this had much effect and by decade's end the intendant Duchesneau estimated that some 700 Canadians did business in the backcountry.

America had a peculiar effect upon people, whether French or English. A sort of freedom flavored the air. In Virginia, this took form in the struggles of Governor William Berkeley and Nathaniel Bacon. In Massachusetts, it appeared in the battles over the founding of the general court. New France never witnessed the political upheavals of the English colonies: Seventeenth-century Frenchmen simply did not think that way. However, the struggle over the backcountry became a conflict about liberty as the French understood it: the freedom to go and come as they pleased, to touch their forelocks to no man. Pierre Radisson, perhaps the greatest of the coureurs, summed it up best when he observed: "We were as Caesars in the wilderness, there being none to oppose us."[21]

It was nevertheless an exacting calling. Radisson described the hardships of his 1660 voyage to Lake Superior: "It is a strange thing when victuals are wanting, work whole nights and dayes, lye downe on the bare ground, and not always that hap, the breech in the water, the feare in the buttocks, to have the belly empty, the weariness in the bones, and the drowsiness of the body by the bad weather that you are to suffer."[22] On the other hand, it could be a wondrous life. For Frenchmen accustomed to the hardships of peasant life, there was the food. Writing of Lake Superior, Radisson observed: "For whatever a man could desire was to be had in great plenty; staggs, fish in abundance, and all sorts of meat."[23] Women were part of the lure as well. Among

Indians, Judeo-Christian notions of sexual propriety, in particular premarital chastity, did not carry much weight, as one French official observed: "The manner in which the girls live among the savages is very convenient. They are mistresses of their bodies until they are absolutely married."[24]

The final attraction was economic. The Saint Lawrence Valley produced only French crops. Tobacco and sugar might make a man rich, as they did in the Chesapeake and the West Indies. Corn, peas, and hogs would not. Moreover, it took a year's backbreaking work for a man to clear an acre of ground for cultivation. Colbert's nascent industries would amount to little as well. From first to last, fur constituted 75 percent of the colony's exports. The trade offered a commoner the only way to get ahead. Even for the less ambitious, the lure of easy wealth proved powerful. When combined with the other attractions of the trader's life, it was an irresistible call for those hardy enough to heed it:

> The Pedlars call'd *coureurs de bois,* export from hence every year several Canows full of Merchandise, which they dispose of among all of the Savage Nations of the Continent, by way of exchange for Beaver-Skins. Seven or eight days ago, I saw twenty-five or thirty of the Canows return with heavy Cargoes; each Canow was manag'd by two or three Men, and carried twenty hundred weight, i.e. forty packs of Beaver Skins, which are worth a hundred Crowns a piece. These Canows had been a year and eighteen months out. You would be amaz'd if you saw how lewd these Pedlars are when they return; how they Feast and Game, and how prodigal they are, not only in their Cloaths but upon Women. Such of 'em as are married, have the wisdom to retire to their own Houses; but the Batchelors act just as our *East India Men,* and Pirates are wont to do; for they Lavish, Eat, Drink, and Play all away as long as the Goods hold out; and when these are gone, they e'en sell their Embroidery, their lace, and even their Cloaths. This done, they are forced to go upon a New Voyage for their subsistence.[25]

In light of all this, it is hard to see how Colbert's plan could have worked. In fact, the peculiar nature of the trade probably doomed it from the outset. The northern nations such as the Ojibwa were hunter-gatherers who migrated from place to place within their territories to take advantage of seasonal products: winter was for hunting, summer for fishing, autumn for the wild

"A Canadian Militiaman circa 1690," Francis Back. Courtesy of the artist. The costume of the *coureurs de bois* would have been essentially the same as the militiaman depicted here.

rice. The farmers to the south also went on extended hunts before and after the harvest. They purchased only as much as they could carry, as possessions were an encumbrance. To expand production, the French needed more customers and this fact would drive them ever deeper into the west.

There were, however, two expedients. The first was brandy. The Great Lakes Indians had no intoxicants. Alcohol is as old as civilization. Indeed, some have argued that farming was as much about beer as bread. Over time, the West had evolved moral and legal strictures to govern drink. The Indians, by contrast, had a long tradition of inducing hallucination through hunger and physical suffering to communicate with the supernatural. As a result, Indians drank hard, and would give all that they owned for liquor. As a commercial lever, then, brandy offered a potent tool to the fur traders. It was a dangerous tool, however. Europeans functioned under a system of external constraints: death or prison for those who broke the statute law and Hell for those who broke the tenets of Christianity. Indian societies had very little of this. They remained largely clan-based and so the execution of an individual could provoke civil war; prison provided a poor deterrent in migratory societies which lived in bark houses; and finally, Indian religion had no real conception of Hell. In place of these, their societies functioned by a system of internal constraints. Honor and reputation were the highest aspirations of these peoples. Behavior that brought shame or disgrace was shunned and one who acted dishonorably was never allowed to forget it. Success in hunting or war brought renown. Failure brought ignominy. The Indians' famed stoicism, in fact, represented a form of ferocious self-control. Indian societies were, thus, powder kegs which needed only a spark to explode.

Alcohol provided the spark: "They are naturally very much inclined to drink and become intoxicated willingly because at this time they believe everything is permitted . . . [them]."[26] In this state, they could also turn violent. Knowing this, chiefs demanded the trade in spirits cease. The Jesuits supported them, having all too often seen years of evangelical labor destroyed in a night. Given the colony's weakness and the church's power, the brandy trade remained forbidden until 1665. In the years which followed, however, the situation became more ambiguous. The Jesuits and traders like the Jolliets continued to oppose it, as did officers charged with keeping peace in the west. Now, however, other voices made themselves heard. Colbert, interested in wine exports, tended to look the other way. Talon, with his dreams of economic growth, declared it a necessary evil. In general, the new imperial administrators supported the trade while the old hands resisted it: a dangerous situation.

A less obvious, but ultimately more important, instrument lay in the nature of the other trade goods. With them, Neolithic people might progress 5,000 years in an afternoon. Iron tools and copper kettles made work more efficient and food preparation simpler. Replacing animal skins with cloth made people more comfortable. Despite this, many Indians were reluctant to trade. The French brought disease, their priests sowed discord, and the time spent trapping and traveling to the trading posts might be better spent in hunting or farming. Factoring these things together, many felt trade goods not worth the cost.

Firearms, however, had a calculus all their own. Expensive to buy and maintain, slower to load, less reliable, and often less accurate than bows, muskets would seem a dubious improvement. Yet they remained in high demand. Part of this was psychological. If your opponent hurls smoke, flame, and thunder at you, you want to hurl it back, particularly as the Indians initially saw guns as supernatural devices and called them "spirits." Another part was a realistic assessment of what a gun did to the human body. A seventeenth-century fusil fired a .50- to .75-caliber ball at 700 to 900 feet per second. Where arrows tended to glance off bone, the soft lead ball would plow right through, removing as much as an inch and sending fragments like shrapnel into muscles and organs. Where an arrow left a relatively neat puncture wound, the kinetic energy of the ball often damaged surrounding tissue. The aftermath was worse. A lead ball wrapped in cloth and lubricated with animal fat invited infection, blood, or lead poisoning. Muskets ultimately sold because they killed better. To spurn the French carried the risk that your neighbors might obtain weapons you did not have. This fear was often decisive, as one trader wrote from Wisconsin: "These peoples held several councils to deliberate whether they should go down to Montreal; they hesitated at first, because they had so few beavers . . . [and] preferred to devote themselves to hunting such animals as could furnish subsistence for their families."

Finally, however, they elected to go, "[reflecting] that if they allowed the Frenchmen to go away . . . , the latter would thereafter attach themselves to some other tribe."[27]

Colbert's idea that he could import alcohol and firearms into the upper country and remain aloof from the consequences was wishful thinking. Worse, the English had now entered the equation. The minister's plan assumed no competition. Indians would simply paddle down to trade as the Huron had. By 1670, this was no longer the case. In 1660, Pierre Radisson and his brother-in-law Medart Chouart des Groseilliers had returned from Lake Superior with a rich haul of furs. They expected a heroes' welcome. Instead the governor seized their pelts as they had set out without permission and clapped Des Groseilliers in jail. The two men sailed for France seeking redress, but found none. The irrepressible Radisson now set on a new scheme. While traveling on Lake Superior, he had learned that only a relatively short canoe journey separated the lake from Hudson's Bay, a region abounding in beaver. He tried to interest French captains in a voyage to the Bay but, failing in this, he went to New England and finally to London, where he found backers. The first trips brought promising returns, and in May 1670, Charles II granted a charter for a "company of merchant adventurers trading into Hudson's Bay." In 1671, Radisson founded a trading post in James Bay, only 400 miles northeast of Lake Superior. If the French did not go west, who would keep the Indians from going north?

To the south, there was more trouble. Until the 1670s the English had really only dabbled in the fur trade. Dealing primarily with local Indians, the commerce was always ancillary to agriculture. Now this began to change. In 1675, a fumbled Puritan landgrab in Massachusetts exploded into a full-scale war. Led by a Wampanoag sachem, Metacomet (King Phillip), the Indians burned villages, killed 600 colonists, and for a time threatened to push the Puritans into the sea. Watching this, Governor Edmund Andros of New York treated with the Iroquois to relieve the pressure and, in a winter campaign, the Mohawk smashed Metacomet. This victory restored Iroquois prestige lost in 1667 and they again emerged as the most powerful nation in the northeast. At Andros's urging, they also adopted many of the refugees fleeing New England. In Virginia, colonists and royal authorities had clashed over Indian policy. Led by Nathaniel Bacon, the small planters had deposed the governor and attacked Indians living between the Rappahannock and Potomac Rivers. Many fled north, seeking asylum among the Iroquois. New France now found itself caught between the Hudson's Bay Company and Andros's resurgent allies.

What made Andros particularly dangerous to the French was his rather different vision of America. New England had posed no great threat, as the Puritans with their burgeoning population had tended to antagonize neighboring Indians. Occasionally, as with the Pequot War in 1632 and Metacomet's War, this had exploded into outright violence. Moreover, Calvinism tended to discourage Red-White interaction. To Puritans the Indians were not souls to be saved, but were rather predestined to Hell. In Virginia, competition for land had already triggered Indian wars in 1622 and 1644 and Bacon's Rebellion in 1675. The Dutch, however, had enjoyed considerable success as fur traders, and Andros would now follow their example. Charles II wanted to contain the independent New Englanders. The Iroquois could arrange it. The King also had an imperial vision for America and wished to cripple the French. The Iroquois could help there as well. The governor now set out to forge an Anglo-Iroquoian alliance. He met with them in a great council, put an end to the trade abuses which had plagued Dutch relations with the Iroquois, and sought to negotiate border problems which distracted them from the task he had in mind: Canada.

ONE

Frontenac and La Salle, 1673–1682

NEW FRANCE AT THE BEGINNING of the 1670s had undergone a remarkable transformation. Near collapse only a decade before, the French had defeated the Iroquois, reconnoitered the interior, and begun a commercial and diplomatic alliance system which would eventually encompass a considerable portion of the continent. It was, however, profoundly divided. The Canadians wished to exploit the interior, while the crown sought to limit expansion. The missionaries wanted control over the region to protect their flocks from the corrosive influence of the traders. For their part, the traders wanted not only access to the west but also freedom from clerical interference. Into this conflict would come two men, Louis de Buade, Comte de Frontenac et de Palluau, and René-Robert Cavalier, Sieur de La Salle. A turbulent pair, they would aggravate these tensions to the breaking point and drive New France into a new and dangerous future.

Born in 1622, Frontenac had spent most of his adult life as a soldier in the Thirty Years War and Italy. He married well, but over the strenuous objections of the bride's parents. A courtier when not on campaign, he never reached any position of note. He liked fine things and, by the 1660s, had amassed debts of more than 300,000 livres. France, unfortunately, suffered under the blessings of peace just then and so Frontenac joined a Venetian expedition against the Turks. He again failed to distinguish himself and the Doge eventually fired him. Two years later Louis XIV appointed him governor of New France, a comment perhaps on the King's opinion of his new colony. In any case, Frontenac apparently leapt at the opportunity to put an ocean between himself and his creditors, or his wife, or both.

Canada must have come as a shock: Its capital Quebec, a ramshackle wooden town of perhaps 600 or 700 souls, stood at the edge of a trackless forest stretching all the way to Hudson's Bay. Nevertheless, he set out to make the best of it, and in so doing managed to antagonize nearly everyone in the colony. French political theory of the time held that the best protection against a local tyrant was to divide authority so that no one person could rule absolutely. In New France the governor attended to military and diplomatic matters, the intendant oversaw the economy, the bishop tended to spiritual affairs, and the Sovereign Council, a group of prominent colonists, advised the governor and intendant on local affairs and tried important court cases. Under Frontenac, this arrangement quickly fell apart. Demanding the title "High and Mighty Lord," instead of the traditional "Monsieur le Governor," he set out to assume sole power.[1] The bishop had departed the year before he arrived and the intendant Talon caught the last ship of the season, fed up with Frontenac's meddling. That left only the council, and the governor immediately set out to appropriate its judicial functions as well.

Frontenac's actions that first fall were high-handed, but his conduct the following year proved rather more serious. In the summer of 1673, he ordered the construction of a fort at Cataracoui near the head of the Saint Lawrence River. Ostensibly a defense against the Iroquois, the governor's post also lay 200 miles upstream from Montreal. To the town's merchants, it appeared that he had built it to drive them out of business. Indians coming down from the upper country would have no need to descend the river to sell their pelts. Adding insult to injury, Frontenac had imposed a *corvée* (labor service) on the town to build it.

At the same time, Frontenac began to sell licenses to coureurs de bois to go up the Ottawa to trade. Some of these openly sold brandy and thumbed their noses at the Montreal officials. When the governor of the town tried to intervene, Frontenac had him arrested. Worse, he now moved to take over the Montreal fur markets. To "protect" the Indians from sharp practice, Frontenac ordered guards to accompany them about the town. The guests then discovered that they had to pay for the service.

Frontenac also insisted upon a council and demanded presents to "open his ears."[2] Gifts were standard in native diplomacy, but Frontenac demanded rather more than symbolic offerings. He also purchased furs on his own account and allowed French merchants to attend the fairs in defiance of the Sovereign Council, which had reserved them for the Canadians.

The *Montrealais* were furious. Having survived Iroquois, ferocious winters, and back-breaking labor clearing the forest, they had no intention of rolling over. In their battle with the governor, coureurs de bois became their weapon of choice. Merchants began outfitting bush runners with goods and fencing their contraband furs. Frontenac retaliated in kind and soon whole troops traveled the west either illicitly or armed with one of the governor's fraudulent permits.

Two events now interceded to make a bad situation considerably worse. In 1675, the King legalized the sale of brandy to the Indians, seeing it as essential to halting English commercial expansion, and granted the entire fur trade to a monopoly, the Company of the Farm. Canadians paid very little in the way of taxes and to defray the administrative costs of the colony, Colbert leased out the right to export Canadian furs to the company for ten years for a fee of 350,000 livres. To prevent gouging he set the price of beaver at a uniform 4 livres, 10 sols to the pound, later amended to 5 livres, 10 sols for *castor gras,* 4 livres, 10 sols for middle-grade pelts, and 3 livres, 10 sols for *castor sec,* or dry beaver.[3] With guaranteed prices, the pace of the trade accelerated. Protected from the laws of supply and demand, the Canadians could dump as much beaver onto the market as they could bring in. In the long term, this practice would nearly bring New France to its knees. In the short term, however, it added considerable snow to what was quickly becoming an avalanche.

In 1667, the Canadians had exported 555,000 livres value of furs to France. There had been no convoys for several years previous and so the trade might have produced 100,000 livres annually. Between 1675 and 1685, these figures exploded. Given the prices paid for the different grades of furs, these figures would indicate an average annual value of some 400,000 livres. It could not last, but clearly prices had had a strong effect on the expansion of the trade.

It was a corrupt, chaotic time of fast money and few rules, and

TABLE 1.1. *Return of Beaver from Canada, 1675–1684*

Year	Beaver Fur in Livres Weight
1675	61,000
1676	70,000
1677	92,000
1678	80,135
1679	68,080
1680	69,000
1681	82,900
1682	90,353
1683	95,489
1684	49,056

Source: "Return of Beaver from Canada from 1675 to 1685," in E. B. O'Callaghan, ed., *Documents Relating to the Colonial History of New York*, 15 vols. (Albany: Weed and Parsons, 1855–1883), 9:287.

in it the coureurs de bois attracted more than their share of rogues and scoundrels. It also produced extraordinarily capable men with a taste for adventure. The first of these, Daniel Greysolon, Sieur du Luth, had been a soldier in Louis's elite King's Guard. Emigrating to Canada, he heard the stories of the west and became fired with the idea of exploration. Du Luth also had a connection to Frontenac: His sister had married Louis de La Porte de Louvigny, an officer in the governor's guards. He set out in September 1678 with seven men for the northwest, intending to go farther than any before. The official status of the voyage was a bit vague: he appears to have had the governor's blessing but no official sanction.

Du Luth wintered at the mouth of the Kaministigoya River on the northwest shore of Lake Superior. By July 2 the next year, he had reached Lac Mille Lac in Minnesota, where he erected a cross and took possession of the country. In September, he called a council of the Sioux, Assiniboin, and other northern peoples to negotiate a general peace. All that winter, he organized hunts and feasts between the different nations to "draw closer the bonds of friendship."[4] He also dispelled rumors of smallpox on the Saint Lawrence which had discouraged the Indians from journeying to the colony.

In the summer of 1680, Du Luth went south from Lake

Superior over the Bois Brulé and Saint Croix Rivers to the Mississippi. Learning that the Sioux held 3 Frenchmen, Father Louis Hennepin, Michel Accault, and one Dugay, as captives, he set out to paddle the 120 miles to the Sioux village: "I went in my canoe two days and two nights, and the next day at ten o'clock in the morning."[5] Walking into a village of 1,000 people, he demanded their release. Spurning offers of peace with a calculated insult, he intimidated the Sioux into releasing the three to his charge and then nonchalantly departed.

Returning to Michilimackinac, he found himself charged as a coureur de bois. Taking advantage of a general amnesty, he returned to the Saint Lawrence to argue that he had worked only for the good of the colony. He had some grounds for this. His negotiations had opened the way for Ottawa traders west of Lake Superior, prevented the diversion of pelts to Hudson's Bay and Albany, and had made it clear to the western nations that they might not trifle with Frenchmen traveling the country. He was nevertheless arrested, but was released a short time later.

Another character of this sort was the trader-interpreter-diplomat Nicolas Perrot. Born around 1644, Perrot came to New France in 1660 as a *donné* of the Jesuits. He first went west to Wisconsin with Father Claude Allouez in 1665. Returning the next year, he found employment as a domestic servant. However, the west had hold of him and the next year he signed on with two other men to trade at Michilimackinac for a tavern keeper Isaac Nafrechoux. He returned to the upper country four years later as one of the interpreters for the Sieur de Saint Lusson's ceremony at Sault Sainte Marie in 1671. Later that year, he married and took up a farm along the Saint Lawrence, but was only marking time. At the beginning of the next decade, he would return to the west as an officer of the King and would figure among the most influential men in the Great Lakes for the next quarter century.

The pivotal figure of this period, however, was the turbulent Norman, René-Robert Cavalier, Sieur de La Salle. Writing a half century after his death, Father Pierre F. X. Charlevoix said of him: "He had a cultivated mind, ambition for distinction, and felt that he had the genius and courage requisite for success. In fact, he lacked neither the resolution to undertake nor constancy to follow up a project, neither firmness to withstand obstacles, nor resources to repair his losses; but he could not win love nor manage those whom he needed, and as soon as he possessed authority he exercised it with severity and hauteur. With such defects, he could not be successful, nor was he."[6] Nearly three centuries later, it remains perhaps the best assessment of La Salle. However, at the time it was not so clear that he would fail. In fact, fear of his enterprise would drive the Canadians into open rebellion and the Iroquois into open warfare. Rarely have the hands of one man touched the springs of so many great events.

Born in 1643 to a Rouen merchant family, La Salle enrolled in the Jesuit seminary. Though bright, he chafed under the discipline. Applying for a post in the American missions, he was turned down and left the order. By joining the Society of Jesus, he had lost his inheritance and was now without means or particular prospects. He did, however, have an older brother, Jean, a Sulpician priest in Montreal. In 1666, La Salle sailed for the New World. The Sulpicians owned lands around the town and offered property on easy terms to any who applied. Through his brother's intercession, he received a large tract and began the business of laying out a village and assigning lands, but his heart was not in it. Too mercurial for the life of a farmer, he sold most of his holdings to finance an exploration to discover a route to the Pacific. He got only as far as Lake Ontario on this first journey, but he would soon make others.

In 1673, La Salle met the newly arrived Frontenac. The governor thought him useful and, in 1675, gave him the post at Cataracoui. This satisfied the Norman for a bit, but he still dreamed of great deeds. In 1677, he proposed to finish the exploration of the Mississippi begun by Jolliet. The following year, he received Colbert's approval. The expedition clearly contravened the minister's plan to limit expansion, but La Salle's proposal had touched on a topic dear to his heart: a warm water port. Quebec, frozen in as much as six months out of twelve, seemed a poor capital for a colonial enterprise. Should La Salle's discoveries include a more temperate location, there might be some value in it. For his labors, he would receive a five-year monopoly on the fur trade of all such lands as he should discover.

In the winter of 1678–1679 La Salle constructed two ships to ferry supplies and men and to haul back furs from his western enterprise. Both sank within the year, the larger of the two, the

Griffon, disappearing in northern Lake Michigan with a cargo of furs valued at 40,000 livres. Despite this, La Salle carried on. Building Fort Crevecoeur on the Illinois River, he returned to Montreal to arrange more credit for his explorations, leaving his lieutenant Henri Tonti in charge. Before departing, he sent the priest Hennepin and the *voyageurs* Accault and Dugay to explore the upper Mississippi. Captured by the Sioux the three disappeared for more than a year, eventually turning up at Michilimackinac with Du Luth. After La Salle's departure his men mutinied, destroyed the fort, and made off with tools, furs, and trade goods. They had received no wages in two years and loss of the *Griffon* made it doubtful they ever would. They had also heard rumors of approaching Iroquois.

La Salle's great lieutenant in this endeavor, the Neapolitan soldier of fortune Henri Tonti, had fled with his parents to France after an abortive rebellion. He joined the army as a cadet in 1668 and served against the Spanish. In his last campaign, he lost a hand to a grenade and was captured. After Tonti was exchanged, Louis XIV awarded him an indemnity of 300 livres and he returned to the fleet. Around this time, Tonti had a prosthetic made: a cast-iron fist which would become legend in the upper country. In 1678, he sought a position at court but had no luck. However, he obtained a place with La Salle. Arriving in Canada, he immediately set out for Niagara, where the explorer was building the *Griffon.*

Tonti, one of those historical figures destined to remain in the shadow of great men, was ultimately the more important of the two. Tough, shrewd, and utterly fearless, he held New France's western flank secure for nearly a generation while La Salle chased his chimeras to Texas and disaster. He remained loyal to his patron always, one of the few who did, but not as the simple follower he often seems. Tonti, the foreigner, had sought preferment at court and despite an admirable military record had found none. La Salle had influence; he did not. It would seem he hitched his star to the explorer's and gave good service in return. This was the way of it in the seventeenth century.

Tonti, upriver at the time of the mutiny, had returned to find the fort burned. Gathering up what little remained of the tools and equipment, he set out with 6 men for the Great Village of the Kaskaskia to await La Salle. All that summer of 1680, they waited. On September 18, an Iroquois force of 500 warriors struck. As the fighting raged, Tonti sought to negotiate a truce, but the Iroquois took him prisoner and the combat resumed. The Illiniwek ultimately retreated downriver all the way to the Mississippi hotly pursued by the Iroquois. French accounts claim that they killed or captured more than 1,200 people with a loss of only 30 men.[7]

The Iroquois, not ready for an open breach with the French, released Tonti and ordered the Italian and his followers immediately from the country. The fugitives had traveled as far as Chicago when one of the missionaries, Father Ribourde, wandered off and was killed by a Kickapoo hunting party. Nearly starving, the five survivors traveled north into Wisconsin hoping to reach the Jesuit mission at Green Bay. Wracked by fever and swollen limbs and living on a few handfuls of leached corn and wild garlic each day, they eventually found a friendly Potawatomi town where they obtained food and assistance. Finally, on June 5, 1681, they reached the safety of Michilimackinac.

Meanwhile, La Salle had made a swift march to Fort Frontenac. The snow still lay on the ground, and at one point, he lost his eyesight to snow blindness. Then the spring thaw came, flooding the country, and La Salle and his men had to sleep in the trees each night. They found signs of Iroquois patrols, and could neither light fires to cook nor dry their sodden clothes. Despite all this, the explorer covered nearly 800 miles in 65 days, arriving at Fort Frontenac in mid-May. Gathering men and supplies, he then set out for the Illinois country.

By October, he had reached Michilimackinac and on December 1 he found the charred ruins of the Kaskaskia town: a ghastly sight, with burned and mutilated corpses amid the wreckage of what had once been a community of several thousand people. La Salle pushed on down the river to the abandoned Fort Crevecoeur and then south to the Mississippi. Along the way, he met no one at all. The Kaskaskias, Peorias, and Michigameas had fled and an eerie silence hung over the long valley. Finally, nearing the confluence, the expedition saw figures standing in a meadow. Landing, they called out and approached only to discover the charred, half-eaten remains of several Illiniwek women still tied to the stakes where the Iroquois had burned them.

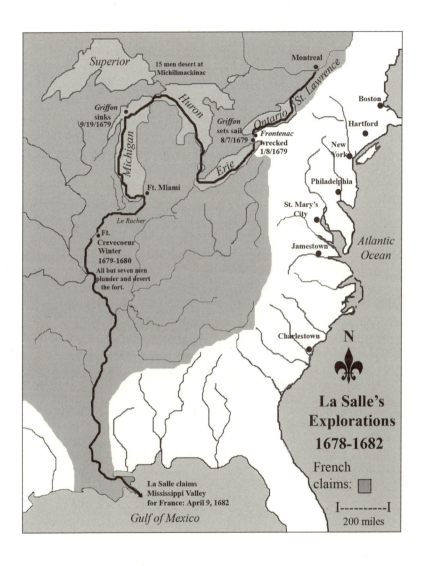

Having found no sign of Tonti, La Salle wintered at the mouth of the Saint Joseph River. During the enforced delay, he worked to repair the damage done by the Iroquois. Rallying the scattered Illiniwek with presents and encouragement, he then distributed presents to the neighboring Miami and screwed up their courage as well. Hearing that Tonti and his men had survived, La Salle again returned to Fort Frontenac to obtain more men, supplies, and credit. By October, he had traveled north to Michilimackinac, where Tonti awaited him. The two, with a party of 30 French and nearly 100 Indians, then made their way down Lake Michigan to the mouth of the Saint Joseph. They paddled to the Chicago Portage around the southern end of Lake Michigan and, finding the river frozen, made sledges to carry the boats south down the Illinois to open water. Traveling nearly 150 miles, they finally found the channel clear at Lake Peoria. Ice again halted them at the mouth of the river for a time, but this finally cleared and they made their way to the Gulf.

On April 9, 1682, La Salle with twenty-three Frenchmen and twenty-two Indians arrived at the mouth of the great river. Firing muskets and chanting "Domine salvum fac Regem," they erected a cross bearing the royal arms and the inscription "Louis Le Grand, Roy de France et Navarre Règne; le Neuvième Avril, 1682." With this raised, La Salle proclaimed to the beach grass, seagulls, and anyone else who might care to know that the Mississippi now belonged to France: "In the name of the most high, mighty, invincible, and victorious Prince, Louis the Great, by the grace of God King of France and of Navarre, Fourteenth of that name, I . . . have taken, and do now take, in the name of his Majesty and of his successors to the crown, possession of this country of Louisiana . . . from the mouth of the great River Saint Louis, otherwise called the Ohio, . . . as also along the river Colbert, or Mississippi, and the rivers which discharge themselves thereinto, from its source . . . [to] the Gulf of Mexico."[8] With the serene arrogance characteristic of seventeenth-century exploration, La Salle had just claimed title to perhaps a quarter of North America.

It was a dramatic moment, yet the response from France would prove lukewarm at best. The King had no use for the project, sharing Colbert's concerns about expansion. By 1682, however, it could no longer be prevented, nor was it clear that to do so would in fact serve any purpose. Over the three centuries since La Salle addressed the seagulls, he has been called a dreamer, visionary, rogue, and madman. He was, in fact, all of these. Yet, in a sense, he saw something his sovereign did not. Writing a year or so after his return he declared, "If foreigners anticipate us they will deprive France of all the advantages to be expected from the enterprise. They will complete the ruin of New France which they already hem in through Virginia, New England, Pennsylvania, and the Hudson's Bay." Like Hudson's Bay, the Mississippi offered a back door to the interior and a highway into the fur country. "They will not fail to ascend the river as high as possible and establish colonies nearest to the savages who now bring their furs to Montreal—they will make constant inroads into the countries of the latter." Moreover, thought La Salle, the problem was imminent. English ships had been sniffing around the Gulf seeking the mouth of the Mississippi. Once the news of his voyage went out they would be back, and soon, "since the Dutch have published it in their newspapers upward of a year ago."[9]

After claiming title to the great river, La Salle turned north. Paddling against the current, they ascended the Mississippi, the Illinois, and the Kankakee, portaged their canoes to the Saint Joseph River, and floated down to his depot Fort Miami on June 15. By July 23, he had reached Michilimackinac. Over the next several months, La Salle pondered what, exactly, he should do with this immense country. In characteristic fashion, he proposed a completely new course for France's colonial endeavor. Canada would never amount to anything, he wrote. The fur trade would remain a marginal industry and the climate would not support crops of any value. The Great Lakes country possessed rich lands, but the waterfalls and rapids of the upper Saint Lawrence and Niagara would prevent the French from ever exploiting them efficiently. For La Salle, then, the future lay in his newfound "Louisiana." It had "everything which has enriched Virginia and New England, and which form the foundation of their commerce and great wealth—timber of every kind—salted meat, tallow, corn, sugar, tobacco, honey, wax, and other gums; immense pasturages, hemp, and other articles with which more than two hundred vessels are freighted every year in New England to carry elsewhere."[10] The broad flat waters of the Mississippi would, moreover, provide a highway through the entire length of the country. He had seen several of its tributaries: the Ohio, Illinois, Tennessee, and Missouri and these seemed to share much the same character. With these, the French could develop a region several times the size of France.

A grand vision of the future, it had rather more immediate consequences. By 1682, La Salle and Frontenac had forts at Cataracoui, Niagara, the mouth of the Saint Joseph, Crevecoeur, and Prudhomme on the Mississippi, and exclusive trade rights to the region. Despite strict instructions, La Salle's men were trading in the north as well. His continental vision seemed to the *Montrealais* an immense boondoggle. The governor and his man had evaded Colbert's restrictions and now used them to take over the fur trade. The merchants could not allow this to stand and outfitted still more coureurs de bois to derail it. Whatever chance Colbert's small-colony plan might have had died with the explorations of La Salle. At the beginning of the decade, perhaps 300–400 coureurs had plied the backcountry. By the beginning of the 1680s, it was estimated that their numbers had doubled.[11]

In 1681, Colbert, bowing to the inevitable, had authorized the distribution of twenty-five *congés,* or trade permits, each year. He thought that rather than risk prosecution, most traders would take their turn waiting for a congé to go up country. These would be awarded to needy families who could then either mount a voyage themselves or sell them to someone who would, and prices could reach as much as 800 to 1,200 francs. Equipped with a license, "The buyer would choose three voyageurs, to whom he gave a thousand écus, which he rated high; these goods would produce about twelve thousand francs profit. The Owner of the Congé had the half of this profit, besides his principle, and the Voyageurs shared the rest."[12] In practice, the twenty-five licenses were a drop in the tide and made no particular difference. With gross profits of nearly 400 percent, it took more dissuasion than Colbert could muster to halt the spread of the French into the backcountry.

The canoe men, however, worked extraordinarily hard for that 400 percent, as one French soldier wrote: "If people could realize the labor which is involved in finding beaver skins they would not think so lightly of this commodity." The canoe men would paddle 12- and 14-hour days, halting periodically to smoke their pipes. By this custom, distances came to be measured in "pipes" of approximately 3 miles. The standard trade craft of the seventeenth century, the "three-and-a-half fathom canoe" was about 20 feet long, carried a crew of 3 and a cargo of perhaps 1,000 livres weight. On one outbound voyage, the provisions consisted of 120 livres of hard bread, 2 bushels of peas, and 20 livres of hog fat. So equipped, the coureurs or voyageurs set out. The Saint Lawrence at Montreal lies some 56 feet above sea level. Lakes Michigan and Huron are 580 feet above and Lake Superior 600. Thus, a trip to the upper country required an ascent of nearly 600 feet in as many miles.

The route to the Great Lakes up the Ottawa and Matawa Rivers, across Lake Nipissing and down French River required forty-two portages and *décharges*. At the former, both canoe and cargo would be carried around the fall or rapid, but the latter required only the cargo be unloaded while the canoe would be dragged up by hand or with long lines known as cordelles. Wearing only their shirts and moccasins, the men "boldly jump into the water and by main strength, all helping one another, they manage to get them along, but not without skinning their feet and legs for the rocks are so cold that their skin sticks to them and the men do not get free without leaving a piece behind them."[13] There was worse, however. When portaging, each paddler had to carry 300 pounds each and make another trip for the canoe. They carried two or three bales of goods weighing as much as 150 pounds suspended by a "tump line," or leather strap worn across the forehead. Moving at a shuffling jog, they would make their way over rough ground uphill and down, where a misstep often resulted in a compound fracture or strangulated hernia. Far from home, such an injury usually meant death.

Barring mishap, the canoe men usually made the 600-mile trip in six to eight weeks. Canoes bound for the Illinois country would follow the north and west shores of Lake Michigan to Chicago or the Saint Joseph River to make the crossing to the Mississippi watershed. At Chicago, the divide lay only 15 feet or so above the level of the lake. In the spring high water, the canoe men would ascend the Chicago River to a marshy pond which actually straddled the divide and enter the west-flowing Des Plaines River, which in turn led to the Illinois River and the Mississippi. The total distance from Michilimackinac to the lands of

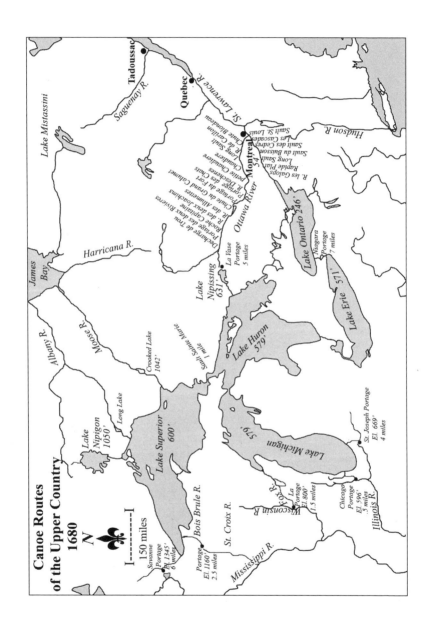

the Illiniwek was perhaps 600 miles and might be covered in an additional six to eight weeks depending on the weather. During most of the year, however, the Chicago Portage and the Des Plaines River were too shallow to permit a passage and the voyageurs had to contend with a nearly continuous portage all the way to Le Rocher, "the Rock," a sandstone butte across the Illinois River from the Great Village of the Kaskaskia, where the deep water commenced. To avoid this, the French would often paddle around the south end of the lake to the Saint Joseph River, ascend this some 50 miles to present-day South Bend, Indiana, and make a 4 mile portage to the Kankakee River, which joined the Des Plaines in northeastern Illinois. A more reliable route, but in the dry months the Kankakee was nearly as shallow as the Des Plaines.

Canoes bound for the northwest would leave Michilimackinac, ascend the Saint Mary's River and coast Lake Superior to Kaministigoya, a distance of nearly 500 miles. The passage required only one portage at Sault Sainte Marie, but storms and headwinds could halt the canoes for days at a time. Eighteenth-century accounts indicate that three to four weeks was common for the passage. By the end of the century, French explorers and traders had pushed west and northwest beyond Lake Superior, crossing from the Great Lakes watershed into those of the upper Mississippi and the Nelson, which flowed into Hudson's Bay. The rivers they used to make the transit were deeper and less seasonal than those in the Illinois country, but the divide above Lake Superior rose nearly 600–700 feet in a distance of 50 or 60 miles requiring a numbing series of portages and décharges.

Canoes returning from the west tended to make made better time. The prevailing westerly winds blew from astern and except for the short 70-mile passage up the French River they were traveling downstream. A canoe generally carried a cargo of 20–25 bales of fur. As one cargo of trade goods usually produced one and a half or two canoe loads of furs, the voyageurs would often obtain a second canoe to carry the extra cargo. Parties would join together and pool their paddlers. The downbound canoes would then be conducted by two men instead of the three required for the outbound journey. It was an easier passage, but it held one great danger: temptation. Rather than endure the hardship and danger of a portage, the canoe men would often elect to run the rapid. In an exhilarating moment or two, they could avoid hours of back-breaking work. On the other hand, the decision could result in a capsize or a stove canoe, a lost cargo, and/or death: "It is difficult to conceive of the dangers to which they are exposed in shooting whirlpools, falls, and rapids which only to think of makes one's hair stand on end."[14] Over the years, most of the major portages came to have burying grounds for the men lost on the trail or in the water and many took their names from the dead. All in all, these fur traders were a tough lot and not to be trifled with.

The traders and the merchants who backed them were not La Salle's only enemies. The explorer had an acid pen and now began denouncing his rivals, among them the stalwart Du Luth. Describing the latter's explorations as a freebooting junket, he declared that Du Luth "went to and returned from the settlements several times, loaded with goods and furs; during that time they exhausted the supply of pelts in the Lake Superior country, besieging it from all sides, and this year they prevented the Outaouacs from going down to Montreal."[15] This blast might seem ungrateful, as Du Luth had rescued his men Accault and Father Hennepin, but La Salle went further. Making reference to the incident, he claimed that it only proved that his men had staked a prior claim to the upper Mississippi.

La Salle also managed to incur the wrath of an even more dangerous opponent: the Society of Jesus. The explorer had little love for the order which had cast him out as a young man, and he had worked to bar them from the lands he explored. The Jesuits thus had reason to despise him and little things began to suggest that they actively sought to oust him from the country. He saw the Jesuits behind a Miami policy of conciliation and even alliance with the Iroquois while they worked to divide the French and Illiniwek. Two years earlier, they had sent ambassadors to the Five Nations proposing war against the Illiniwek. The Miami chief Monceau had spread rumors to the Illiniwek that the explorer "was a brother to the Iroquois, that I was breathing their breath, that I ate the serpents of their country, that they had given me a net to hem them in from one side while the Iroquois came from the other."[16] La Salle had managed to scotch these for the time being, but the intrigues remained.

Behind the Miami, thought La Salle, stood the Jesuit Father

Claude Allouez. A veteran of nearly twenty years in the western country, Allouez was a formidable character. Born in Saint Didier, France, in 1622, he had joined the order at seventeen. Arriving in Canada in 1658, he spent the next seven years ministering along the Saint Lawrence. In 1665, he received orders to evangelize the Ottawa on Lake Superior. In 1669, Marquette replaced him and he set up a new mission, the Mission of Saint Francis Xavier, in Wisconsin, to minister to the Potawatomi and Sauk. The following year, he established the missions of Saint Mark among the Fox nation and Saint Michael among the Menominee. In 1676, he was relieved and established an itinerant mission to the Illiniwek, Mascoutin, and Miami. Along the way, he had been abandoned by his guides on the Ottawa, lost his way in the forest and nearly died, overturned "pagan" idols wherever he encountered them, circumnavigated and mapped Lake Superior, and, by his death in 1689, would claim to have instructed 100,000 Indians and converted 10,000. Unlike the cheerful, curious, much-loved Marquette, Allouez was a Counter-Reformation soldier and capable of many things in God's service.

Whether the Jesuits plotted La Salle's destruction is unclear. On the other hand, he had cause in assuming he had few friends in the order. After leaving the Society of Jesus he had allied himself with the Franciscan and Recollet orders, both eager to break up the Jesuit monopoly on the western missions. La Salle's "Louisiana" now threatened to cut the Jesuits off from vast new fields of converts, the Montreal merchants from vast new supplies of furs, and the Iroquois from new allies and client peoples. La Salle had a tendency toward paranoia, but sometimes even paranoids have good reason to worry. A great number of people hated him just now.

In this frame of mind, La Salle came up with a plan. In October, he wrote to a friend, "It is very desirable that this war between the Iroquois and the Illinois should come to an end. If we had opposed it from the outset, the former tribe would not have become so presumptuous from the victory they have obtained." Rumor had it that the Iroquois planned to return, provoked by La Salle's enemies. "It seems that those who should prevent it are bringing it about, by inciting the Indians who are our allies . . . to begin the war, in the hope, . . . that the war would ruin me."[17] To check this, he would build a fort strong enough to rally the Illiniwek and deter the Iroquois. La Salle had originally planned to build his base on the Saint Joseph but Le Rocher better suited his purpose. More than 600 miles from Michilimackinac, it would assuage accusations that La Salle sought to take over the northern fur trade: "The fear that I should be charged with profiting by furs which ought to go down to Montreal, has caused me to remove it to a greater distance, in order to deprive those who are jealous of me of every kind of pretext of slandering me."[18]

By December 1682, La Salle had returned to the Illinois country, and during the winter, he, Tonti, and the forty-five French and Indians in his party built their fort atop Le Rocher. That first winter at Fort Saint Louis must have been a happy time. Through sheer will and physical stamina, La Salle had overcome misfortunes that would have broken lesser men. Here at the Rock, as the year ended, he could see the beginnings of his dreams coming true. However, storms began to darken the eastern sky, storms which would leave him a bleeding corpse in an east Texas thicket and plunge the Great Lakes country into war for nearly a generation.

All this began with the recall of Governor Frontenac in 1682. Over the years, he had continued his running battle with the Sovereign Council. By 1681, it stood in outright rebellion and blocked him at every opportunity. In March, he lost his temper and caned the son of one of his opponents. Charges and countercharges flew and Frontenac arrested a member of the council. The situation had grown impossible, and in May Louis ordered Frontenac home. La Salle had now lost his patron.

Frontenac's recall, though probably inevitable, came at an awkward time. Colbert's great plan for a compact farming colony was coming apart. Whether the King approved or no, the French were committed to intervening in the affairs of the western country. They really no longer had a choice. In 1681, Intendant Duchesneau dispatched a "Memoir on the Western Indians," which summed up the problem. In the north, he said, the Ottawa "are those of the greatest use to us, because through them we obtain Beaver; and although they, for the most part, do not hunt and have but a small portion of peltry in their Country, they go in search of it to the most distant places, and exchange it for our merchandise which they procure at Montreal."[19] This was clearly a useful arrangement for the French, but there were troubles as the remoter nations "occasionally come down to Montreal, but usually do not do so in great numbers, because they are too far distant, are not expert in managing canoes, and because other Indians intimidate them, in order to be the carriers of their Merchandise and profit thereby."[20] Thus, the French needed the Ottawas, but would have to prevent them from bullying potential customers.

Another concern was brandy. In 1679, the King had reversed his position on the trade in spirits, but the coureurs continued hauling it west with disastrous consequences. This trade threatened the whole endeavor: "Our principal interest, and what alone will crown all of our designs with success, is . . . to establish Religion on a sound basis among those people who have any disposition thereunto. This would succeed, were those in authority in this country to chastise such as set the Indians a bad example, and to forbid . . . the conveying of Brandy to the Natives, inasmuch as drunkenness is, among them, the chief obstacle to religion, destroys both their health and substance, and gives rise among them to quarrels, batteries, and murders, that cannot be remedied on account of the distance."[21]

Finally, there was the most serious matter of all. The Iroquois attack upon the Illiniwek in September of 1680 had made it clear that the Peace of 1667 had fallen apart. Moreover their crushing victory and attendant atrocities had sent a chilling message to the rest of the western nations. If left unchecked, France's new allies might defect en masse to the Five Nations and the Albany traders. Therefore, the intendant wrote, "'Tis our interest to keep these people united . . . to watch carefully that none of them terminate without our mediation, and to constitute ourselves, in all things, their arbiters and protectors." Duchesneau also saw an opportunity in this. The Iroquois menaced all of the western peoples and, properly managed, this fear could be turned to advantage. French assistance could bring them, as the intendant wrote, "into total dependence."[22]

By 1681, affairs in the upper country had reached a critical pass. For the trade to prosper, the Canadians needed to regulate the commerce in brandy and the cupidity of the coureurs de bois. They also needed to smooth over ethnic disputes. Lastly, the

Iroquois again posed a potentially mortal threat. As Duchesneau observed, most of these problems could not "be remedied on account of the distance." The time was quickly coming when the French would actually have to occupy the country itself. The next fall, La Salle would build his Fort Saint Louis des Illinois. The following summer, Du Luth and Olivier Morel, Sieur de La Durantaye, would build a post at the Straits of Michilimackinac and reoccupy the fort at Kaministigoya. The lilies of France would now fly over the upper country and the Mississippi Valley and Louis XIV would have a North American empire whether he wished one or no.

The French were about to embark on an imperial experiment unlike anything the world had seen before. A handful of Frenchmen would attempt to enthrall a continent by means of trade and alliances. England, however, had embarked on an experiment of its own. King Charles II owed large sums to a certain Admiral Penn. In lieu of payment, he granted his son William a considerable tract of land in America. As a Quaker, the younger Penn had a particular vision for his American holding: a haven for religious outcasts. In his "Charter of Privileges," he would write, "Noe Person or Persons, inhabiting in this Province or Territories, who shall confess and acknowledge One almighty God . . . shall be in any Case molested or prejudiced, in his or their Person or Estate, because of his or their conscientious Persuasion or Practice."[23] He had his plan for freedom of conscience printed in French, German, and Swiss and distributed on the continent. Within a year, his new colony had 3,000 inhabitants and within five some 12,000. Pennsylvania now outnumbered New France. In 1682, King James II instructed the governor of New York, "You shall permit all persons of what Religion soever quietly to inhabit within your Government without giving any disturbance or disquiet whatsoever."[24] Five years later, the governor observed the effect of James's edict: "Here be not many of the Church of England, [and] few Roman Catholiks, but abundance of Quakers —preachers, men and women, especially—singing Quakers, ranting Quakers, Sabbatarians, Anti-sabbatarians, some Anabaptists, some Independents, some Jews; in short of all sorts of opinions there are some, and the most part none at all."[25]

Penn's motives were largely altruistic. The Stuarts' were not. By the 1680s, England was running out of Anglicans willing to indenture themselves for America and the Puritan migrations had about run their course. By opening their ports to dissenters of all nationalities, the Middle Colonies would attract some 150,000 German Pietists, Scots-Irish Presbyterians, and Irish over the next century. Trapped within Louis XIV's dictum "one law, one faith, one king," Canada could not draw on any of these. La Salle had set out to claim the continent, but the Stuarts had set out to people it. It remained to be seen who would win.

TWO

The Great Turtle and the Rock, 1683–1687

COUNT FRONTENAC DEPARTED CANADA in the fall of 1682 after a term best described as stormy. Yet for all of his cupidity, arrogance, and ambition, he had a presence, or *majesté,* which allowed him to retain the respect of many of the Indians, if not the Whites. His successor shared much of his avarice but without the grandeur to quite pull it off. He would prove, in short, a small man.

He was the aging naval officer, Joseph Antoine Le Febvre de La Barre. Sixty years old and an undistinguished bureaucrat for much of his career, he enjoyed patronage from some quarter and had received a naval commission. He led a successful expedition against the Dutch in 1664 and became governor of Guyana. Accused of cowardice in action in 1667, he nevertheless served with distinction against the Dutch in 1673. The following year, he had a command in the Mediterranean. In May 1682, Louis appointed him governor-general of New France. Arriving in September, La Barre took an immediate interest in the fur trade. Assuming he would remain for only a term, he wished to make what he could while he might. The Canadians tried to warn him of the danger of the Iroquois, but he seemed uninterested. Given the critical state of things, events would prove that he had neither the youth nor the temperament the times demanded.

Unfortunately, the same month that La Barre arrived, Thomas Dongan received his commission as governor of New York and events would prove his temperament eminently suited to the times. Born in Ireland, Dongan became a soldier and served some years in the French army. In 1667, Charles II invited him back to England and made him lieutenant-governor of Tangiers. An intelligent, dynamic figure and friend to the King's brother James, the Duke of York, Dongan enjoyed favor at court. On September 30, 1682, James sent him to America. As a soldier of considerable talent, he understood the stakes involved in the Great Lakes country as few had.

Dongan's policy was simple: dismissing French territorial claims, he sarcastically wrote "Tis a hard thing that all the countries a Frenchman walks over in America must belong to Canada."[1] The English would trade wherever they wished. Further, Edmund Andros's negotiations had made the Five Nations subjects of the English crown. It was a fiction, but a useful one: the Iroquois had driven all of the Indians from Ohio, southern Michigan, Indiana, and recently Illinois. All the lands south of the Great Lakes thus belonged to England by right of conquest. Planting crosses and singing *Te Deum*s as the French had was a thin claim to sovereignty. Possession by force of arms carried more weight. Dongan was playing a good game of imperialism. With such a man in New York, confrontation became inevitable.

In response, La Barre moved to consolidate France's position in the west and simultaneously line his own purse. The upper country lay in some disarray just then: rebellious Potawatomi, increasing numbers of Indians taking their pelts north to Hudson's Bay, and intertribal warfare between the Fox, Sioux, and Ojibwa, all threatened to disrupt the fur trade. To address this, La Barre needed a real French presence in the west. He dispatched Du Luth to Lake Superior with a party of fifteen canoes and perhaps fifty men to establish trading posts which would stanch the flow of furs northward to the Bay. Stopping off at Michilimackinac, Du Luth rounded up all of the traders there and fortified the Jesuit mission to deter trading ventures from New York. Later that summer, Captain Olivier Morel, Sieur de La Durantaye, arrived with thirty men to take command and Du Luth pressed on to Lake Superior, where he built Forts La Tourette, on Lake Nipigon, and Kaministigoya, on Thunder Bay.

La Durantaye was a formidable character. Born in 1640, he had reached the rank of captain in the Regiment de Carignan-Salières at only twenty-five. He marched against the Mohawk in

1666, returned to France in 1668, but sailed for Canada once again in August 1670. He apparently had reason: only a month later he married Françoise Duquet, a widow of some means. For the next thirteen years, he served in the garrison of Quebec, dabbled in the fur trade, obtained a *seigneurie,* and began a family of ten children. Prickly but able and impeccably honest, he would make Michilimackinac the most important French outpost in the western country. The place took its name from a high, humpbacked island nearby. Michilimackinac, "great turtle" in Algonkian, did, indeed, resemble an immense turtle. The post lay in a cove on the north shore, where the town of Saint Ignace stands today. Baron La Hontan, who arrived there a year later, wrote: "Michilimackinac, the place where I am now is certainly a place of great Importance. . . . Here the Hurons and [Ottawas] have, each of 'em, a Village; the one being severed from the other by a single pallisadoe. . . . In this place the Jesuits have a little house, or college adjoining to a sort of a Church, and inclos'd with pales that separate it from the Village of the Hurons. . . . The Coureurs de Bois have but a small settlement here; though at the same time it is not inconsiderable."[2]

This junction of Lakes Michigan, Huron, and the Saint Mary's River had become a significant place in the wake of the Iroquois invasions. The Huron had settled there with Father Marquette in 1671. Two years later, the Ottawa had begun a village as well. The Indians, in turn, attracted the coureurs de bois. The Straits Indians grew large fields of corn, pumpkins, peas, and squash. For meat, they hunted, but the large population quickly emptied the forests close by. La Hontan reported that by 1684 "they are obliged to travel as much as twenty Leagues in the Woods, before they can kill any Harts or Elks." The real staple of the place was fish: "Trouts as big as one's Thigh," and a seemingly endless supply of white fish.[3]

The settlement lay in a large sandy cove perhaps a mile in circumference. Just back from the water the ground rose sharply to a bluff some 90 feet high. The French town, at the south end of the cove, was a ramshackle affair of a dozen or so log houses 15 or 20 feet square, rudely built with perhaps an attic and roofed with cedar bark. Four hundred yards to the north the Jesuits had their mission house, surrounded with a palisade. Next door, stood a Huron town of perhaps 500 people, also palisaded, but in the Indian fashion with an outer picket some 30 feet high of crossed stakes and a solid inner wall 15 feet high with loopholes for muskets or bows. Within the enclosure stood bark longhouses 100 feet long by 24 feet wide by 20 feet high laid out in regular streets. Separated by a log palisade, the Ottawa village stood just to the north, arranged in much the same manner.[4]

The commandant's duties at Michilimackinac were complex. He regulated the fur trade, kept the peace among the Indians, and recruited warriors for the King's service when required. These last two were no easy task, as the cove seethed with tensions and intrigue. The Hurons, once the principal allies of the French and the dominant player in the fur trade, had become a people without a country and an ethnic minority in the midst of an Algonkian majority. Worse, their neighbors the Ottawas had assumed their position as the principal fur supplier to the French. Antoine Laumet, Sieur de Cadillac, gives a good picture of the Huron: "They are cunning men, intriguing, evil-disposed and capable of great undertakings, but, fortunately their arm is not long enough to execute them; nevertheless since they cannot act like lions they act like Foxes and use every possible means to stir up strife between us and our allies."[5]

Two years before La Durantaye's arrival, the Huron had managed to stir up a great deal of "strife." In September 1681, some Green Bay Indians had captured Annanhac, a Seneca chief, holding him hostage against the return of some of their own captives. For some reason, they brought him to Michilimackinac. The Hurons one day came upon his slave—an Illiniwek girl taken the year before—attempting to escape and brought her back to their village. They had then taunted a band of visiting Illiniwek, calling them cowards if they did not kill Annanhac and recover the girl. The visitors soon rescued her and brought her to Henri Tonti's cabin, where he was staying awaiting the arrival of La Salle for their journey down the Mississippi. The explorer offered tobacco and lent one of the Illiniwek his knife to cut it for their pipes. Just then the Hurons arrived with Annanhac. The chief declared the girl his slave and the Hurons resumed their taunting until one of the Illiniwek seized Tonti's knife and killed the Seneca. The Hurons then sent off word to the Iroquois that the Illiniwek had assassinated Annanhac, with Tonti's knife, and in his presence. This seeming treachery enraged the Seneca against both the French and the Illiniwek.

There were other tensions as well. The Ottawa village originally stood directly adjacent to that of the Huron. In 1687, however, four young Ottawa murdered a Huron chief and they removed their town 1,000 yards to the northeast. Traders charged high prices for their wares, and the Indians responded in kind, as Baron La Hontan observed: "Sometimes these savages sell their Corn very dear, especially when the Beaver trapping happens to not take well: Upon such occasions they make sufficient reprisals upon us for the extravagant price of our commodities."[6] The Jesuits had ministered to the Indians at the Straits for more than a decade, but had made little headway. Most, at best, tolerated the priests.

These, however, were not La Durantaye's only problems. Two hundred and fifty miles to the west lived the Wisconsin nations: the Fox, Ojibwa, Sioux, Sauk, Menominee, and Potawatomi. The Iroquois Wars had driven nearly 20,000 Indians into the region from farther east and friction between them kept La Durantaye commuting back and forth between La Baie des Puans (Green Bay) and Michilimackinac resolving conflicts and keeping the canoe routes open. A commandant was equal parts diplomat, judge, soldier, recruiter, and travelers' aid society. Unlike many of his successors, who employed creative bookkeeping methods, La Durantaye kept meticulous records of his expenditures, and these provide a striking portrait of the daily life and responsibilities of a western post commander. On July 2, 1683, La Durantaye distributed six pounds of tobacco to the "four nations of Michilimackinac." On August 5 he presented the Potawatomi with tobacco, waistcoats, shirts, and stockings. On August 26 he hired eight Potawatomi to paddle him to Wisconsin to reassure the Fox nation after an Iroquois attack. While there, he presented a Fox chief a gun, a waistcoat, a shirt and stockings, and two blankets. On September 25 he hired three Indians to guide him to La Salle's post in the Illinois country. On October 5 he hired another to take him home. On November 20 he distributed eleven pounds of tobacco to the Wisconsin nations to encourage them to go to Montreal to meet with the governor and hired two men to paddle him back to Michilimackinac. The following summer he was recruiting Indians to go south against the Iroquois, rescuing stranded voyageurs, and equipping them with canoes, provisions, and equipment to get home. In addition, he provided presents upon the deaths of notable Indians, a custom known as "covering the dead."[7] Much like the ward-heelers of a later day, funerals constituted an important part of his duties.

Despite his best efforts, the unified command of Michilimackinac and La Baie proved too much for one man and a later governor would appoint Nicolas Perrot commandant in Wisconsin. His first task was to resolve a war between the Sioux, Ojibwa, and Fox. The latter had inflicted a heavy blow against the other two and the situation looked as if it might become much worse. The Ottawa stood ready to intervene on behalf of their Ojibwa kinsmen and, should this happen, the war might become general. The largest impediment to a settlement, Perrot discovered, was an Ojibwa girl held by the Fox. Despite offers of ransom, they intended to burn her alive. Perrot went alone to their town and requested the girl be spared and released. Restoring the captive to her father, he then arranged a peace. That fall he went west to the Mississippi and established Fort Saint Antoine among the Sioux on Lake Pepin.

Under La Durantaye, Du Luth, and Perrot, the new forts proved their value almost immediately. They acted as impartial brokers in local disputes, serving the interests of all concerned. They also rode herd on the fur traders. La Durantaye, a man of good character, expected the traders at his post to follow his example. "If any voyageur Were obliged," wrote the missionary Father Étienne de Carheil, "through any extraordinary necessity, to lodge for any time in the village of the savages, He notified the commandant and the missionary, so that he might be assigned a cabin about which there was no suspicion, that he might lodge there without scandal."[8] Finally, the forts had an important influence on the fur trade itself. The English often sold their goods at cheaper prices, but the new posts allowed the French to provide goods far more conveniently. This apparently mattered a great deal. In 1686, Du Luth's brother the Sieur de La Tourette reported that 1,500 Indians visited his post on Lake Nipigon and that he had quickly run through his stock of goods. Since his fort lay on the main canoe route from Lake Superior to Hudson's Bay, La Tourette had just cost the English a great deal of money.[9]

Ironically, La Durantaye's most delicate diplomacy that first summer had nothing to do with Indians. La Salle's five-year monopoly had lapsed and, given the King's general dissatisfaction with his patron Frontenac, La Barre felt emboldened to seize Forts Frontenac and Saint Louis des Illinois for himself. The governor instructed La Durantaye to escort his traders and one of his officers, the Chevalier de Baugy, to Illinois. La Salle's men might retain their personal property and Tonti could remain to keep an eye on La Salle's goods, but the fort now belonged to La Barre. It was a large convoy of 30 canoes and 90 or 100 men which made its way down Lake Michigan that summer. Encountering La Salle on his way back to Montreal, La Durantaye presented him with the news. There was little the explorer could do, and so he acceded gracefully and then set out for France to get his fort back. Stopping at Chicago, he wrote a last letter to his men instructing them to behave until he could appeal to the King: "Whatever you write, speak always with great respect of the governor and be very punctual in obeying his orders. . . . Finally do nothing which looks like plot or party. You will gain by obeying and lose by murmuring."[10]

About the time La Salle wrote his farewell, La Durantaye, Baugy, and the governor's men arrived at Fort Saint Louis. The site, a sandstone butte some 125 feet high on the south bank of the Illinois 80 miles southwest of Lake Michigan, was perhaps the strongest place in New France. "It is situated," La Salle wrote "on a rock steep on all sides . . . which is six hundred feet in circumference. It is accessible only on the one side where the rise is still quite steep. The neighboring rocks are all lower than this one and the nearest one is two hundred paces away, the others more."[11] The fort itself was equally formidable. La Salle had not built the usual palisaded trading post. It lay in the path of the Iroquois and perhaps even the bellicose Governor Dongan. The explorer knew that he had a fight on his hands, and had built accordingly. Guarding the vulnerable east side stood "a palisade of white oak posts from eight to ten inches in diameter and twenty-two feet high, flanked by three redoubts made of squared beams set one upon the other, and situated so that all defend one another." Four more bastions and pickets 15 feet high guarded the remainder of the perimeter. The most striking feature of the defenses was a "parapet of big trees laid lengthwise one on the other to the height of two men, the whole filled with earth; and at the height of the palisade is a sort of 'cheval de frise,' the points of which are iron to prevent climbing over."[12] The presence of a 12-foot earthen parapet tells a lot about what La Salle thought he might be up against. Such a wall would have required a great deal of labor and so would not have been constructed casually. Earthworks could absorb the shock of cannonballs. Indians had no cannon, but Englishmen did, and so it is reasonable to assume the explorer thought a confrontation with the English likely.

Henri Joutel, who wintered there in 1687, mentions other features probably original: "The river passes at the foot [of the cliff] and M. Tonty has had four big squared timbers placed so that one may draw water from on high in case anyone came to attack it. . . . There are several houses built of squared timbers and the others, more temporary, which are only of stakes."[13] La Salle had brought two gunsmiths, Pierre Prudhomme and Nicholas Doyon, and the two had a forge in operation by the summer of 1683. There was also a storehouse, or *magazin*. All of the buildings stood along the perimeter of the compound with what Joutel describes as "a spacious esplanade or place des armes" (parade ground) in the center.[14]

Completing the fort, Tonti had sent messengers to spread the news: "I invited all of the neighboring tribes to come to it. There needed no great pains or art to get them to come hither." There was good farmland and hunting on either bank of the river and within the year some 500 Indian lodges had sprung up along the valley. This would be the capital of La Salle's Louisiana: "The beauty of the country, the fruitfulness of the land, and the conveniency of a fine navigable river, the nearness of about a hundred different nations, and of those little lakes or rather little seas, which make a fit seat for all the commerce of North America, and reach from the Saint Lawrence to the Gulf of Mexico."[15]

La Salle had come to stay and even before he had completed the fort began assigning seigneurial grants to his men. On December 1, 1682, he deeded Michel Disy 170 acres. The following April, La Salle awarded several more land grants along the river. Jacques Bourdon, Sieur d'Autray, and four associates—the gunsmiths Doyon and Prudhomme and the voyageurs Jean Filastreau and André Hunault—received some two and half miles of river frontage extending downstream from the fort and inland an eighth of a mile. D'Autray would have exclusive rights to the hunting, fishing, and to 250 acres of forest except for such timber as the fort might require. He further received rights to a house lot twenty feet square within the fort.[16]

On August 11, La Salle granted Prudhomme nearly a mile and three-quarters of frontage on the north bank. "In recognition of the services that he has rendered both in the discovery of Louisiana and in the construction of Fort Saint Louis."[17] The grant ran a like distance inland. Prudhomme would enjoy the same privileges as D'Autray, but La Salle reserved to himself access to the slate and clay deposits on the property. It is doubtful that any of these estates ever came to anything. The local Indians probably helped build the fort, as it protected them as much as the French. The speed with which Tonti and La Salle completed it makes it clear that they must have had a great deal of local labor. However, it seems unlikely that the Indians would have helped clear fields as well.

Settling in, La Salle and his men now took stock of this Illinois country. Like most Europeans, the climate took them by surprise. Bathed in warm moist air off the Gulf Stream, France enjoys a remarkably temperate climate. Fort Saint Louis lay on the same latitude as Naples. Illinois, however, was no southern Italy. "Planting is done here only once a year and that is in the month of May, as there is always a hard freeze in April. It is true that the mildness of the month of January . . . at first caused us to believe that this country would be as mild as Provence, but since then we have learned that the winter is not less severe than that of the Iroquois in as much as on March 22, the [Illinois] River was still frozen; and [Lake Michigan] was again as full of ice along the south shore."[18]

Then there was the prairie. In French, the word meant "meadow," which scarcely began to describe its American iteration: broiling hot in summer, blasted by winter winds, swept by wildfires, alternately parched and flooded, it was something altogether different. "It should not be supposed that these lands of which we speak in the country of the Illinois are lands to which one only has to put the plow, for the greater part are drowned by ever so little rain. Others are too dry, and the best require considerable labor to clear off the aspens [poplars] which cover them as well as the marshes which comprise large areas."[19]

Yet, for all of that it was a wondrous country, a virtual paradise compared to the north: At Michilimackinac, the ice remained as late as May. In Illinois, it often broke up at the end of February. Tonti's nephew, Pierre Liette, declared: "The Illinois country is undeniably the most beautiful that is known between the mouth of the Saint Lawrence and that of the Mississippi, which are a thousand leagues apart." Part of its charm lay in the extraordinary variety of things to eat. At modern Joliet, he wrote, "you begin to see the buffalo. As for turkeys, there are quantities of them. There is a game bird, that is abundant, which is a good deal like a French pheasant, and very good." Below the confluence of the Des Plaines and Kankakee Rivers, he declared "you begin to see the beauty of this country both for the soil, which yields bountifully, and for the abundance of animals." In those days, the Illinois Valley was a maze of ponds, sloughs, and swamps. Here, wrote Liette, "you find marshes which in spring and autumn are full of bustards, swans, ducks, cranes, and teal."[20]

There were also oddities: Liette describes, with both zoological and gastronomic interest, his first encounter with possums "as big as a French cat, which have white fur inclined to reddish, as long as that of a marten. . . . They have tails a foot long and as thick as a finger, just like that of a muskrat. . . . They are very good to eat. They are very heavy, and there is no need of running after them for when they see anyone they do not flee; they only open their mouths and you smash their heads with a stick."[21] He also describes "a great abundance of stinking animals" and from his account it would seem that skunks have changed little in the last three and a half centuries. The river provided an abundance of food as well. In the seventeenth century, the Illinois was a clear, fast-running stream, home to some extraordinary fish, as Joutel describes: "There are carp much better than we have in France, two feet long and six inches thick. A savage, in good weather, spears as many as sixty of them in a day. There are brills [channel catfish] of monstrous size. I have seen one of them whose two eyes were sixteen inches apart and whose body was as big as the biggest man."[22] Tonti, however, assured him that they were often eighteen inches between the eyes. One day, a soldier had hooked one and the enormous fish set out for the Mississippi towing man, canoe, and anchor.

Finally, there were the Indians who inhabited the valley. To make money, which La Salle sorely needed just then, he needed customers. To make allies for his great imperial venture, he needed Indians as well. Therefore, the fort served as a store, a fortress, and a repair facility for iron goods and weapons. Given the special interdependence of Fort Saint Louis and its neighbors, the French and Indians interacted with a kind of intimacy unknown on the English frontier.

The nearest and most numerous neighbors, the Illiniwek, lived across the river. By 1684, the French reckoned their village to possess 1,200 warriors. Assuming one warrior to every four to six inhabitants, this produces a figure of nearly 5,000–7,000 people. At the mouth of the Vermilion River, just downstream stood a Shawnee village of 800 to 1,000. Of the Illiniwek, Liette observed: "You can see no finer looking people. They are neither tall nor short usually; there are some you could encompass with two hands. They have legs that seem drawn with an artist's pen. . . . They have faces as beautiful as white milk, in so far as this is possible for Indians of that country. The have the most regular and the whitest teeth imaginable."[23] Fond of tattoos, they adorned much of their bodies with them. In summer the women wore only a knee-length skirt of doe skin or French cloth and moccasins, often finely embroidered with quills. In summer, the men went nearly naked wearing only a loincloth. In winter the Illiniwek donned buffalo robes, often highly decorated.

Primarily farmers, the Illiniwek augmented their crops with hunting and fishing. Theirs was a rich land and they exploited it with considerable skill. During the winter months, they would scatter to hunt, returning to their village at the end of March. Spring planting took place in early May. In June, they "hilled up" the corn, and then set out for a month or more to hunt buffalo. In July and August they harvested their corn along with crops of pumpkins, beans, and watermelons. The Illiniwek also gathered a variety of roots, wild onions, and berries, particularly blackberries.

For the French, however, life at the fort was more leisurely, as Joutel describes: "[Each day] the Indian women brought in something fresh, We wanted not for watermelons, Bread made of Indian corn, bak'd in the Embers, and other such Things and we rewarded them with little presents in return. Indian hunters often came bearing game to sell as well." The clerk of the fort's store, the Sieur de Boisrondet, experimented with growing wheat on Plum Island just downriver and the French actually ate white bread more than 1,000 miles from the Saint Lawrence. As Joutel observed: "We had good Bread and as good Fruit, and had there been any Thing to drink besides Water, we'd have fared well."[24]

The French also enjoyed a variety of diversions. Tonti liked cards and many evenings were spent in high-stakes games of chance. They frequently went out to hunt and fish, both for food and sport. In spring, before the Illiniwek set out to hunt buffalo, they would stage great lacrosse matches in which the whole tribe, both men and women, took part. Using rackets of walnut laced with buffalo sinew and a pinewood ball, they erected two forked saplings on the prairie and points were scored when one team would "go and return" with the ball.[25] Contact rules were at best rudimentary:

> They strike [their opponents'] legs in such a manner that they are crippled sometimes, especially when someone manages to get the ball in hand so as to send it very far so that it has a reasonable chance for getting an impetus and then strikes a player's legs in front. This makes them fall in such a manner that it might be supposed that they would never get up again. I have seen men in this state who were thought to be dead. The players pass over them without any heed; only the women, their relatives, come and carry them off in a deerskin. It is at times as much as two months before they can make use of their legs, and often they break them.[26]

Limbs were broken, eyes put out, and players knocked unconscious: the sort of sport a seventeenth-century European could appreciate.

There were other diversions, some less savory than the good clean mayhem of lacrosse. Inveterate gamblers, the Illiniwek took particular delight in a game of straws where immense sums were wagered. "They are addicted to this game in a degree which cannot be exceeded," reports Liette. "Some of them have staked their sisters after they have lost all of their personal property."[27]

The French took servants from among the local women, and these arrangements often involved more than cooking and cleaning, as Joutel reports: "Adultery is not reckon'd any great crime among them, and there are Women who make no secret of having had to do with French Men. Yet they are not sufficiently addicted to that vice to offer themselves, and they never fall, unless they are sued to, when they are none of the most difficult in the World to be prevail'd on."[28] Joutel misspoke here. Premarital chastity counted for little among the Indians, but adultery *was* a "great crime." Marquette observed that husbands among the Illiniwek were extremely jealous and would cut off the noses of unfaithful wives. Liette wrote that a chief came to him to complain that his wife had gone to the cabin of the Frenchman's servant. Liette went to the man's house with the chief and ordered him to open the door. After some delay, the woman finally emerged carrying "a bit of paper containing some vermillion. Her husband laid hold of her and led her off behind one of the bastions of our fort, where there were twenty young men who did not spare her."[29] The Frenchman reported that he knew of 100 women scalped for adultery in his time in Illinois.

The traders sometimes paid a price for their free-and-easy ways as well. Jean de Broyeux, a veteran of the Ottawa country, first appeared in Illinois in 1684 and eventually became *commis*, or clerk, of Tonti's warehouse at Fort Saint Louis. In the 1690s, he returned home to find himself the most famous cuckold in the colony. Tested by his long absences, his wife Marguerite succumbed to the attentions of Captain François Desjordy, a soldier, and the two took up lodgings. The arrangement lasted several years, and finally the authorities intervened. Denied communion and threatened with excommunication, they stood their ground. Frontenac tried to mediate and sent Desjordy to command at Fort Frontenac. Marguerite, however, went to court and the whole affair ascended the French bureaucracy, ending up before the King's Privy Council. In 1699, poor Jean died in Montreal. Madame Broyeux, however, lived on in Batiscan for another thirty years.

The new commandant of Fort Saint Louis, Lieutenant Louis-Henri, le Chevalier de Baugy, had arrived in the colony as part of La Barre's escort, and the governor selected him to go west with La Durantaye to command at Le Rocher. Although the date of his birth is unknown, his rank and the fact that he lived until 1720 indicate that he was still a young man in 1684. His military record indicates considerable talent, and his surviving correspondence and reports show him a man of some wit and education. Over the course of that first year, he would have need of all these traits.

The personality of a post commander tended to set the tone for his fort. Baugy does not seem to have concerned himself with the moral rectitude of his men as La Durantaye had; he had bigger things to worry about. Half of them were actually La Salle's and Tonti outranked him both in seniority and prestige among his own men and the neighboring Indians. The latter particularly admired the iron prosthetic Tonti wore where his hand had once been, and called him *main de fer,* or "Iron Hand." However, Baugy does not seem to have felt any great loyalty to La Barre: He was simply a young officer obeying orders. He and Tonti appear to have gotten on well enough and he seems to have genuinely admired the Italian. His discretion in these matters would bear fruit.

The winter of 1683–1684 passed quietly. By late February, stores at the post had run low, but the river was breaking up and Baugy could expect the arrival of a supply convoy shortly. A party from Montreal had wintered on the Kankakee River and with open water the party was expected to appear any day. On February 28, therefore, Baugy sold off most of what remained of his gunpowder to the Illiniwek across the river. They wished to go hunting, and with the weather improving and fresh supplies on the way, the Chevalier saw no harm in granting their request for powder.

Two voyageurs loaded a dugout and paddled across the river, and upon reaching the far bank they began unloading. Suddenly, gunfire erupted off to the west in the direction of the Shawnee town. A little while later a number of Shawnee and their families came running up the bank toward the fort. The Iroquois had returned. The Miami and Loup camped nearby came up the rock as well. Baugy and Tonti now had to move quickly. They ordered a dugout brought up to the fort to store water, and the Chevalier had shots fired to warn the men across the river. These ran back to their canoe and attempted to load it to return. However, the Iroquois now appeared, hundreds of them, close behind the fleeing Shawnee. Dumping their cargo on the far bank, the two

The Great Turtle and the Rock 59

men just managed to reach the safety of the fort before the Iroquois arrived at the foot of the Rock.

The place could not be carried by assault, but the Iroquois had come some 600 miles from western New York in winter snow and their blood was up. They had overrun the Shawnee village earlier, and the pursuit up the bank had wrecked any semblance of control the chiefs might have had. The warriors swarmed up the trail into a storm of musketfire. The attack failed as quickly as it had begun and the Iroquois withdrew with a loss of perhaps twenty men. The attackers now settled down to a siege. Tonti, Baugy, and their men must have been relieved when the first attack petered out, but they remained in considerable danger. The fort now held 24 Frenchmen, 22 Indian warriors, and their families: perhaps 80 or 90 people. They had neither food nor water for so many, but they had another problem: With most of the remaining powder in the bushes on the north bank, they had little to defend the place. Baugy gave orders that no one should fire unless he could count on a hit. Eventually he had to halt even this to hoard what remained of the ammunition in case the Iroquois tried another assault.

Just how many Iroquois they faced is a question. Baugy never made a guess. Tonti said 200. On the other hand, according to the Iroquois themselves, somewhere around 500 men had laid siege to the Rock. These were daunting odds, but their numbers now became a liability. The Iroquois traveled on foot and so could carry few provisions. They would have sent out hunters and foragers, but feeding so large a stationary force in late winter in north-central Illinois proved an impossible task. Unaware of Baugy's problems, the Iroquois tried to lure the defenders out. They bragged of the captives they had taken and sang rude songs to mock the French. Finally, they sent negotiators to try to get Baugy to withdraw: "Twenty more Iroquois braves [asked] to enter the fort which [was] granted to them, without weapons." However, the French allies "as quick as they could, made them sit down and one by one cut them into pieces throwing their heads and arms over the palisade."[30] With this, what had once been an Indian war now became an emphatically French war as well.

The Iroquois withdrew on March 8, but Baugy had no idea whether they might return and sent word to Michilimackinac asking for assistance. When his letter reached the Straits, La

Durantaye rounded up 60 coureurs de bois and set out for the south. Rescuing 24 with 60 from 500 might seem questionable odds, but La Durantaye was that sort of man. By the time he reached Illinois on May 21, however, the invaders had departed. On the other hand, he had brought with him a new threat: the glowering Jesuit, Allouez. With La Salle gone and Frontenac ousted, the Society of Jesus saw an opportunity to recover the Illinois country for God and their order. For the next three years, Allouez tended to his converts without interference, but wanted Tonti and his people out entirely. Reports filtered back to Quebec of the goings on at the fort which were duly forwarded to Paris, with Allouez the most likely source: "Every 8 days they marry squaws after the Indian fashion of that country, whom they purchase from the parents at the expense of the merchants. Those fellows pretending to be independent and masters on their distant lands."[31] The missionary's carping did no good, for La Salle's star had risen once again and the old priest would flee Illinois on hearing rumors of the explorer's return. The Iroquois killed him in southern Michigan in 1689.

The Jesuits routinely proclaimed themselves the protectors of Indian women and gained converts and support thereby, but the impact of the priests was actually more ambiguous. Pierre Liette tells a story of the arrival of the first White woman in Illinois. Madame Le Sieur, "very tall, slender, blonde, and who has a well-shaped face, caused a sensation and was mobbed with visitors for two whole days." Liette, encountering a woman he knew in the throng, asked what she thought: "I wish she had never come to this country. I believed that our women and girls could hold their own for beauty with other natives . . . ; but . . . we are only monsters compared with your women. . . . Her little children are like the little Jesuses that Father Gravier shows us every day."[32] It is interesting to consider who caused the more harm: the amorous voyageurs with their brandy and presents or the missionaries with their Caucasian virgin and her blond child.

While all of this went on, La Salle had taken ship for France in late 1683 and had pled his case before the King that winter. Mightily displeased with La Barre's actions, Louis rebuked him in a scathing memorandum. He began by noting that he had abused Colbert's licenses: "I see by your letters that the person named Du Luth and the Chevalier Baugy have permission to trade for a whole year with a large number of canoes which are accompanying them, that these permissions have been signed only by yourself." The King also took exception to La Barre's seizure of La Salle's property and declared that he should "return all that belongs to him to the Sieur de La Forest, who is returning by my orders to the said country with the men engaged by the said La Salle."[33] La Salle himself, however, would never return. With his properties secured, he now hatched a plan to found a colony at the mouth of the Mississippi. Everything went wrong, as so often happened with his projects, and he was murdered by his own men on the coast of Texas in 1687.

La Barre was now in trouble. His handing of La Salle and his subversion of the fur trade had raised the King's ire. Events the following summer would send him packing. The attack on Fort Saint Louis des Illinois presented the governor with a serious problem. Up until that point, the Iroquois had confined their aggression to the Illiniwek, which gave the French maneuvering room to seek a diplomatic solution to the war. Now the situation had changed. The Iroquois had fired on the French flag and the King's honor required retaliation. The Canadians, moreover, saw this as further justification for the war they had urged on the governor since he had arrived. La Barre, therefore, reluctantly began to organize a punitive expedition. He sent word to La Durantaye and Du Luth at Michilimackinac to assemble the western nations and meet him on Lake Ontario. The governor, for his part, would ascend the upper Saint Lawrence with a force of French regulars and Canadian militia.

The Iroquois made preparations as well. On August 2, a delegation of Onondaga and Cayuga met with Dongan and Lord Howard, the governor of Virginia, at the town hall of Albany to request assistance:

> Brother Corlaer [Dongan]:
> Your Sachem [the King] is a great sachem and we are but a small people, when the Manhatans . . . , Virginia, and . . . Maryland were but a small people and we a great people, and finding that they were a good people we gave them land and treated them civilly, now since you are a great people and we are but small, you will protect us from the French, which if you do not, we shall lose all of our hunting and Bevers [sic], The French will have all the Bevers, and are angry with us for bringing any to you.[34]

The Iroquois were clearly concerned and the English might have used the situation to bind the Five Nations to them more closely. Dongan, however, missed the opportunity. He offered help but on terms too dear for the Iroquois and his high-handed manner temporarily strained the alliance.

In the end, however, it did not matter much. La Barre's plan went badly from the start. The year before, he had requested 600 regulars to defend the colony. The King had sent 150 green recruits, defective muskets, and worthless swords instead. La Barre also had no cannon small enough to be carried by canoe. Despite this, he did his best and by mid-July he had some 800 troops and militia and 400 mission Indians assembled in Montreal. Now, however, he panicked. He squandered ten days writing Governor Dongan to propose a joint expedition against the Iroquois to avenge the murder of some colonists or, failing that, he suggested, New York remain neutral in the war. There was precious little chance of this happening, and it cost La Barre time he could ill afford to lose.

Arriving on Lake Ontario, the Iroquois managed to totally befuddle the poor governor with alternating threats of war and peace and dragged him into protracted negotiations. Supplies ran low, influenza broke out, and sensing victory, the Iroquois negotiators began to bully the hapless governor. Deathly ill himself, La Barre finally agreed to a treaty in which the Iroquois promised not to plunder French traders and would leave Fort Saint Louis unmolested, but could continue their war against the Illiniwek. The next day, La Durantaye and Du Luth arrived with 150 coureurs de bois and 600 Indians. The governor ordered them to return home, much to the disgust of the western nations, who saw the campaign as a way to finally halt Iroquois depredations.

La Barre's treaty was a disaster. The western nations had long feared that the French would sell them out if push came to shove. The Huron plot to kill Annahac at Michilimackinac had sought to force the French into open war with the Iroquois. The massacre of their negotiators at Fort Saint Louis came out of the same concern. Now, despite their best efforts, the French had, in fact, abandoned them. The Illiniwek were clients of the King of France. If he could not protect his Indian allies, they would have no reason to remain allies and New France would have no reason to exist.

Sifting through his annual reports, Louis recognized that the fate of the Illiniwek and New France were intimately linked. In March 1685, the King graciously wrote La Barre: "Having been informed that your years do not permit you to support the fatigues inseparable from the duties of your office..., I send you this letter to advise you that I have selected Sieur de Denonville to serve in your place."[35] He wrote to the intendant De Meulles in a blunter vein: "His abandonment of the Illinois has seriously displeased me, and has determined me to recall him."[36] Taking up a third sheet of paper, the enraged King then set down instructions to his new governor-general which left no doubt as to his intentions: "He must humble the pride of the Iroquois, give assistance to the Illinois and the other Indian allies whom Governor La Barre has abandoned, and begin by a firm and vigorous conduct to teach the Iroquois that they will have everything to fear for themselves if they do not submit to the conditions which he may wish to impose upon them."[37]

Louis would take no chances; he would have no more La Barres. Instead, he chose Jacques-René de Brisay, the Marquis de Denonville. The Marquis, fifty-eight years old, came from a noble military family. A veteran of the Dutch Wars, he was tough, competent, and energetic. An invasion of the Seneca country would require an expedition operating nearly 400 miles from Montreal and involve coordinating the movements of French and Indian auxiliaries spread over more than 1,000 miles of country. It was an operation on a scale not seen since the days of the *conquistadores,* and in many ways more difficult. However if the thing could be done, Denonville appeared the man for the task.

The King's appointment of Denonville would set great events in motion, but at Fort Saint Louis the removal of La Barre had more comic repercussions. That spring, a Frenchman appeared announcing himself as Captain Richard Pilette and presented a commission from the new governor to assume command of the post. Tonti, thinking the man an imposter, refused and Pilette ordered him arrested. Furious, Tonti swung at him with his famed iron hand and knocked out the man's front teeth. He then ordered the charlatan thrown out of the gate. The path down from Fort Saint Louis, always steep, was icy with sleet just then. Unable to recover his balance, Pilette slid to the bottom shredding his trousers and cutting himself on the rocks and brambles.

Apparently none daunted, he resumed his actual career as a coureur de bois, settled nearby, and raised a large Indian family. For the next two centuries, the Pilettes proudly related the story of their family's "descent."

A funny story, it also helps explain something important. The Indian alliance would survive La Barre's blundering, and much of the credit should go to the post commanders: La Durantaye, Du Luth, Perrot, and Tonti. Down the centuries, they have remained larger-than-life characters and would have seemed such to the Indians. Each had a distinct style: La Durantaye's steadfastness and stern piety, Perrot's subtlety and skill with oratory, and Du Luth's utter indifference to danger. Tonti's iron prosthetic became his signature. The story of Pilette's teeth would have quickly spread, and though the Indians thought La Barre a fool, "Iron Hand" remained worthy of respect. It was on these personal ties that the French alliance now rested.

THREE

War in the Wilderness, 1687–1701

IN THE WINTER OF 1686–1687, an aide prepared a memorandum for the Marquis de Seignelay summing up the situation in New France: "Canada is encompassed by many powerful colonies of English who labor incessantly to ruin it by exciting all our Indians, and drawing them away with their peltries for which the said English give them a great deal more merchandise than the French."[1] The Iroquois were again loose in the west as well. Caught between the Hudson's Bay Company, the Iroquois, and Albany, New France was indeed "surrounded."

The tone of the memoir was as important as its content. On Denonville's expedition, it declared, "depends either the ruin of the Country and of the Religion if he be not assisted, or the Establishment of Religion, of Commerce and the King's Power over all of North America, if granted the required aid." Only twenty years had passed since Colbert had cautioned against expansion. His son, Seignelay, would now place before the King a plan for a continental empire. La Salle's great vision had taken hold in France. Thomas Dongan had raised the stakes as well, declaring, "That if [the Iroquois] are attacked by Monsieur de Denonville the latter will have to do with him."[2] As English subjects, an attack on Iroquoia amounted to an attack on England. North America was becoming a dangerous place.

News crossed the Atlantic slowly, and so the author had not yet heard of events which had changed the complexion of things in Canada. To begin, the menace of the Hudson's Bay Company had vanished. In March 1686, the Chevalier de Troyes had led 30 regulars and 70 militia and coureurs de bois north to burn out the English. In an epic 85-day journey up the Ottawa and down the Abitibi, they overwhelmed Moose Factory, Rupert Fort, and Albany House and secured the trade of the country for the French.

De Troyes's campaign was important for another reason as well. The Chevalier, new to the country, knew nothing of the wilderness. However, as a man of considerable wit, humor, and psychological subtlety, he devised an ad hoc command structure which smoothly merged his military experience with the Canadians' woodcraft. He had with him three young colonial officers, all brothers: Le Moyne d'Iberville, Maricourt, and Saint Helene. Rather than risk making a fool of himself in the rapids and on the portages, he left them to command day-to-day operations. After a near-mutiny, he removed most of the regular army discipline, keeping only basic things like the posting of sentries, and reduced penalties for infractions. In return, the Canadians paddled nearly 2,000 miles for him, overcame ice, snow, and forest fires, stormed forts, hijacked ships, and relieved the Hudson's Bay Company of something like 50,000 prime beaver pelts worth £75,000. Clearly the Canadians had a marked talent for this sort of thing and de Troyes's arrangements began a new style of command which could harness it.

The reduction of Hudson's Bay had secured New France's northern frontier, but a new danger had appeared. In 1686, Governor Dongan had tested France's monopoly of the Great Lakes trade by sending a party of Senecas and renegade coureurs de bois to Michilimackinac. The Ottawa and Huron, delighted with their prices and angered by La Barre's bungled campaign two years earlier, had welcomed them. Having done a lively business, Dongan's party got away without Captain La Durantaye being able to do anything about it. This success led Dongan to write: "The great difference between us is about the Beaver Trade, and in truth they have the advantage of us in it & that by noe other means than by their industry in making discoveries in Ye Country before us. . . . Before my coming hither, noe man of our government ever went beyond the [Seneca] country." Dongan's expedition to Michilimackinac changed all that. Encouraged by his success, he wrote, "I am sending a Scotch gentleman called

McGreger (that formerly in the French service) along with our People hee has orders not to disturb or meddle with the French, and I hope they will not meddle with him."[3] The French would most assuredly "meddle with him." The Canadians could not match English prices and, with their Indian policy in disarray, Albany traders traveling the lakes posed a mortal threat.

The Iroquois remained defiant as well, and Denonville proposed an immense pincer movement against them involving simultaneous attacks against the Mohawk and Seneca. The largest military operation in the colony's history, it would involve nearly 4,000 French regulars, militia, coureurs de bois, and Indians. Messages went out in the fall of 1686 to Du Luth, La Durantaye, and Tonti to recruit all of the coureurs, voyageurs, and Indians they could and bring them south to Lake Ontario the following June. Denonville also sent Tonti 150 muskets and La Durantaye another 300 to arm their expeditions. An ambitious project, it fell apart almost at once. The King vacillated about sending reinforcements and the planned assault on the Mohawk went by the board. Nevertheless, Denonville persevered, assembling provisions, hiring canoes, and building bateaux (large wooden rowing boats) for the regulars.

Denonville's great expedition departed Montreal on June 13. Twice the size of the Regiment de Carignan twenty years before, it comprised 800 regulars, 800 militia, 400 Indians, and 100 voyageurs and bateaumen. For two and a half weeks Denonville's army worked its way up the Saint Lawrence to Fort Frontenac, arriving on June 30. Resting a few days, the governor resumed his advance along the south shore of Lake Ontario. On July 10, he met up with La Durantaye, Du Luth, and Tonti with 180 coureurs de bois and 400 Indians and the combined force landed at Irondequoit Bay. Building a stockade to protect the stores and boats, they prepared to march inland.

On July 13, Denonville formed his column for the final advance on the Seneca town of Ganondagan. In front he placed three companies of coureurs de bois, 170 men under La Durantaye, Tonti, and Du Luth. On either flank, he placed western Indians. Behind these came the regulars and militia, with the remaining Indians in the rear. All went well until they neared the town. Ganondagan stood atop a 200-foot hill with a marshy stream in front. The Seneca had learned of the French plan from two Indian deserters and made their stand at the foot of the hill. Placing 500 men behind the creek to block the French advance, they hid 300 warriors in the swamp and planned to let Denonville's men pass through the marsh and then attack them from the flank and rear.

Initially, the plan seemed to work. The coureurs passed with their Ottawa, Potawatomi, and Huron flankers without detecting the Seneca. Now, however, the defenders made a mistake. Instead of waiting for the main force, they attacked the rear of La Durantaye's men. This mistake may have saved Denonville's army, but the attack was nevertheless shattering. The Seneca had picked their ground well. The weather had turned hot and the French column had become strung out along the road. No one could see more than twenty yards in the tall grass and black powder smoke, and in the noise and confusion few could hear the shouted orders of the officers. Rushing blindly forward, the main body fired into the advance party. A portion of La Durantaye's Indians fled, leaving the coureurs to deal with a force four or five times their number. A company of Canadian militia, coming to their aid, broke and fled to the rear. The regulars panicked and fell back as well. The coureurs' position was now critical. Tonti's company alone had lost seven men. Father Enjalran from Michilimackinac, who had marched with the Indians, fell, too, castrated by a ball.

Now, however, the tide began to turn. The fleeing militia ran into the men of Montreal coming up, and their captain Dugué rallied the panicked men. Christian Mohawks and Hurons from the Saint Lawrence stood firm as well. The loss of three chiefs testifies to the ferocity of their fight. One, La Cendre Chaude, had been with the Mohawk who attacked the mission of Saint Ignace in 1649. Long since a Christian, he died now in the service of the French. The stand of the Montreal militia and Christian Indians bought the army critical time. Denonville and his lieutenant Captain Hector de Callières arrived and took charge of the field. Spurning cover, the two paced about in their shirtsleeves giving orders and restoring confidence. Having steadied his main force, Denonville ordered an advance which broke through to La Durantaye's hard-pressed men and the Seneca fled.

The governor had a victory of sorts, but now squandered it. Despite warnings from Thomas Dongan of the impending invasion, the Seneca had done little to prepare and their women, children, and elderly remained in the town. If Denonville had pressed his attack, he might have captured a sizable portion of the Seneca nation. Instead he halted for twenty-four hours. According to La Hontan, the ambush had left the governor badly shaken and he used the excuse that he needed to secure his wounded. Frantic with the delay, the allied Indians offered to carry them on their backs if only the governor would attack. This he declined to do and the Seneca escaped, bloodied but intact. Denonville later stated that he halted his men for lack of intelligence. He had dense undergrowth before him, no idea of how many men he faced, and no map of the country through which the pursuit would have to take place. A heavy rain further delayed the French, and it was not until the 14th that the French actually entered the town. By then only two or three old women remained.

The Seneca gave a somewhat different account. According to one sachem, they had evacuated the town well before the French arrived and most of their warriors had left to escort the women and children south. By the time Denonville set out from Irondequoit Bay, only about 100 men remained. These called for reinforcements and some 350 returned, mostly young warriors brave enough but undisciplined. The rest roughly matches the French version, with a bloody hand-to-hand fight in which the French and Indians first broke, withdrew 150 yards, and then came on again.

> The [Seneca] Continued the fight with there [sic] hatchets but Perceiving at Last that the French were too Numerous and would not give ground some of the [Seneca] begun to Retreat, whereupon the French Indians Cryed out the [Senecas] Runn and the rest heareing that follwd the first party that gave way . . . [they] in there retreat were followed about half an English mile. And if the enemy had followd them further, the [Seneca] would have lost abundance of People, because they carried off there [sic] wounded men, and were resolv'd to Stick to them and not leave them. . . . There was amongst the 450 [Senecas] five women who Engaged as well as the men, and were Resolv'd not to Leave there husbands but live and dye with them.[4]

Estimates for the casualties at Ganondagan vary wildly. Denonville reported 22 killed and wounded with the Seneca losing just over 100. The Seneca reported 16 dead, having killed 12 French and their allied Indians. La Hontan lists 110 French and allies dead with 20–30 wounded and a Seneca loss of 80. Whatever the losses, one thing seems clear: the peculiar character of wilderness fighting had unnerved a European general. He had little faith in his coureurs de bois or Indian auxiliaries, and little sense of how to use them. So ended Denonville's great campaign, begun with such hopes that spring. In the end, he contented himself with razing Seneca crops and villages. In two weeks, the governor estimated that he had destroyed 400,000 bushels of corn. The expedition returned to Montreal declaring victory, but had accomplished little. The Seneca suffered famine and hardship, but this only hardened their resolve.

That winter, the Seneca blockaded the French fort at Niagara and 89 of the garrison of 100 perished from scurvy and fever. They also attacked Forts Frontenac and Chambly. Faced with this, Denonville tried to patch up a peace with the Iroquois, but now events intervened. The Huron chief Kondiaronk at Michilimackinac had promised the governor that he would bring his people down to attack the Iroquois, and in the spring of 1688, he set out for the south. Arriving at Fort Frontenac, the commandant informed him that the governor was negotiating peace and that he should return home. Kondiaronk, outraged, determined to destroy the peace before it happened. As always, he feared that the French would abandon their allies to protect their colony. The Huron had supported both La Barre's and Denonville's abortive attacks on the Seneca. With the French out of the equation, what would prevent them retaliating?

Before departing, Kondiaronk made discreet inquiries as to the route the Iroquois diplomats would take to Montreal. Then, ostensibly setting off for home, he laid an ambush for them at Famine Bay on Lake Ontario. A few days later, the ambassadors passed that way and Kondiaronk kidnapped them. Returning to Fort Frontenac, he announced that he had just wrecked the peace and that "we shall see how Ononthio will get out of this business."[5] (The Chevalier de Montmagny replaced Champlain in 1636. The Iroquois translated his name as Ononthio, or "Big Mountain," and this word became a generic term for French governors.) Returning to his men, Kondiaronk met with one of the Iroquois emissaries. The man demanded he be released as a

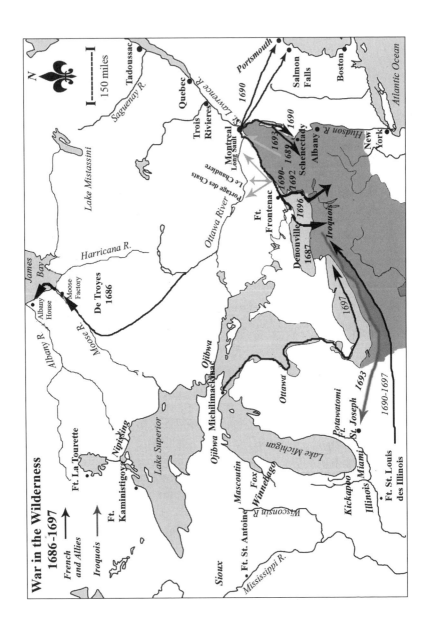

diplomat on a peace errand. The Huron feigned surprise and told him that he knew nothing of peace. The French had sent him to kill them. With this, he immediately released all his captives but one and sent them home with apparently heartfelt apologies. Kondiaronk then returned to Michilimackinac with the remaining prisoner. Arriving at the Straits, he turned the Iroquois over to La Durantaye. The captain, ignorant of Denonville's peace initiative, had him shot. Kondiaronk then freed another Iroquois prisoner and sent him home to tell his people of the treachery of the French. The governor's peace was over.

The next year, 1689, England declared war on France and Dongan renewed his support for overt Iroquois aggression. On August 5, 1,500 warriors attacked the village of La Chine near Montreal. English ships bearing the news from Europe had arrived at New York months before those bound for New France, and so the blow caught the village completely unprepared. The French reported that the attackers had killed, burned, or carried off more than 300 people, though modern scholars say the number was more like 24 dead with 80 taken captive. In any case, the raid stunned the French. Up to this point, the Europeans had tried to exempt their people from the horrors of Indian-style warfare. The French, English, and Dutch had usually ransomed White captives and arranged their return to their respective colonies. After La Chine, the French wasted little time on such niceties. Dongan's use of Indians against Whites initiated a kind of ferocity never seen before in colonial conflict but which now became common until the fall of Quebec some seventy years later.

In October, a ship arrived at Quebec carrying Count Frontenac with orders recalling Denonville. The former governor had spent the past seven years lobbying to obtain a post and when Denonville had requested a replacement due to age and ill health Louis sent Frontenac to Canada once again. No one was particularly happy to see him, nor he them, as he had actually hoped for something better than the wilds of North America. Still, the governor and the Canadians were stuck with each other. Out of this dubious union, ironically, would come New France's finest hour.

In the winter of 1690, the French struck back. In February, 210 French and Indians under Nicholas d'Aillesbout de Manthet

War in the Wilderness 73

and Jacques Le Moyne de Saint Helene marched south from Montreal toward New York. They had no specific orders, but hoped to attack Albany. The Indians, however, preferred the village of Schenectady, a few miles upriver. The invaders found it asleep with the gates open and unguarded. Within two hours, they had overwhelmed the place, killed 60 people, and destroyed 80 houses, livestock, and grain stores worth 400,000 livres, and led away thirty English captives. A month later a second party destroyed the town of Salmon Falls, New Hampshire, burning 27 houses and killing 2,000 head of cattle. A force of 200 English militia from nearby Portsmouth attempted to cut off their retreat, but the French ambushed and routed them, escaping with little loss. Meeting up with another party from Quebec, the combined force then laid waste to Casco, Maine, and returned to Quebec.

The French had wrought havoc on the English colonies, but in the upper country a disaster loomed. News of La Chine had filtered west and, like most rumors, it grew with each retelling. By the time it reached Michilimackinac, Montreal, not La Chine, had fallen. The Indians at the Straits, fearful of being caught on the losing side, began to make overtures to the Iroquois and by the spring of 1690 it appeared that the whole French alliance might unravel. To counter this, Frontenac dispatched a "great convoy" of trade goods, gifts, and weapons to Michilimackinac to restore confidence and resupply the Indians at the post.

The convoy departed up the Ottawa on May 22 under Louis de La Porte de Louvigny. He brought with him 140 coureurs de bois and an escort of 30 men who would accompany him to the Calumet Portage 150 miles above Montreal. The Iroquois knew of the convoy and had sent 60 men in 13 canoes to intercept it. Below Portage des Chats, 12 days out, De Louvigny's van of 30 men in 3 canoes paddled into an ambush and took a galling fire at close range which killed or wounded 8. The rest got ashore, but were pinned down by Iroquois firing from the forest. Hearing the musketry, the main body came ashore some distance downriver. De Louvigny wanted to march his men up and take the Iroquois in the flank. Nicolas Perrot, the party's negotiator and titular commander, refused, however, fearing the Iroquois might capture the goods left behind by the main party. Frantic, De Louvigny begged him to release his troops before the Iroquois wiped out the men pinned on the bank. Perrot finally relented and the French charged up the shore and routed the Iroquois, killing 30, taking a few captives, and driving the rest in headlong flight back to their canoes.

The convoy arrived at Michilimackinac to find the Indians close to open rebellion. Sensing the urgency, Perrot put on a show based upon his twenty-five years experience in the country. He sent news of their impending arrival and La Durantaye lined up his hundred soldiers and traders, their muskets loaded with blank charges, to fire a salute. However, the captain took the precaution of ordering each man to carry a ball in his mouth in case anything went wrong. "The canoes then came into view, at their head the one in which was the Iroquois slave; according to custom, he was made to sing, all the time standing upright. The Nipissings who had accompanied the French to the fort kept time by loud shouts of 'Sassakoue!' followed by volleys of musketry."[6] They paddled past the Ottawa and Huron villages but did not land until they came to the French town. They fired a salute to the shore, and La Durantaye's men fired returning the honor. Suitably impressed, the Huron and Ottawa took no action.

Perrot then held a council at the Jesuit house and gave a lengthy speech. He first dismissed La Chine as no more than a raid. He then said that they should consider the French "a great river which never ran dry, and whose course could not be checked by any barrier. That they ought to regard the five Iroquois nations as five cabins of muskrats in a marsh which the French would soon drain off, and then burn them there."[7] The pageantry, oratory, and presents did the trick. The Huron and Ottawa renewed their loyalty, and the rest of the western nations followed suit. With confidence restored, the tribes assembled a great convoy, 300 warriors in 110 canoes loaded with 100,000 crowns worth of furs, and went down to Montreal to renew their fidelity to the governor.

The convoy had also delivered dispatches from Frontenac ordering La Durantaye to turn over the post to De Louvigny. Why the governor should have replaced a distinguished, experienced commander with a far less accomplished man is hard to fathom. Frontenac declared the change necessary to protect Michilimackinac from the Iroquois. As La Durantaye had successfully defended his post from just this danger for nearly a

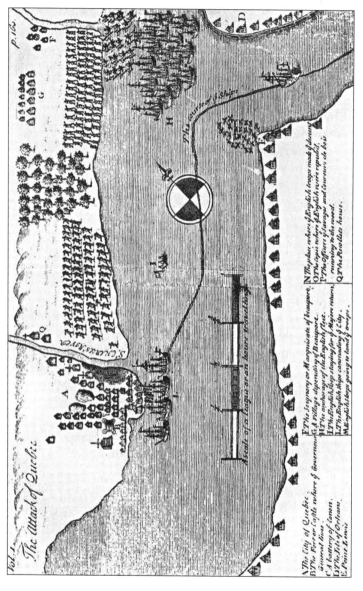

"The Attack of Quebec," from Reuben Gold Thwaites, ed., *The Baron Labontan's New Voyages to North America* (Chicago: A. C. McClurg & Company, 1905), 316–317.

decade, this claim is absurd. The intendant thought that De Louvigny had offered to pay an annual fee of 500 livres for the post. This, however, seems too low a figure to have interested the Count. More likely, De Louvigny was a young officer on the make with an interest in the fur trade. That same year, he took out a land grant at Fort Saint Louis in the Illinois country. It would seem the governor picked him as a more pliable candidate than the stern La Durantaye. De Louvigny's successor, Antoine Laumet, Sieur de Cadillac, would prove even more cooperative.

In the fall, a new threat emerged. Outraged at the sacking of the New England frontier and casting covetous eyes on the French fishery, Governor William Phips of Massachusetts organized an expedition against Quebec. He sailed for the Saint Lawrence on August 20 with 32 ships and 2,000 militia. Headwinds, weather, and the shoals of the lower river slowed his progress, however, and the fleet did not arrive until October 16. The delay probably saved the town, as it had only 200 defenders when the English reached the mouth of the river. By the time they arrived, however, Frontenac had hurried east from Montreal and assembled three battalions of French regulars and a large force of Canadian militia and Indians, nearly 3,000 all told. Phips delivered an ultimatum demanding the surrender of the town and Frontenac responded contemptuously that he had no reply "save from the mouths of my cannon and from my musketry."[8]

On October 18, Phips landed 1,200 militia on the north bank of the river east of the city. These were to attack Quebec from the east while he landed a second smaller force in the lower town covered by fire from his ships. The plan collapsed almost as soon as it had begun. Frontenac kept nearly all of his troops in or near the city and sent only 200 coureurs de bois and allied Indians under Jacques Le Moyne de Saint Helene to harass the landing. At age thirty-one, he was already an experienced wilderness fighter. In 1684, he had marched with La Barre on his disastrous expedition against the Iroquois. In 1686, he and his brothers had accompanied De Troyes's expedition to burn the English out of Hudson's Bay. The next year, he had commanded 300 Indians in Denonville's expedition. In February 1690, he had marched against Schenectady. The New Englanders had never encountered anything quite like him before.

The English came ashore in sixty pinnaces. Saint Helene, lacking the men to oppose a landing, posted his force in a rocky thicket about a mile to the west. The Massachusetts men advanced in European order with flags and drums. All went well till they came to the woods: "We suffered them to enter, and then fir'd upon 'em, lying flat upon the ground till they fir'd their pieces; after which we sprung up, and drawing into knots here and there, repeated our fire with such success, that the *English* Militia perceiving our savages fell into confusion and disorder, and their Batallions were broke."[9] Crying, "Indians! Indians!" the Puritans fled back to their boats. Nothing happened the next day, but on the 20th the English landed four cannon to renew the attack. There was no panic this time, but they could not dislodge the French and Indians. The English withdrew to their boats the next day, leaving behind their guns and equipment.

It had been a bloody fight. La Hontan estimated the English losses in the hundreds while the French suffered 40 casualties, including Saint Helene, who died of an infected leg wound. English estimates were considerably lower, but whatever the number, they had been roughly handled. Phips departed downriver a few days later, defeated by 200 French frontiersmen and a handful of Indians. A planned expedition from New York never got farther than the south end of Lake Champlain.

Except for desultory raids, the attack on Quebec effectively marked the end of King William's War in the east. The Canadians had accomplished a great deal with limited resources, but had also benefited from events beyond their control. In 1686 James II, with war clearly in the offing, had sought to strengthen his American colonies against a possible Canadian attack. He united the Puritan colonies into one large province, the Dominion of New England, under a royal military governor. In 1688 he added New York and the two Jerseys (East and West) and placed Edmund Andros in charge. The move made sense at a variety of levels. The governor had strong ties to the Iroquois, essential in any war with New France. Despite his colony's numerical weakness, the governor of New France effectively commanded all of the resources of Canada and could mobilize them far more easily than could any one English colony. The Dominion and its viceregal governor now cancelled that advantage. In his commission, the King gave Andros "full power and authority to levy arme muster and command or employ, all persons whatsoever residing within our said Territory and Dominion of New England and, as occasion shall serve, them to transfers [*sic*] from one place to another for the resisting and withstanding all enemies pyrats and rebells, both at land and sea."[10] Frontenac had enjoyed such authority and it had allowed him to throw 3,000 men in front of Phips on short notice. The arrangement, however, did not last. The colonists resented the Dominion, as it rode roughshod over their colonial charters. Worse, Andros was diligent in enforcing the Navigation Acts along his coasts and in stamping out smuggling. For a year, the Americans fumed. In 1689, however, they had an opportunity to overthrow this perceived despotism.

At the beginning of 1689, William of Orange became King of England, ousting the Catholic James Stuart. In New York, a German immigrant, Jacob Leisler, took advantage of the anti-Catholic hatreds of the colony to launch a rebellion against James's officers. Francis Nicholson had succeeded Thomas Dongan as governor in 1688, but the Irishman had remained in the colony to advise him. Leisler seized control of New York in the new King's name and Nicholson fled. The rebels then arrested Dongan. In Massachusetts, the Puritans arrested Edmund Andros as well. William sent a new royal governor, Henry Sloughter, but Leisler refused to relinquish his authority. He finally surrendered and went to the gallows for treason in 1691. This upheaval may have rescued American liberties from Stuart absolutism, but it deprived the colonists of their two best Indian diplomats, divided authority for the war between New York, Connecticut, Rhode Island, and Massachusetts, and replaced the old Stuart hands with inexperienced men of limited ability. William Phips's performance at Quebec made it clear that he was no Andros, and the fiasco of the New York attack on Montreal only reinforced the point. In 1692, the situation became worse. An epidemic of witchcraft accusations broke out in Massachusetts and spread until even Governor Phips's wife stood under suspicion. All of this played to the Canadians' advantage. With the English effectively out of the war, they could now turn their attention to the Iroquois.

But how? With France at war on the Continent, Louis could not send troops to America. Therefore, there could be no grand stroke like the campaigns of the Regiment de Carignan or Denonville's march against the Seneca—perhaps not a great loss as these had not worked terribly well. "Experience has demonstrated, by the trifling impression made by three thousand men on the Iroquois in 1687, that it is very difficult to derive much advantage from going in quest of them, laying aside the very heavy expense and the hardships attendant thereupon which bring very little benefit to the French colony."[11] The military proposed various expedients: fleets of rowboats to patrol the Saint Lawrence, elaborate ambush tactics to trap the Iroquois as they approached the colony, and so on, none terribly practical and most exorbitantly expensive. Moreover, by 1691 nearly half of the 1,300 regular troops in Canada had died of wounds or disease and the colony had lost nearly 2,000 men all told. Given this, Frontenac really had little choice and adopted the most obvious tactic: French and Indian parties would invade Iroquoia in a guerrilla campaign of attrition. The command structure of this war stood in marked contrast to previous conflicts as well. Governor Frontenac, now seventy and too old to go bushwhacking, assumed an essentially ceremonial role as commander in chief. This represented a marked change from La Barre and Denonville, who had actually taken the field. Tough, competent Hector de Callières became the theater commander at Montreal. The actual fighting, however, was left to a remarkable group of junior officers, many of them Canadians with experience in the upper country.

The Achilles' heel of New France remained the Ottawa River, the main artery of the fur trade and the critical supply line for arming and equipping the western Indians. The success of the convoy of 1690 had probably saved the colony. However, in the years which followed, the river would remain a battleground. In 1691, most of the fighting took place around Montreal Island, with Iroquois parties raiding outlying towns and Indian villages. Two convoys for Michilimackinac departed Montreal for the west without interference. The next year, things would not be so simple.

In early 1692, a patrol from Fort Frontenac clashed with an Iroquois hunting party and took prisoners who declared that 100 Senecas had gone hunting near the Chaudière on the Ottawa. They planned to spend the summer there and 200 Onondagas under Chief Black Kettle would march to join them as soon as the snow melted. Together, they would cut the route to Michilimackinac. Callières expected the spring fur convoy from the west soon and so he sent an officer and forty coureurs de bois with an armed escort of three canoes to go upriver to the Chaudière to warn them. The canoes reached the falls without incident, but further north at Portage des Chats, they found evidence that Black Kettle and his Onondagas had arrived, and they returned to Montreal as quickly as they could.

Reinforced, they tried again, but encountered 60 Iroquois canoes at Portage des Chats and fled south. About this time a party of 60 Indians arrived in Montreal, having eluded Black Kettle's patrols. After selling their furs, they asked for an escort to the Chaudière and a French party of 30 accompanied them upriver. As they made the portage of the Long Sault, Black Kettle and 140 Onondagas burst from the forest with a blast of musketfire. Some of the French were lining their canoes along the bank while the rest shuttled the cargo on shore. The Iroquois cut through the Indians screening the trail and drove the French into the river. Attempting to climb into the canoes and escape, they upset them and the wretched men were swept downstream with the Iroquois running down the bank firing on them. In the fight, the French lost 21 killed and 30 captured. Equally serious, Black Kettle had taken a large store of merchandise, arms, powder, and shot, "which will render them more insolent, and furnish them with the means to carry on the war against us with greater vigor."[12]

Black Kettle, however, now disappeared. But then, on July 15, he struck again, raiding a village on Montreal Island and carrying off 18 prisoners. A force of 100 regulars set out after him, but he escaped and resumed his blockade. A French captive slipped off and made his way to Montreal to report that Black Kettle had cached two canoe loads of furs taken along the Ottawa near the Long Sault. A French force accompanied by 120 Indians went out to recover the pelts and if possible bring Black Kettle to battle. Finding the Onondagas a few miles above the Long Sault, the French and their allies stormed into their encampment, but the Iroquois fought back fiercely until nightfall, and then escaped. It had been a nasty little battle: the Iroquois killed eleven French against a loss of ten of their own men. The French, however, had recovered some of their prisoners and captured 14 Iroquois and were content to let Black Kettle go. Among the captives, they discovered Black Kettle's wife. Four hundred French and Indians came down from Michilimackinac to Montreal that summer, but brought no furs, as they feared encountering the Onondaga. In dispatches from De Louvigny at Michilimackinac, however, the governor learned that nearly 800 western Indians had gone to war that year, killing or capturing 42 Iroquois.

The following May, Frontenac sent 20 picked volunteers with several Christian Indians and an escort of 27 voyageurs to Michilimackinac with orders for De Louvigny. After Black Kettle's depredations, he found it necessary to pay a bounty to both the French and Indian paddlers to induce them to go. The couriers got through without incident, but the escort was ambushed on its way home, losing its commander and four others.[13] The message to De Louvigny ordered him to assemble the 200 coureurs de bois then in the west and send them down to Montreal with the furs piling up at the Straits. These arrived at Montreal in a spectacular convoy of 200 canoes on August 17. As they came ashore, the town erupted: "It is impossible to conceive the joy of the public on beholding such a vast quantity of riches. For several years Canada had been impatiently waiting for this prodigious heap of beaver, which was reported to be at Michilimackinac. The merchant, the farmer, and other individuals who might have had peltries there, were dying of hunger with property they did not enjoy. Credit was exhausted and the apprehension universal that the enemy would become masters, on the way, of the last resource of the country."[14] The expedition, moreover, had been accompanied by a number of western chiefs and Henri Tonti from Fort Saint Louis. Frontenac entertained the allied leaders at a feast on September 6. Amid singing, dancing, and the distribution of gifts, the western chiefs recounted their feats against the Iroquois.

This feast would pay unexpected dividends down the road. Frontenac was apparently in fine form that night. Alternately jocular and dignified, he teased, joked, and flattered his Indian guests with his seemingly august attention. European monarchies had progressed a long way since the days of warrior kings like Clovis and Charlemagne. The power of the institution could survive madness or deviants like Henry III of France or the dull-witted, deformed Charles "the Impotent" of Spain. Indians had not. They awarded trust to those who merited it. As the most important war chief of the Hurons, Kondiaronk probably attended the feast and apparently came away with a favorable impression which would last the rest of his life. It would prove to be Frontenac's greatest legacy to New France.

The arrival of this convoy marked the turning point of the war. The Ottawa River blockade had ultimately failed. Black Kettle had caused the French considerable trouble but, as in 1690, when the French applied their full strength to opening the river, the Iroquois could not close it. The economy of the colony continued to function, the French could maintain their forts in the west, and the Indian allies could obtain their necessaries. The Iroquois could afford none of these outcomes and so their failure to cut the river had likely cost them the war.

On the other hand, they could do little about it. The incompetence of the English had allowed the French to turn their full fury on the Five Nations. By 1690 New France had perhaps 10,000 inhabitants to the Confederacy's 12,000. However, the Canadian success in holding together their alliance changed the equation. The western nations together represented perhaps 40,000–50,000 people. Lavishly equipped with French arms, these pounded the western territories of the Iroquois. To make matters worse, smallpox had struck. By the time it had run its course, disease and battle deaths had reduced the Five Nations by nearly half.

In addition, the French had won a smashing victory earlier in the year. In January 1693, the Sieurs de Manthet, Courtemanche, and Lanoue led a force of 600 men in a winter campaign against the Mohawk, storming a town, killing 30, and capturing 300. A Mohawk force, determined to recover the captives, pursued them, but the French beat them off with a loss of only 15 wounded. In the west Tonti and his coureurs de bois, Illiniwek, and Miami had conducted a series of murderous raids against the Seneca. He estimated that since 1690, they had killed nearly 450 people.[15] By the end of 1693, the crisis which had begun at La Chine four years earlier had passed. One grisly sign of this was a royal order terminating the bounty paid for Iroquois captives and scalps: 10 écus for each Indian killed, 20 for each captured, half for women. The body count and number of captives taken had reached such a scale that the King could no longer afford it. The allies sensed the change as well and their attitude hardened. The French had awarded Black Kettle's wife to the Christian

Oneida chief Tataconière. Discovering that she intended to escape, the Oneida split her skull open with an axe. "He then struck his hatchet into the gate as a sign that he would not grant pardon to anyone, and invited his brethren to do likewise."[16]

There were other signs. In September 1691, Liette, at Fort Saint Louis des Illinois, received instructions to "sound out the Illinois regarding the abandonment of their village, for which they have shown a desire because their firewood was so remote and because it was so difficult to get water upon the rock if they were attacked by an enemy."[17] Assembling the chiefs, Liette asked for their thoughts and they recommended they move to Lake Pimitoui (Peoria), the "Fat Lake," named for its abundance of game, and the French consented. The new fort, Saint Louis de Pimitoui, a rectangle of 1,800 pickets, containing four buildings —a storehouse, barracks, commandant's house, and a chapel— was built on the shore of Lake Pimitoui. Substantial enough by French standards, it hardly compared with the citadel of Le Rocher and could never have withstood the Iroquois attack of 1684. However, by now, the Iroquois could no longer strike such a blow.

For the first time in its history, New France had the luxury of manpower and Frontenac was quick to use it, this time against the Seneca, the "Keepers of the Western Door." The English were treating with the Miami of southwestern Michigan, and to put a stop to this and check the Seneca, he sent a force of French regulars, coureurs de bois, and militia to Fort Saint Joseph under De Manthet and Courtemanche. They were to serve under Tonti and received stark instructions: "Think more of fighting than of trading."[18] In addition, Frontenac sent Nicolas Perrot to the Kalamazoo River to counter the maneuvers of the English and Iroquois. All these measures served to reassure the western allies and, during 1694–1695, 900 western Indians would again take the field.

The French spent 1695 securing and rebuilding Fort Frontenac and took little offensive action. Nevertheless, the Ottawa route remained undisturbed. Some 80 canoes came down and Lieutenant La Forest led the regular June convoy to Michilimackinac without incident. In the west, moreover, the French scored a considerable success. Three or four hundred Seneca raiders descended upon the Miami, sacking villages and carrying off captives. Emboldened, they attacked Fort Saint Joseph. Advancing under cover of darkness, "They had already stuck their guns through the palisades when they were repulsed so vigorously and fired upon so briskly that they retreated to their camp in disorder, leaving some of their men dead at the foot of the stockade."[19]

In 1696, an Ottawa and Potawatomi force led by chiefs Mickinac, Onnaské, and Wilamak attacked a large Iroquois hunting party in southern Ontario, killing 72, capturing 32 prisoners, and seizing 500 beaver pelts. In July, Frontenac, borne in a litter, accompanied a force of 2,150 regulars, militia, and Indians against the Onondaga, in the very heartland of the Five Nations. They captured a town and burned crops in a wide swath across the country. In 1687 the Iroquois could have survived something like this, but not now.

To the north at Michilimackinac, however, trouble was brewing. In response to the steady deterioration of their military situation, the Iroquois had undertaken a frantic diplomatic effort to break up the French-Indian alliance. Playing on old resentments, they had begun to drive a wedge into the heart of the upper country. A Huron chief called "the Baron" had used this tension to make himself the leader of the pro-Iroquois faction. Unbeknownst to Cadillac, the commandant, he had sent his son to meet with the Seneca and had returned with a treaty. For the next two years, the commandant could get little service from either the Huron or Ottawa. Kondiaronk, however, seems to have had no part in these plots. Although careful never to let the French take the Huron for granted, he seemed to have finally bound himself to Frontenac to the finish.

Three things may have affected his policy. The first was that famous feast in 1692. The second was far grimmer. An Ottawa chief Kichinabé had formed a war party ostensibly to march against the Iroquois. Kondiaronk's son had joined the band and went south with them. A few days out, they had encountered a Huron family in their canoe returning to the Straits. The Ottawa "massacred them remorselessly and [Kondiaronk's] son shared the same fate."[20] They then returned to Michilimackinac with the victims' scalps and presented them as Iroquois trophies. The Huron smelled treachery and sent men to investigate. These soon discovered the hastily dug graves of the butchered family.

War in the Wilderness 85

Both villages took up arms, but the commandant arranged a truce and the matter was sent east to Frontenac for judgment. It may be that the murder drove home to Kondiaronk that his people remained an alien minority in an Algonkian land and that their best protection lay in close ties to the French.

The final factor may have been the Jesuit priest Father Étienne de Carheil of the Mission of Saint Ignace. A man of considerable intelligence, he struck up a lasting friendship with Kondiaronk. Well over sixty years old, Carheil had begun his mission work among the Iroquois. He had made few converts, but was apparently universally admired. Fluent in Huron and Iroquois, he was sent by his order in 1686 to Michilimackinac, where he developed a close relationship with La Durantaye. After Frontenac replaced the captain with De Louvigny and then Cadillac, the brandy traders had a much freer hand and the old priest spent much of his time trying to protect the Indians from their alcohol and sharp practice. Carheil understood that the Indians associated baptism with the epidemics which ravaged them and tempered his proselytizing with a genuine concern for the well-being of his charges. Something about this practical, patient, saintly man appealed to Kondiaronk. Out of this relationship, the Huron became a Christian. Whether he truly found faith might be questioned, but he clearly admired Carheil, as he once said "that there were but two men of talent in Canada—Count Frontenac and Father de Carheil."[21]

In 1697, Kondiaronk with 150 warriors defeated an Iroquois force of 250 in a canoe battle on Lake Erie, killing, drowning, or capturing some 60 of them. That same year, the Iroquois suffered another crushing blow. Black Kettle and a party of 40 warriors appeared near Fort Frontenac. Taking a captive, they withdrew to the Bay of Quinte. A force of 30 Algonquins surprised them, killed Black Kettle, his new wife, 4 other chiefs, and 14 warriors. Their scalps, along with a half dozen prisoners, were sent downriver to Montreal. His death demoralized the Iroquois; "it is always certain that the death of one of their great chiefs disconcerts all of their projects; that they require time to recover from it, and that they appear, in their sorrow to forget what they previously proposed."[22]

At the end of August, Cadillac arrived in Montreal with a fur convoy from Michilimackinac. His party of 62 canoes manned by perhaps 150 coureurs de bois and 35 Ottawa craft delivered a cargo of 176,000 livres weight. By now, the Iroquois could do nothing to stop the traders hauling furs from the north. Three weeks later, England and France signed the Treaty of Ryswick, ending King William's War and with it such help as New York provided. In 1689, the Iroquois could field 2,800 warriors. By 1698, disease, battle deaths, and men lost to capture had reduced this to barely 1,300. These losses, moreover, had not been evenly distributed. The Mohawk and Seneca, exposed to the full fury of the French and their allies, had suffered worse than the rest. The Seneca, in particular, had grown disillusioned under the attacks of Kondiaronk and the western nations and threatened to make a separate peace with the French. The war had finally run its course.

In the summer of 1701, 1,300 Indians from forty nations gathered at Montreal to hammer out a general peace. Nothing like it had ever been seen before, and no one quite knew what would happen. Some of the belligerents had been at war for a century, and all had scars and scores to settle. In this tense situation the French found themselves peculiarly blessed. Frontenac had finally passed away at the end of 1698 and Callières had replaced him. In a sharp departure from the traditions of his predecessor, the new governor ordered the taverns closed for the duration of the council and the ambassadors settled down to the protracted business of ending a hundred-year war. The worst stumbling block lay in the matter of prisoners. The French allies had brought their captives down to Montreal, the Iroquois had not. It was a serious matter, and for a time it seemed that the council would break down over the issue.

Through it all, Kondiaronk strove to hold the council together. For a decade he had worked toward this day, first by forcing the French to honor their obligations to his people, then by leading the western nations to victory over the Seneca. It had cost him his son's life to Ottawa treachery and would shortly cost him his own, but he would see the thing through. Speaking for the assembled allies he addressed the governor: "Our Father! It is not without many perils that we have attempted this long voyage. What chutes, rapids, & the thousand other obstacles have we not surmounted in the desire we had to see you at the assembly here. We have found many of our brothers dead along the river, our spirit has become sick, word had spread that the sickness was great in Montreal. All these corpses eaten away by the birds which we found at every moment were sufficiently convincing proof of it. But we made a bridge of all these bodies on which we marched firmly."[23]

On August 1, a Huron named Quarante Sols rose to address the assembly. As he spoke, Kondiaronk collapsed. He recovered consciousness a short time later, and Governor Callières had him placed in a comfortable chair. As the assembly gathered close, he gave an eloquent speech on the peace and how it would benefit each of the nations assembled. He knew all of their concerns and addressed each separately. He then called upon Governor Callières to uphold the terms of the agreement. The governor promised to do so, and Kondiaronk was silent. The representatives all applauded, even his enemies. He died at 2 o'clock the next morning. Befitting his role in getting the treaty signed, Kondiaronk was laid in state in the uniform of a French captain. A funeral procession of sixty soldiers with guns reversed, sixteen Huron warriors, and the clergy escorted his coffin borne by six chiefs. He was buried to volleys of musketry in the great church of Montreal in a tomb which bore the simple inscription: "Here lies the Rat, a Huron Chief."[24]

Kondiaronk's speech apparently turned the tide, for on August 4 the assembled nations agreed to ratify the great treaty. Governor Callières, obviously relieved, then addressed them: "I am exceedingly rejoiced to see all my Children assembled here at present; and as you have, both the one and the other, deposited your interests in my hands, that I can cause you all to live in quietness. . . . I invite you all to smoke the Calumet of Peace, which I begin first to do, and to eat some meat and drink some broth that I cause to be prepared for you, so that I, like a good Father, may have the satisfaction to see all my Children united together."[25] The thirty-eight signatories then drew their marks in the form of animals: birds, beavers, otters, and moose. The great war was now at an end.

FOUR

The Foxes, 1701–1736

THE GREAT PEACE OF 1701 marks the high noon of New France. In the long war which began at Fort Saint Louis, the Canadians had crushed the Five Nations and humiliated the English. Even as the conflict raged, French expansion went on steadily. In 1689, Nicolas Perrot had claimed the upper Mississippi, completing the annexation begun by La Salle. That same year, Jacques de Noyon had paddled west from Lake Superior all the way to the Lake of the Woods. Finally, in 1698, Jacques Le Moyne d'Iberville began a new post on the Gulf of Mexico. The Great Peace, however, also marked the end of Canada's "Heroic Age." The wars of the new century would be grimmer, more brutal, and fought for less lofty aims. New France had become an empire with everything that implied.

Already there was trouble. In the 1690s, the Canadians had fought for their lives. The English colonies, by contrast, had scarcely noticed the conflict outside of New England, and even there it did not pose a mortal threat. By 1701, the population of English America had grown to nearly 250,000, while that of New France had reached perhaps 12,000. The defeat of the Five Nations had ended the military threat to the colony but created another. In the closing years of the war, the allies had wanted to destroy the Iroquois utterly and open the road to Albany. Knowing the Canadians could not compete with English prices, Governor Callières had sought a treaty which left the Iroquois crippled but intact and still blocking access from Lake Ontario to the

Hudson. La Hontan summed up this policy: "Those who alledge that the destruction of the Iroquois would promote the interests of the Colonies of New France are strangers to the true interests of that Country; . . . Tis in the interests of the French to weaken the Iroquois, but not to see them entirely defeated."[1] This clash of interests would exacerbate relations for the next half century.

To make this worse, in 1698 the King had ordered the fur trade closed and the western posts abandoned. The colony produced four times as much beaver as the market would bear, and the monopoly lost vast sums each year paying a fixed price for fur it could not move. Informed that the monopoly would be relinquished when it lapsed in 1697, Louis was presented with a considerable dilemma. He stood to lose a half million livres if no one picked it up and so he ordered the trade closed until the glut could be absorbed. It would be difficult to persuade the Indians not to go to the English when the French had nothing to sell.

Strangely, the most immediate threat was the coureur de bois, Jean Couture. A carpenter from Rouen, the Norman had come to New France with the army. In 1683, he had gone west to work at Fort Saint Louis. A man of some ability, he was picked by Tonti to command a small trading post at the mouth of the Arkansas River. Around 1692, however, he had a falling out with his employer. Instead of heading north as a coureur de bois, he made his way to Charlestown in the Carolinas. It might seem a strange destination, but the Frenchman had learned a good deal about the affairs of the lower Mississippi Valley. The Carolinians would have considerable interest in what he had to say.

In 1663, Charles II had granted a group of courtiers an immense territory extending from 31 to 36 degrees north latitude with no western boundary. In April 1670, 150 settlers arrived at the mouth of the Ashley River to begin a village named for their sovereign, Charles Town. Carolina soon became an enterprise unlike any the English had undertaken before. The Spanish in Florida wanted them out. Powerful Indian states surrounded them as well. Last but not least, the great Appalachian barrier which hemmed in the English colonies to the north dropped away into low hills to the west of Charles Town. To survive and turn a profit, the colony looked westward to the Indian world in a way no other English colony yet had.

By 1674, the proprietors had begun trading in hides and furs. In 1679, they dispatched explorers west across the Appalachians. Beaver proved scarce, but the backcountry had immense herds of deer. By the beginning of the eighteenth century, the Carolinians exported more than 50,000 deer skins annually. In 1680, a new and more vicious commerce began as well: slave trading. The Spanish had sought to build an Indian alliance which would oust the English, and the Carolinians used this as a pretext to go to war against the Westo people. Their real motive was slaving. Exploiting existing Indian conflicts or promoting new ones, they moved west into Georgia, Alabama, and eastern Tennessee looking for deer hides and captives. By 1700, Indians constituted a third of the colony's slaves and it had exported many more to New England and the West Indies.[2]

It was to this colony then that Jean Couture paddled bearing tales of furs and gold mines. In 1698, Thomas Welsh retraced Couture's journey to the mouth of the Arkansas, becoming the first Englishman to reach the Mississippi. In 1700, a group of Carolina merchants sent the Frenchman down the Tennessee River to claim the Mississippi Valley for England. Led by Welsh, Thomas Nairne, and Price Hughes, the Carolinians would use the Tennessee as a highway in an enterprise aimed at nothing short of driving the French out of the west entirely. Their instrument would be the Chickasaw nation, which lived between the Great Bend of the Tennessee and the Mississippi.

Tonti and La Salle had encountered the Chickasaw on their voyage down the Mississippi in 1682: "They have 2000 warriors, the greatest number of whom have flat heads . . . , the women taking pains to flatten the heads of their children, by means of a cushion which they put on the foreheads and bind them with a band to the cradle, and thus make their heads take this form, and when they are fat their faces are as big as a large soup plate."[3] Clearly a powerful tribe, these *Tetes plat,* or "flat heads," harbored no particular hostility to the French. This would change. In 1698, the Jesuits reported: "The [Shawnee, Chickasaw, and Kickapoo] had attacked the [Cahokias] . . . about five or six leagues below the mouth of the Illinois . . . , and that they had killed ten men and taken nearly one hundred slaves, both women and children."[4] Armed with English weapons, the Chickasaw now menaced the Mississippi Valley. The Carolinians planned to follow up these victories with commercial ventures into Illinois, and for a time it seemed that they might take control of the entire region.

Now, however, the French struck back. Jacques Le Moyne d'Iberville had established a settlement at Biloxi in 1699 and another Fort Saint Louis at Mobile Bay in 1702. Tonti had come south in 1700 hoping to become governor of the new colony. As always, his lack of patrons put an end to his ambitions and he went to work as an Indian agent and diplomat. D'Iberville and Tonti negotiated alliances to dislodge the Carolina traders in Alabama. Thanks to the Tombigbee River, the French could reach the interior more cheaply than the English, who had to rely upon pack animals. The Indians, moreover, feared the slavers, and the French allied themselves with the powerful Choctaw as a counterweight to the Chickasaw. In 1702, Tonti succeeded in forging a peace between the two which gradually extended to the Illiniwek. The crisis had been averted and the Yamassee War of 1716–1717 would further slow the Carolinians, but the fact remained a new Indian power had emerged in the Mississippi Valley and stood clearly in the English interest. This would mean trouble.

The Chickasaw-Choctaw peace proved Henri Tonti's last act upon the frontier stage he had dominated for a quarter century. At fifty-two, the old soldier retired. In 1704 a supply ship, the *Pelican,* arrived at Mobile carrying twenty-one young *Filles du Roi* and Tonti now assumed the unaccustomed role of suitor. Though one of the last to choose a wife, by the end of August he was engaged. Sadly, the *Pelican* also brought yellow fever. It ran its course through the ship's company, but the young woman survived. The disease flared up again, however, among the colonists. Tonti contracted it in the middle of September and died three weeks later without marrying his bride.

The upper country would miss him. The closing of the fur trade had made a shambles of Indian relations, and French expansion into the upper Mississippi Valley had created a serious problem. As traders passed out of the Great Lakes watershed to the Mississippi, they left the lands of the Algonkians, their traditional allies, and entered the territory of the Sioux, enemies of the Algonkians for nearly half a century and the particular nemesis of the Fox nation. For the trade to grow, the French had to do business with the Sioux. To retain their alliance system, they had to keep peace in Wisconsin. An insoluble problem, it would ultimately plunge the Great Lakes into war for more than a generation.

The Fox, a fierce, proud people, had few friends, Red or White, and sought none. They took offense easily and could bear a grudge for years without regard for the consequences. In 1670, Father Allouez reported that "they are held in very low estimation, and are considered by the other Nations as stingy, avaricious, thieving, choleric, and quarrelsome."[5] This reputation probably cost them little sleep, as they did not like anyone else either. At a council in Quebec in 1695, a chief of a neighboring nation claimed that they "despised not only the French, but all other nations."[6] That same year, the Sioux had massed a force of 2,000 warriors and the Fox fled the country for some months, planning that fall to move to the Wabash River permanently. The French opposed this, as it would place them "in a position to effect a junction easily with the Iroquois and the English, without the French being able to prevent it."[7] The commandant at Michilimackinac apparently persuaded them to stay, but could do little about the Sioux threat.

As the new century began, tensions mounted. In 1699, the Fox closed the Fox-Wisconsin canoe route. The missionary Saint Cosme, on his way to the Mississippi, had to use the Chicago Portage, as "the Renards [Foxes] who live on that little river that one ascends . . . to reach the Ouiskonsin will not suffer any person to pass lest they might go to the Sioux with whom they are at war, and consequently have plundered several Frenchmen who wished to go by that road."[8] In 1701, they took more direct action, plundering a trading post in the Sioux country and killing three men. In 1702, the Fox waylaid eight canoes on the Fox River and demanded a toll of 1,000 crowns in goods to let them pass. The Fox also plundered coureurs de bois around La Baie des Puans and lorded it over their neighbors. With the trade closed and the garrisons in the west for the most part withdrawn, the French could do nothing.

In 1700, Cadillac, at Michilimackinac, obtained permission to move his garrison to the narrows, or *detroit*, at the southern outlet of Lake Huron. His plan called for a post to guard against English penetration while reducing the number of troops in the region. On a map, the plan seemed sound. The upper country had only two portals from the east: Montreal guarded the Ottawa River and Detroit would now block access through the lower lakes. Cadillac proposed to invite the allied nations to come settle, and obtained permission for a limited trade to induce them to make the move.

The idea seemed elegant. In practice, it proved disastrous. Bringing the western nations, alternately friends and mortal foes for centuries, together at such close quarters invited trouble. Equally serious, Detroit lay within easy distance of the Iroquois country. The Five Nations could no longer make overt war against the French, but they had lost none of their skill at diplomacy. To lure over the Indians at Detroit would make good the losses they suffered in King William's War. Finally, there was Cadillac himself. As commandant of Michilimackinac, he had replaced La Durantaye's stern, just, efficient regime with a venal corruption which had reduced the most sensitive post in French America to a dram shop and brothel. According to Father Carheil, "The two infamous sorts of Commerce which have brought the missions to the brink of destruction [are] the Commerce in Brandy, and the Commerce of the savage women with the French. . . . All the villages of our savages are only Taverns, as regards drunkenness; and Sodoms, as regards immorality—from which we must withdraw, and which we must abandon to the just Anger and vengeance of God."[9]

Cadillac founded Detroit in the summer of 1701 and from the outset controversy raged. The Canadians saw it as another boondoggle à la La Salle, the Jesuits had little use for Cadillac, and the Company of the Colony, which controlled the fur trade, fretted over the expense. Charges and countercharges flew, but the King stuck by his decision. Initially resistant to leaving Michilimackinac, some of the Ottawas and Hurons moved south and the Miamis came to settle as well. It could not end happily. In 1706, the Miamis murdered several Ottawas, including a headman of some stature. The Ottawas then appealed for justice. Cadillac assured them that he would look into the matter and then promptly left for Quebec. The Ottawas waited, but nothing was done and Cadillac would not return until the following spring. Fearing that the French would let the Miamis destroy them, the Ottawas went to Captain Bourgmont, the acting commandant, who brusquely ignored them. Sometime later, his dog bit an Ottawa. The man beat the animal and Bourgmont beat the man—to death. It now seemed clear that the French wished them ill and the Ottawa took matters into their own hands. Meeting up with six Miamis, they murdered five of them but the sixth escaped and ran to the fort crying, "The Ottawas are killing us!"[10] Seeing the Ottawa pursuing the lone survivor, the garrison opened fire. The rest of the Miamis, fleeing to the protection of the fort, now arrived. A battle ensued and a missionary and a soldier died in the cross fire. When the smoke cleared, thirty Ottawas, France's most important allies, lay dead.

Events now moved from bad to worse. The next year, the Miamis killed three Frenchmen. Cadillac gathered the garrison, militia, and Indians and set out to punish the culprits. Through mismanagement, his force of 400 was defeated by 60 warriors and the commandant had to call a council. The Miamis returned some Ottawa captives taken the year before and paid Cadillac a hefty bribe of 50 bales of pelts, but never turned over the murderers. The commandant, nevertheless, ordered his men back to Detroit. The expedition lost four dead and nine wounded and Cadillac's cupidity seemed plain to all.

In 1708, the King sent the Sieur d'Aigremont to Detroit on an inspection tour. He spoke with the officers, *habitants,* and Indians and quickly drafted a devastating report. The blacksmith and the armorer complained that Cadillac extorted fees and services and that they intended to pack up and leave if the abuses did not cease. The post had nearly 300 acres under cultivation. The Hurons owned 125, and Cadillac held 131 in his own name, while the 63 habitants owned only 39 between them. House lots within the fort went for exorbitant rents payable to the commandant. He also owned the only mill and charged comparable fees to grind the habitants' corn. There was, as well, a tax for the right to trade with the Indians. When not busy extorting fees, rents, and taxes, he reported, Cadillac exploited a monopoly on brandy, which he sold to both the French and Indians at a markup of 500 percent. His chicanery regarding the fur trade was comparable. Indian diplomacy was not helped by the fact that the post's interpreter had better political connections than linguistic skills.

There were other problems as well. "Our allies the Hurons,"

the inspector wrote, "even now carry their peltries through to the country of the English; and they have also introduced to the English the Miamis."[11] As evidence, he noted that "Detroit has not sent to the office at Montreal more than 700 weight of beaver this year, while Michilimackinac has sent forty thousand pounds. It is certain, however, that the Detroit tribes have traded as much as usual, therefore the rest must have passed to the English."[12] Given Detroit's proximity to the English posts, the French could do little about the southern trade, but the soldier also made an ominous prediction about the north: "If Michilimackinac is abandoned and the [Ottawas] go to Detroit, as [Cadillac] intends, it is certain that the low price of the English goods will cause the trade in beaver to pass into their colony, without our being able to prevent it. We should also lose the beaver from the north of Lake Superior, which is the best there is; it will pass to the English of Hudson's Bay."[13]

English prices provided a powerful incentive, but there were other issues. The French now, in effect, reaped what they had sown in their generous treaty with the Iroquois in 1701. Writing in 1702, Father Carheil had foreseen this trade. "In speaking of the detroit Establishment, I forgot to tell you that, during the whole time while the war lasted, the savages desired That Establishment at detroit; because They always supposed that the destruction of the Iroquois was desired, and that by his Destruction They would peaceably enjoy all the lands in his Country." Things had not worked out quite that way. Instead of the fire-and-sword ending they had hoped for, the French "thought only of sparing and Preserving [the Iroquois]; of befriending him, by giving him land in what they considered As their own country; and by Restoring the fort of Cataracouy for his benefit." Given the apparent equivocation of the French, southern Michigan had actually remained Iroquois country, "an Enemy's country, where they can have no Wish to dwell, and where there can be no security for them. . . . Those of the huron nation who remain Here, and who do not wish to go to detroit, mistrust Those who have gone to Settle there, and Think that they intend to go there in order to Surrender to the Iroquois, so as to join in the Trade with the English."[14]

Making all of this worse, England and France had gone to war once again. In 1701, the King of Spain died without an heir and

Louis proposed his grandson Philippe as his successor. England, opposed to the union of Habsburg Spain and Bourbon France, supported the claim of the Arch-Duke Charles of the Holy Roman Empire. In this War of the Spanish Succession, the armies of England and a coalition of German states under the Duke of Marlborough and Eugen of Savoy inflicted stunning defeats at Blenheim, Ramillies, and elsewhere, but could not wear down the immense staying power of France. The conflict deteriorated into a stalemate and the belligerents would finally reach a negotiated settlement in the Treaty of Utrecht in 1713. As in 1689, the war spilled over into North America and proved as indecisive there as it had in Europe. The Canadians resumed their bloody border raids and the New Englanders floundered about trying to respond. In 1711, a British fleet of 84 vessels and 7,000 troops under Sir Hovenden Walker attempted to capture Quebec. The fleet met with disaster, however. Eight transports were wrecked in the lower river, drowning more than 800 soldiers, and the British withdrew.

With the Iroquois out of the equation, the war did not spread to the Great Lakes. Governor Callières died in 1703, replaced by Philippe Rigaud de Vaudreuil. Originally one of the King's Musketeers, he had made a name for himself against the Iroquois. His years of service in Canada had made him keenly aware of their importance, and he carefully avoided a confrontation with New York and the Five Nations. With the memory of Schenectady still fresh, New York proved more than willing to cooperate and essentially sat out much of the war. Unfortunately, with Canada's fur trade closed, this neutrality opened the way for its Indians to smuggle large quantities of furs to the Albany traders. The Iroquois, for their part, used the cessation of hostilities to open diplomatic contacts among the western nations. Gauging the hostility of the Fox toward the French, the Iroquois made them a particular object of their attentions.

In 1712, all of this erupted when more than 1,000 Foxes arrived at Detroit under their chiefs Pemoussa and Lamima. They ominously raised their lodges 50 yards from the fort, and no one knew quite what they had come for. Rumors, however, abounded. Some said that they had received gifts from the English to "destroy the post of Fort Ponchartrain [Detroit], and then cut our throats and those of our allies, particularly the

The Foxes 97

Hurons and Ottawas."[15] There was little, however, that the commandant, Captain Dubuisson, could do just then. He had only 30 troops and 8 Miamis in the town, as the Hurons and Ottawas had not returned from their winter hunt. Sensing this, the Foxes began stealing poultry and livestock from the surrounding farms. Worse, a group of them walked into the fort announcing that they had come to kill a Frenchman and a young woman of the village.

Dubuisson ordered them out and closed the gates and an uneasy quiet fell over Detroit. Shortly thereafter, word arrived that the Ottawas and Potawatomis had killed 50 Mascoutins, allies of the Foxes, near the Saint Joseph River. A Christian Fox went to Dubuisson to inform him that his people planned to burn the fort in retaliation. Sending word to the Hurons and Ottawas at their hunting grounds, the captain prepared for a siege. The Foxes attacked a few days later, and for a time all seemed lost. On May 13, however, a small party of French traders managed to slip into the fort. Soon after, word arrived that the Hurons, Potawatomis, and Ottawas were on their way. Loading his two cannon with scrap metal, Dubuisson grimly prepared to hang on till help came. However, with no certainty that they would arrive in time, the village priest gave communion and prepared a general absolution in case of need.

A few days later, a shout went up. Climbing a bastion, Dubuisson looked out upon an extraordinary scene: "Casting my eyes toward the woods, I saw the army of the nations of the south issuing from it. They were the Illinois, the Missouris, the Osages, and other nations yet more remote. There were also with them the Ottawa chief Saguina and also the Potawatomis, the Sacs, and some Menomonee's. Detroit never saw such a collection of people."[16] With standards raised, they halted at the village of the Hurons, who ran to meet them, crying: "You must not encamp. Affairs are too pressing. We must enter into our Father's fort, and fight for him. . . . don't you see that smoke also. They are the women of your village, Saguina, who are burning there, and your wife is among them."[17]

With this, the host roared and charged the Fox and Mascoutin villages. The defenders rushed out to meet them, hoping to buy time while their women and children escaped. The bluff failed and they fell back. The French and their Indian allies besieged them there for nineteen days. Dubuisson distributed all the ammunition he had and purchased an additional 200 pounds of powder and 300 pounds of lead from the local traders. The desperate Foxes raised red Albany trade blankets on poles and declared themselves children of the English and that the allies should join them. Using fire arrows, they set the thatched-roof houses within the fort afire, but the garrison quickly put them out. After two and a half weeks, the frustrated besiegers began grumbling. Dubuisson's men became discouraged as well and suggested that they abandon the fort and retreat to Michilimackinac. It was all the commandant could do to hold the siege together.

The Fox, however, had reached the end of their endurance. Pemoussa, Lamima, and some Mascoutin headmen requested a council, where they declared, "My father, I speak to you, and to all the nations who are before you. I come to demand life. It is no longer ours. You are the master of it. . . . I am not afraid to die. It is the life of our women and children that I ask of you."[18] Dubuisson asked his chiefs for their opinion and they responded bluntly: kill the chiefs and the rest will surrender soon enough. An honorable man, the captain would have none of it. He sent the Fox back to their villages and the siege resumed. On the night of the nineteenth day, the Fox fled under cover of a rainstorm. At daybreak, the besiegers set out after them and caught up about five miles up the Detroit River. The Fox fought on for four more days, but it was hopeless and they finally surrendered. The enraged allies, in no mood for mercy, having lost 60 men killed and wounded, slaughtered all of the men and carried off the women and children as slaves, 1,000 people all told. Only 100 escaped.

Detroit had survived and the allies returned home in triumph with captives and tales of great deeds, but the battle had been a fiasco. The alliance upon which New France depended had begun to tear itself apart: first Ottawa against Miami, now virtually everyone against the Fox. Barely a decade after the Great Peace, very little peace remained, and there was worse. When word of the massacre reached Wisconsin, the surviving Fox went on a rampage. With several other La Baie nations they raided as far east as Detroit, north into Lake Superior, and south into the Illinois country. The allies demanded French aid, but with the trade closed and the garrisons withdrawn, Governor Vaudreuil could offer little assistance.

Almost as a finishing touch, word reached New France in the spring of 1713 that England and France had signed a peace treaty in the Dutch town of Utrecht. Most of the document concerned itself with the European settlement, but one clause, Article 15, concerned the upper country: "Both sides . . . shall have full Liberty of going and coming on account of Trade as also the Natives of those Countries shall, with the same Liberty, resort, as they please, to the British and French Colonies."[19] Thomas Dongan had pursued this policy thirty years earlier. With the stroke of a pen, some distracted diplomat had conceded what the Canadians had fought nearly two decades to deny. With their cheap goods, the Albany traders would make short work of the French alliance. The Carolinians, pushing up out of the Tennessee River Valley, would take care of whatever remained.

It was, however, an agreement largely concocted out of indifference. England and France, reeling from ten years of war and bloodbaths like Malplaquet, where 40,000 men fell out of 180,000 engaged, had sought to hammer out some sort of agreement at Utrecht. No one had much interest in the affairs of a few savages and uncouth woodsmen, and so they drafted a seemingly innocuous solution to the problem. Governor Vaudreuil doubted if anyone would go to war over Article 15. The Great Lakes would go to whoever took them and he intended it to be the French. Using the Fox emergency to justify his actions, the governor began moving troops and trade goods to the old western posts. For nearly twenty years, the glut of beaver had depressed the market and crippled both the trade and France's western policy. In 1714, however, Vaudreuil learned that the masses of unsold furs had rotted or succumbed to vermin. Demand rose sharply and the governor could now move openly to restore the trade and secure the upper country.

In 1715, he dispatched Marchand de Lignery to Michilimackinac. Intensive farming had exhausted the fields around the old post and the Iroquois no longer posed a threat in lower Michigan, and so he erected a new one on the south side of the Strait. In 1717, Vaudreuil built posts at La Baie des Puans and Kaministigoya and the following year another at Chequamegon. During the 1720s, he would build two more on Lake Superior at

Nipigon and Michipicoten to check the Hudson's Bay Company. The Miami, now in the English interest, posed a problem south of the lakes and Vaudreuil built Fort Miami at the head of the Maumee River in 1712 to protect the portage to the Wabash. In 1714, however, the situation became more complicated. The governor received a disturbing letter from Liette in the Illinois country. Three coureurs de bois, Bourmon, Bisaillon, and Bourdon, had hatched a plan to guide a party of Carolina traders to Illinois. If these "Criminals" should succeed, the intendant wrote, "It is to be Feared that they may draw away from the Illinois a part of the other [northern] nations into the interests of the English of Carolina for both commerce and war." More than 1,500 miles from Quebec and 1,000 from the Gulf settlements, it would be hopelessly isolated. "Judge from that, Monseigneur, the condition to which the colony would be reduced; since we and these nations when united have difficulty in maintaining ourselves during war. Judge in what manner they would act if war were declared, when they are aided by their former enemies."[20]

Clearly then, the upper country's southern frontier would require as much attention as the north. Over the next decade, Forts Miami, Ouiatanon, Saint Joseph, and Kaskaskia would go up as a barrier to English expansion from the south. Vaudreuil received particular orders for these posts: "It is of the utmost importance to establish those on the southern frontier where the English of Pennsylvania, Carolina, and Virginia are anxious to introduce themselves, which would ruin the Commerce not only of Canada, but of Louisiana, on account of the easy communication furnished by the rivers that empty into the great River Mississippi."[21] The Appalachian barrier which had protected the French through most of the seventeenth century had begun to crumble.

The work of securing the perimeters of the upper country would go on throughout the 1720s, but the problem of the Fox remained. Opinion, however, was divided over what exactly should be done. Nicolas Perrot, now in his sixties, thought war folly. Even if the French won, "still other wars would arise.... There is not one of those peoples which does not feel itself justified in waging war against the others; accordingly we can only expect successive and inevitable wars, unless we do something to prevent them. But I fear ... that the fire is kindled so brightly that it cannot be extinguished."²² Others shared his assessment. Dubuisson, having replaced Cadillac only a year before, lacked experience but was a good soldier, and modern historians have tended to accept his version of the Detroit battle. However, another account, much more sympathetic to the Fox, made the rounds of Montreal and Quebec that fall. In this telling, they had moved to Detroit in good faith. The Hurons and Ottawas there, fearful of their ties to the Iroquois, conspired to kill them. The Indian army, which conveniently arrived in the nick of time, had actually been summoned beforehand by the Hurons to finish them once and for all. They had duped Dubuisson into the plot and during the siege one of the Fox chiefs called out to him from their besieged fort: "What does this mean, my Father? Thou didst invite us to come and dwell near thee. . . . And yet thou declarest war against us. What cause have we given for it? . . . But know that the Renard is immortal; and that if in defending myself I shed the blood of Frenchmen my father cannot reproach me."²³ In this telling, the Fox massacre was an Indian affair and no business of the French. Dubuisson had failed to keep the peace and had misrepresented the incident to cover his incompetence. In any case, as Perrot said, there was no point in further embroiling the French in an Indian dispute. The best course lay in patching up some sort of peace between the Fox and French and let the Indians work the rest out among themselves.

Governor Vaudreuil and his senior western commander Captain de Louvigny seem to have shared these doubts. Both had spent much of their careers in Frontenac's service. The old Count had come to New France a debtor and died a wealthy man, a fact not lost on either man and the path to wealth in New France lay through the fur trade. Governor Callières had, in fact, arrested De Louvigny for illegal trading at Fort Frontenac. As the colony's two senior officials, civil and military, it was now their turn to reap the benefits to which their rank and dignity entitled them. A protracted war in the upper country could disrupt this, perhaps for years, and neither had so many of these left them.

As experienced wilderness soldiers, they knew something else as well. In the aftermath of the Thirty Years War, European princes had sought to reduce the violence of warfare. Conflicts were now fought between professional armies, preferably by maneuver—as soldiers cost money—until one side or the other recognized the futility of continuing. Corps of diplomats, most of whom knew each other from repeated conferences, would then negotiate a reasonable transfer of towns and provinces. Calling in a musician such as George Handel to compose something tasteful, the conflict would be declared over. Wilderness war did not work that way, as the formal campaigns of La Barre and Denonville had proven. Moreover, an invasion of Wisconsin would involve moving men and equipment 900 miles from Montreal and back again in a single season, nearly three times the distance which had stymied Denonville. Given all of this, a war in the upper country would resemble the worst of the campaigns of the Iroquois Wars: the burning of crops, the slaughter of warriors and noncombatants alike, torture, and the wholesale enslavement of prisoners. It was not clear that such a thing could succeed, nor that even if it did it might not sow hatreds which would defeat the whole purpose of the war. This ambivalence would produce one of the most peculiar military expeditions in American history.

Governor Vaudreuil sent a force against the Fox in 1715. Arriving at Michilimackinac, it discovered that provisions ordered from Detroit had not been sent and the invasion degenerated into a drunken trade fair. The next year, however, De Louvigny led an expedition into Wisconsin. Leaving Montreal on the first of May with 225 French troops and militia, he traveled by the Lake Ontario–Niagara–Lake Erie route to Detroit, where he picked up additional French and Indian forces, and then to Michilimackinac, where he rendezvoused with a third force of voyageurs, coureurs de bois, and Indians. All told, 425 French and about 400 Indians then paddled west toward La Baie. They ascended the Fox River to Lake Butte des Morts and laid siege to the village of the Foxes.

The town's defenders consisted of 500 warriors and 3,000 women, "who on these occasions fight desperately."[24] The village, surrounded by a triple palisade and a ditch, presented a serious obstacle. Undaunted, De Louvigny set to work. He had brought two cannon and a grenade mortar and used these to pin down the defenders while his men dug approach trenches under cover of darkness. By the third day it was clear that De Louvigny would mine the wall and blow his way into the fort, and the defenders surrendered. De Louvigny offered remarkably generous terms, ordering the Fox to make peace with the allied nations, force their allies the Kickapoo and Mascoutin to do the same, return all captives, make war against distant nations for captives to replace those they had killed, and trap enough beaver to repay the costs of the war. Taking hostages against the fulfillment of the agreement, De Louvigny departed for Montreal in triumph.

It is a dramatic story, but for nearly three centuries there has been something suspect about it. Perhaps the most striking feature of Governor Vaudreuil's account is that it fails to mention casualties. Obligatory in any military report of the time, they are glaringly absent here. Sappers trenched, cannon roared, and mortars shrieked, but it is unclear that anyone actually died. Secondly, why did the Fox stand and fight against so powerful an opponent? The Iroquois certainly never did, and after the massacre in Detroit four years earlier the Fox would have had ample grounds to flee. The simplest explanation is that Vaudreuil and De Louvigny never intended to kill anyone. They arranged a sham battle, imposed terms the Fox could accept, and came away with approximately the situation Perrot had advocated. Another clue appears in Vaudreuil's report, which disingenuously declared that "the munitions of war, the presents, and the necessary provisions were carried by the French at no cost to the King."[25] The governor had liberally awarded trading licenses to anyone willing to haul supplies for the campaign and the expedition became a traveling bazaar as much as a military campaign.

In Illinois, by contrast, the French had waged real war. In 1715, a party of eighty Christian Mohawks, Potawatomis, and Detroit Hurons marched west to Le Rocher. They were to rendezvous with a force from the Illinois country and attack the Mascoutins and Kickapoos hunting along the Rock River. The officers assigned to lead the expedition fell ill and command passed to a young cadet, the Sieur Pachot, and a trader named Bisaillon. The two led their force north and on November 20 trapped the Kickapoo on a steep rock overlooking the river. Forcing their entrenchments, they killed more than 100, captured 47 warriors, and a number of women and children. The allies then marched downriver toward the Mississippi. Eleven days after the battle, 400 Foxes stormed their camp just at sunrise. Pachot and his men defended themselves from dawn until midafternoon and finally drove them off. Taking seven heads as trophies, Pachot's men then pursued their attackers for several hours. The expedition had performed a considerable feat of arms, but it had cost them 26 killed and 18 wounded. Pachot received an ensign's commission for his service.

The campaigns of 1715–1716 had the desired effect. In May 1717, De Louvigny returned to Michilimackinac and sent an emissary to the Foxes who assured him that they would keep the peace, but they had just sold all of their pelts to some passing coureurs de bois and so could make no reparations that year. De Louvigny accepted this second bit of news gracefully and then declared an amnesty for the coureurs de bois, who assured the captain that they would return in the spring. Having accomplished his mission, the captain wrote, "The result of these two Voyages has been the establishment of peace among all the Nations with whom the French trade . . . and an Extraordinary abundance of rich and valuable peltries, of which we have never Seen so great a quantity, with a great deal of fat Beaver."[26]

Unfortunately matters were not so simple. The Kickapoo and Mascoutin whom Pachot had trounced in 1715 remained at war with the Illiniwek. The Fox honored their promises for a time, but quickly found themselves victims of Illiniwek raids. To cope with this, Vaudreuil appointed De Louvigny commandant-general for the upper country in 1720. He quickly found that the war threatened to become general. The Potawatomi, Ojibwa, and Miami wanted to intervene. On their side, the Fox had grown increasingly angry at the depredations of the Illiniwek. Ouachala, a Fox chief committed to peace, reported that his people despised him as a friend of the French and that "the Young men have lost their Senses, and that he would be constrained to abandon the [peace]."[27] De Louvigny, however, refused to intervene. "It is more expedient for the repose of all the Europeans to let the Savages who have a war between themselves fight it out. . . . We should reserve to ourselves only the quality of mediators."[28]

In 1721 the Jesuit Father Charlevoix, journeying from Montreal to the Gulf of Mexico, reported that the Fox had allied themselves with their old enemy the Sioux and had closed the Fox-Wisconsin Portage and the upper Mississippi to French traders. Fox raiding parties had also made the upper Illinois River unsafe for travelers. In 1722, one of their war parties pushed south as far as Fort de Chartre, but were roughly handled by the French and fled the way they had come. In 1723, however, another force marched south and defeated the Peoria at Le Rocher. The survivors fled downriver never to return. The Fox destroyed the Illiniwek village at Pimitoui as well. By the end of the year, the Fox and Ojibwa had resumed their war.

Vaudreuil was now in a delicate position. By closing the Fox-Wisconsin route and the Illinois River, the Fox had effectively cut New France in half. On the other hand, the Fox had not attacked Canadians, the western posts remained secure, and the fur trade was booming. War might change all of that. The problem was Louisiana. Illinois had become part of the new colony in 1717 and New Orleans complained that Vaudreuil vacillated only to protect the interests of the Canadian merchants and his own purse. In 1725, Claude Charles Du Tisné, the commander of Fort de Chartre wrote: "We are killed everywhere by the Renards to whom the Canada supplies weapons and powder. . . . The Beaver in Their district cause this Great carnage among us; and we shall obtain no relief unless you give orders in regard to this affair." The commandant concluded his missive with the ominous remark that "if no more succor be sent to us from the Sea, we shall be compelled to abandon this post."[29] The Jesuits were even blunter: "Monsieur de Vaudreuil will amuse the Court by writing that it is our fault If we do not have peace. He seems to have no other desire than to have the vein of beaverskins to flow."[30] Pressure now mounted for war. Vaudreuil and his lieutenant delayed as long as they could, but the old governor died in 1725. That same year, De Louvigny drowned when his ship *Le Chameau* struck a rock off Cape Breton Island and sank with the loss of all aboard. In a real sense, the Fox nation died with them.

The new governor, Charles de La Boische, Marquis de Beauharnois, arrived in 1726. Knowing what was expected of him, he moved quickly. In 1727, he built a new post, Fort Beauharnois, on the upper Mississippi at Lake Pepin to provide the Sioux with trade goods and woo them from the Fox. Any expedition into Wisconsin would fail so long as the Fox could retreat westward into Minnesota, out of range of the French army. The following year, Beauharnois ordered Marchand de Lignery to Wisconsin with a force of 400 regulars and militia and 900 Indians supported by a force of 500 French and Indians from Illinois to strike "a Signal blow that may lower the pride of the Savages and overthrow the projects of our enemies."[31]

Everything went wrong that summer. The expedition set out from Montreal on June 4, a month late for an enterprise of this sort. Ascending the Ottawa, it quickly ran into problems. Moving 400 men and canoes over the 42 carrying places between Montreal and Lake Huron would have created endless traffic jams and so the canoes traveled independently to a rendezvous at La Prairie, a meadow at the mouth of the French River. It took seven weeks for all of them to arrive, a trip normally accomplished in four. They made a swift passage to Michilimackinac, arriving on August 4, but De Lignery had fallen nearly two months behind schedule.

At Michilimackinac the army halted to wait for the Indian allies to assemble, bless its banners, and bury its dead. Sickness had broken out and others had succumbed from the hardships of the journey. On August 10, De Lignery, now commanding nearly 1,600 men, set out for La Baie. Crossing the mouth of Green Bay on the 14th, a number of canoes were destroyed when a squall rose. The French lost more time sorting cargoes and reassigning men to the remaining craft. The next day, the expedition brushed aside a small force of Menominees allied to the Fox and swept up the Bay to Fort Saint Francis near the mouth of the Fox River.

That night De Lignery attacked the Sauk villages upriver on the chance that they might harbor Foxes, but found them nearly empty. Ascending farther, he tried to surprise a Winnebago village, but its inhabitants too had escaped. Going on, De Lignery lost more canoes in the rapids and more time reassigning crews and cargoes. Finally arriving at the Fox towns, the French found these deserted as well. From one of the few captives taken, De Lignery learned that the Fox had fled four days earlier, retreating westward. The Illinois contingent had halted near Chicago after an indecisive skirmish and never got to Wisconsin at all. Like Denonville 40 years earlier, De Lignery had to content himself with burning towns and crops before he began the 1,000-mile journey back to Montreal. On his way he burned Fort Saint Francis, which had become untenable under the circumstances. Fort Beauharnois would have to be evacuated as well, but the Sioux, declaring themselves "Foxes in the heart" burned it for him.

The governor hauled De Lignery before a court-martial for the fiasco, but could find little fault with him. Wisconsin was simply too far to go. As in the Iroquois Wars, the French now changed tactics. Beauharnois ordered his western commanders to recruit allied raiding parties to strike the Fox whenever and wherever they could. In 1729, Beauharnois reported that they had killed 30 warriors and 70 women and children. In March 1730, the Foxes were beaten near the Kaukauna Rapids on the Fox River, with a loss of 15 killed. Later that year, 200 Ottawas, Ojibwa, Menominees, and Winnebagos ambushed a Fox hunting party as the hunters returned home in their dugout canoes, killing 80 warriors and taking 300 women and children. After two years of such pounding, most of the remaining Fox attempted to flee to the Iroquois.

Passing south of Lake Michigan, they skirmished with the Illiniwek near Le Rocher. The Illiniwek sent for help, and French troops, traders, and Indians from Forts Miami, Ouiatanon, and Saint Joseph and the Illinois settlements began to converge from three directions. Blocked in their passage east, the Fox marched nearly 100 miles southeast to get past. It was no good. A scouting party of horsemen under the Sieur de Vincennes particularly terrified the Fox and the fugitives went to ground in a stand of trees near the headwaters of the Sangamon River. Digging rifle pits and shelters, they prepared to fight it out: 200 warriors with 600 women and children. The Sieur de Saint Ange with the Illinois contingent, a mix of French regulars, habitants, armed African slaves, and Indians, arrived first on August 10 and the Sieur Coulon de Villiers arrived from Fort Saint Joseph on the 17th. The Sieur de Noyelle and Vincennes encamped shortly thereafter. The force now numbered some 1,300 men.[32]

The outcome was inevitable, yet the siege dragged on for twenty-three days in the late summer heat. As the Fox hung on, they won the admiration of the allied Indians, who began smuggling provisions to them. On the night of September 9 a great rainstorm blew up and the besieging Indians withdrew their pickets. Taking advantage, the Fox attempted to flee but the crying of their children gave them away. At sunrise, the French and their allies set out after them and a massacre ensued. Around 600 men, women, and children died, with the rest distributed among the attacking Indians. The French took a number of slaves as well. The Fox War had seemingly come to an end.

Or had it? In 1731, Beauharnois rebuilt Fort Saint Francis at La Baie and a company of traders reestablished Fort Beauharnois. The French need only round up the remaining Foxes and finish the business. The governor reckoned their numbers at no more than 50. That fall, however, a force of Mission Iroquois (Catholic converts who had settled in Canada) and Detroit Huron came upon a Fox band dug in atop Maramec Hill on the Fox River west of Chicago. After some skirmishing, the allies concluded that the place was too strong to attack and negotiated a vague promise from the Foxes to come in and surrender. Alarmingly, the Indians reported that the defenders had with them a number of former captives.

This incident should have sounded a warning, but the next year Beauharnois sent Coulon de Villiers, now called "the Destroyer of the Foxes" for his victory in 1730, with a party of 60 French and 200 Indians to La Baie to round up the Foxes. Marching up to the village of the Sauks near Fort Saint Francis, De Villiers demanded they turn over any fugitives they might have. The Sauks responded to his ultimatum with a blast of musketfire, killing him. A battle ensued and three days later the Sauks and their Fox guests escaped, fleeing up the Fox River hotly pursued by the French, who caught up with the fugitives about twenty miles upriver. In a drawn, bloody battle, the two sides fought from midafternoon till sunset and the Sauks then withdrew under cover of night.

Beauharnois still did not have his final victory, and the battles at Maramec and La Baie had resulted in humiliating reverses. Learning that the Fox and Sauk had fled west into Iowa, he dispatched the Sieur de Noyelle with 84 troops and militia and 200 Mission Iroquois to finish them. Crossing the Mississippi on March 12, they arrived at the Fox fort, but found it empty. De Noyelle then pressed on to a second camp, also deserted. His food running out, he finally found the Fox strongly entrenched on an island in the Des Moines River, then clogged with drift ice. Instead of the handful of fugitives he expected, he counted 50 lodges defended by perhaps 250 Sauks and Foxes. One of the

Christian Mohawks declared, "My French and Indian Brothers, we are dead men, but we must sell our lives dearly and not let ourselves be captured."³³ After a desperate fight, De Noyelle managed to extract his men and they escaped back across the Mississippi to La Baie, eating their dogs, packhorses, and moccasins along the way.

The war was falling apart and the allies were releasing Fox captives and sending them home. In a letter to Paris, a dejected but wiser Beauharnois observed: "You may imagine, Monseigneur, that the Savages have a policy as we have ours, and that they are not greatly pleased at seeing a nation destroyed, for fear their turn may come."³⁴ In the spring of 1737, a delegation of western chiefs descended to Montreal to demand that the war cease. The governor tried to put the best face on it he could and grandiloquently declared: "My Children, since you have asked me for the lives of the Foxes and Sakis [Sauks], and assure me that the evil hearts have been destroyed, I am willing to grant this to you out of consideration for you, to prove to you that I desire to see you tranquil on your mats, and that I am glad to give you the means of hunting in peace so that you may provide for your families."³⁵ In his official report, he wrote more frankly: "The position of affairs did not permit me to hesitate for a moment to grant them what they urgently requested of me."³⁶

Beauharnois's assessment contained a fair measure of truth, but there was more. Algonkians, as warrior peoples, fought with an implacable fury when the cause seemed just. However, this question of justice was critical. They waged war as vengeance for perceived wrongs and the degree of injury dictated the level of revenge. To kill more of the enemy than the insult warranted violated this, and carried with it the threat of retaliation from the spirit world. Beauharnois's campaigns of 1729–1733 had gone far beyond anything justifiable in the traditional scheme of warfare. In doing so, he had struck at the very foundations of the Algonkians' moral universe.³⁷

The French paid a price for the Fox Wars. The wholesale slaughter of a people, the captives deported to the West Indies, made the Indians see the French in a new and grimmer light. The experience of dictating terms, as the western nations did in 1737, also showed the French far weaker than the Indians had imagined and the French would never again enjoy the Promethean stature they once had. The great alliance begun by Champlain now became only a marriage of convenience on terms set, to a great extent, by the Native peoples themselves. At the same time, the closing of the Fox-Wisconsin and Chicago-Kankakee Portages for nearly two decades convinced the French to rely more heavily on the shorter, less-vulnerable Maumee-Wabash-Ohio route as the principal line of communication to Louisiana. By 1726 already, one official had referred to the Wabash as "one of the most important rivers on this continent."[38] The most vital artery of New France now lay more than 300 miles closer to the English of New York and the Carolinas.[39]

FIVE

Illinois and the Chickasaw Wars, 1700–1740

BETWEEN 1700 AND 1740, Illinois became the most substantial French settlement between Montreal and the Gulf of Mexico. Though largely colonized by Canadians, it bore little similarity to Canada or the trading posts of the north. Despite its ties to Louisiana and the Caribbean islands, it never really resembled these either. Instead it became a peculiar, and not entirely successful, fusion of the two. The contradictions inherent between them would render the Illinois country vulnerable in a war which would, for a time, threaten to bring Louisiana and even the whole of New France to its knees.

Despite the dreams of La Salle, Louisiana never amounted to much. By the 1750s, the population would reach only 10,000 or 11,000 people. The swamps of the Gulf coast discouraged farming, the semitropical climate took a savage toll, yellow fever regularly decimated the colony, and until 1708, Louisiana remained dependent upon France for provisions. In 1711, fogs and humidity took the wheat crop at Mobile, and the British Navy plundered Dauphin Island. The founding of new settlements, always a difficult business, required strong leaders: Quebec had the indomitable Champlain; Jamestown, the capable John Smith; and Massachusetts Bay, stern-eyed John Winthrop. In its hour of need, poor Louisiana had only Antoine Laumet, Sieur de Cadillac.

During his disastrous tenure at Detroit, Cadillac became something of a dilemma for the French Minister of Marine,

Jerome Phelypeaux, Count de Ponchartrain. Cadillac clearly had to go. But where? To simply sack him would require that Ponchartrain admit to a serious blunder. Therefore, the minister had to put him somewhere. If he could not consign him to oblivion, the next best thing was to make him governor of Louisiana. Cadillac wanted no part of the miasmal failure along the Gulf and stalled for three years. In the end, however, there was nothing for it and he set out for Biloxi in 1713.

Cadillac and his employer the Sieur de Crozat, who had received a sixteen-year monopoly to develop the colony, set out to open a trade with Mexico and prospect for mines. The Spanish, however, had no interest in French interlopers on the Gulf and nothing came of the first scheme. Cadillac went north to the Illinois country and returned announcing that he had discovered silver. This proved apocryphal, and the colony's only exports remained laboriously hand-sawn planks, produce, and furs brought down by Canadian voyageurs. The northerners also sold Indian slaves, who the colonists put to work clearing fields and felling timber.

Crozat, seeking to extract a profit from his fledgling venture, began to set prices so low on products the colonists sold to his agents that they made next to nothing. The Canadians disappeared, taking their furs back to Canada or to South Carolina. Cadillac quarreled with all and sundry and meddled in Indian affairs with the same ineptitude he had exhibited in Detroit. In despair, Crozat fired him in 1716 just before he surrendered the colony back to the Crown. The Duc d'Orleans, Regent of France, then awarded a new twenty-five-year monopoly to the Company of the Indies under the direction of the Scots financier John Law. To sweeten the deal, he added Illinois, with its rumored mines, to Louisiana. In exchange, Law promised to import 6,000 colonists and 3,000 African slaves.

A complex character, the Scot arrived in France with Dutch and English techniques of banking and credit unknown to the French. Nearly bankrupt in the aftermath of the War of the Spanish Succession, France hailed him as a miracle worker and he effectively ruled the economy for a time. He also understood advertising. To promote Louisiana, he published glowing accounts of silver mines in Illinois, silks woven in Mississippi, and pearl fisheries in the Gulf of Mexico. Cadillac, back in France,

Illinois and the Chickasaw Wars 113

denounced them as fairy tales and found himself in the Bastille for his trouble; the Crown had no intention of allowing the truth to interfere. Law recruited colonists all over Europe and swept France's prisons and orphanages as well. Delivered in chains to the seaports, some committed suicide. Yet, to those not sent to the docks, all seemed well. Investors lined up to buy shares in his Company of the Indies and speculators made paper fortunes of 2,000 percent. Then, in 1720, the whole Ponzi scheme collapsed and Law fled.

In 1722, the reorganized company moved its headquarters from Biloxi to a new settlement on the Mississippi named in honor of the regent, New Orleans. That September, however, a hurricane flattened the church, the hospital, and thirty newly built houses and damaged everything left standing. The storm obliterated Biloxi to the east: houses, crops, and shipping. The hurricane wrought havoc, but the colony had actually suffered few casualties and the people were able to rebuild. Louisiana's real problem lay elsewhere. Like Quebec, it needed a staple export and, like Jamestown, the labor to produce one. The climate could support tobacco, rice, sugar, and indigo, but required slave labor, as the torrid summers drove the French from their fields. Indian slaves, however, proved unsatisfactory both as workers and for their tendency to escape at the first opportunity. The settlers clamored for Africans, and between 1719 and 1721 the colony imported nearly 2,000 and another 6,000 over the next decade. The French also needed land. Much of the Gulf coast was too low and its rivers too brackish for settlement. During the 1720s, the French began pushing up the Mississippi in search of higher, drier ground.

In 1716, the French had built Fort Rosalie as a trade depot and listening post. The local Natchez Indians, allied to the Chickasaw, took slaves for the Carolina market. By 1729, the fort had grown into a considerable settlement and relations with the Indians had disintegrated. The French wanted Natchez land for tobacco and their heavy-handed attempts to secure it had angered the Indians, who, accordingly, began to make plans to oust the Whites. Some Frenchmen learned of the plot and reported it to the commandant, but the bumbling Sieur de Chépart had them clapped in irons for spreading malicious rumors. On the morning of November 28, the Natchez attacked. Claiming they intended to go hunting, they purchased or borrowed French guns and dispersed themselves around the fort. Upon a signal shot at 8 o'clock in the morning, they burst into the cabins killing 100 people, and capturing 130 women and children and 80 slaves in two hours. Governor Étienne Périer responded quickly, mobilizing troops, militia, Blacks, and Indian allies and by the middle of February, he had laid siege to the Natchez town. The Indians, however, still had captives and so things dragged on for weeks as the French tried to recover their people. In the end, the defenders agreed to give up their hostages if Périer withdrew, but threatened to burn them all if he did not. Finally, an exchange was arranged and the Natchez fled inland on the night of February 29.

The Natchez retaliated with a series of raids and Périer ordered an expedition to destroy them. The French inflicted a crushing blow and the survivors fled to the Chickasaw in northern Mississippi. The governor demanded the fugitives, but the Chickasaw rebuffed him and joined in the Natchez raids. Most of these consisted of attacking traders and Indians on the Mississippi, but the war began to spill into the north as well. In 1732, the King encouraged Governor Beauharnois to recruit Indians against the insurgents and cooperate with Louisiana in bringing them to heel. As the Fox Wars absorbed most of Canada's attention just then, however, Louisiana would have to go it alone.

All during Louisiana's early struggles, the Illinois country prospered. In 1698, the French established a mission to the Tamaroa which quickly became the nucleus of the village of Cahokia. The mission's founding reflected a religious turf battle which quickly engulfed the new colony. That May, the Seminary of Foreign Missions and its Canadian headquarters, the Seminary of Quebec, had received a commission to evangelize the tribes of the Mississippi Valley among nations the Jesuits had not yet reached. One of these, the Tamaroa, lived on the Mississippi, too remote from Fort Saint Louis de Pimitoui for the Jesuits to do much with them. However, the order refused to relinquish their claim to jurisdiction. The argument soon spread to France, where the two orders fought over the souls of the unsuspecting Tamaroas. Both finally received permission to found missions among them.

In 1700, the Christian Kaskaskias and the Jesuit Father Gabriel Marest departed Fort Saint Louis de Pimitoui and built a new village on the River De Pere in Missouri. Three years later, they moved farther south to the mouth of the Kaskaskia River. The region also became a haven for the less apostolic. In 1715, a report reached Quebec that

> about a hundred Frenchmen, who secretly went up to Michilimackinac two years ago, after consuming the wares of the merchants who had equipped them, went to the Thamarois on the Mississippi, where 47 were already established. . . . they are living there at their ease; as grain thrives in that region they have built a mill, and have a great many cattle. They get as many savage slaves as they wish on the River of the Missouris, whom they use to cultivate their land; and they sell these to the English of Carolina. This settlement is a dangerous one, serving as a retreat for the lawless men both of this colony and of Louisiana.[1]

With the transfer of Illinois to Louisiana, the country became that much more attractive to persons needing to depart Canada in a hurry and the defections continued. The commandant, the Sieur de Boisbriant, encouraged them by a liberal use of trade permits. The Canadians quickly learned they could obtain these more easily in Illinois than in the upper country, where the post commanders held their forts as regional monopolies. Even unlicensed coureurs de bois found a welcome. Louisiana considered Canada's trade restrictions none of its business and the smugglers found easy access to trade goods in the new colony instead of the floggings and terms in the galleys which awaited them in Quebec.

One of the earliest accounts of the new colony comes from an unlikely source. In a bloody French assault on Deerfield, Massachusetts, in the War of the Spanish Succession, the French captured a young New Englander, Joseph Kellogg. Marched to Canada along with the other captives, he spent a year with an Indian band. Ransomed, he spent the rest of the decade in Montreal. New France did not really have the money to keep prisoners of war and so Kellogg had to find a job. Seeking employment in the fur trade, in 1710 he signed on with a party of voyageurs for a trip to Michilimackinac and the Illinois country. After Montreal, it seemed "a New World, Compar'd with the River of Canada. . . . The climate Temperate, everything gay and pleasant, abundance of fine fruit trees, Stocks of Small parrots in the Woods. . . . The

Winter is here so moderate that the Snow Seldom Lies above 24 hours, and no more than two or three inches deep." The French "raise excellent wheat, very good Indian Corn, have a Wind Mill, and have a Stock of Cattle, make a very good sort of wine." In addition, Kellogg reported, "The Land produces excellent melons, good beans, turneps and all sorts of Garden erbs." All said, he thought it a "noble country."[2] Exchanged in 1714, Kellogg returned to Massachusetts and wrote an account of his travels which corrected current English maps of the Mississippi Valley. The governor forwarded it to the Royal Society of London, where it joined the growing body of information the English had about the lands beyond the Appalachians.

Nominally excluded from Canadian territory, the Illinois traders began pushing up the Missouri looking for furs and slaves and by 1720 had reached at least the mouth of the Platte River in Nebraska. The volume of their slave trading can be seen in the fact that the generic Canadian term for an Indian slave became *Panis,* named for the Pawnee captives the Illinois French obtained from the nations upriver. That year, the Spanish at Sante Fe heard that French traders had appeared on the Missouri. Alarmed, they sent a party of cavalry to investigate. The Illinois men met them with an Indian force and wiped out the entire patrol.

In 1720 Philippe François Renault, formerly a banker and presently mining director for the Company of the Indies, began a lead mining operation at the mouth of the Meramec River across the Mississippi from the new settlements. He brought miners with him and the company promised to send him 25 African slaves each year to assist in the work. All told, between exporting foodstuffs to the Gulf settlements, fur trading, and Renault's mines, French Illinois became a remarkably dynamic community. By 1726, its colonial population had grown to 512 people and the village of Kaskaskia alone had 80 houses and 4 mills. The Fox threatened for a time, and raiders from Wisconsin made their way south as far as Kaskaskia on several occasions. Renault complained that if this did not cease he would have to close his mines. After the siege on the prairie in 1730, however, the threat had largely passed. By 1732, an incomplete census gave the population of the colony as 699 souls, a quarter of whom were African slaves. By 1737 the number of Blacks had doubled to 314. The lure of rich soil, mild winters, and easy trade licenses

Illinois and the Chickasaw Wars

exerted a strong pull on the Saint Lawrence. By 1734, Beauharnois was denying permission to Canadians wishing to move to the Illinois country, and the governor of Louisiana complained that he had prevented more than 100 families from immigrating.

It was, in truth, a rich country. By 1732 the French had nearly 354 acres under cultivation growing wheat, corn, garden vegetables, and melons, and more than 650 oxen, 600 cows, 2,400 pigs, and 310 horses. In 1731, the colony shipped 100,000 livres weight of grain to New Orleans. The next year, it shipped 200,000 livres weight in wheat. By 1738 and 1739, this figure had risen to 300,000 and during the 1740s one Louisiana official reported that New Orleans had received 800,000. It also exported smoked or dried venison and bear meat, lard, and hides. Yet, for all of its ties to New Orleans, Illinois remained a part of the upper country. Agriculture became the central part of the economy, but furs remained important. Some pursued them full time, but farmers would also set out on trading voyages after the spring planting and return in time for the harvest. Furs taken during the winter season could not be shipped to New Orleans, as the torrid summers tended to rot the pelts before they reached market. Thus the enterprising Illinois traders, working as far west as the Great Plains and perhaps the Rocky Mountains, still moved their pelts across the Chicago and Kankakee Portages to the lakes and Montreal. Until the very end, Illinois would remain the aggressive, bumptious cousin of Canada.

By the 1730s, there were five villages along the Mississippi from Cahokia in the north down through Prairie de Rocher, Fort de Chartre, St. Philippe, and finally the largest at Kaskaskia. In Canada, habitants built their homes directly on their farm lots as close to the Saint Lawrence as possible. Despite the danger of Iroquois attack, they had clung tenaciously to their farmsteads even when the governors sought to move them into the towns for safety. So far from home and confronted with warring Foxes and later Chickasaws, this pattern was replaced by one of relatively concentrated villages. The French had little choice as the Foxes tended to lie in wait for men who wandered too far from town. "Relative," however, was the operative word. House lots in Kaskaskia tended to run between 160 and 192 feet on a side with the house at the front and stables, gardens, and even small orchards behind. If the habitants could not live out on their farms, they simply brought their farms to town. None of these were ever walled, as at Detroit or Michilimackinac, despite repeated instructions from New Orleans to do so. They were simply too big. Like their Canadian kinsmen, the Illinois French remained an independent lot and changed their ways only as far as they thought they needed.

Like the colony itself, these villages were both Canadian and Caribbean. Most houses, built of upright logs either trenched into the ground or upon a stone foundation with roofs of bark or wooden shingles, resembled those at Detroit or Michilimackinac. There were differences, however. Illinois had far warmer winters than Canada, but the colonists paid for this in summer when the temperature soared to over 100 degrees with humidity to match. To deal with this, the settlers borrowed from the West Indian planters, constructing broad covered porches which surrounded the buildings and shaded the windows. Those who could afford it built detached summer kitchens. In the worst of the heat, the inhabitants would sleep outside to catch whatever breeze there might be.

In terms of materials, the frontier French towns differed little from their English counterparts. Illinois had but one stone house in the early days, built by the miner Renault in the 1720s. Estate records from the villages, however, list a mixture of imported furniture and implements and locally produced goods. Walnut tables and chests, glassware, and table services from France would share space with homemade objects. Clothing differed from American homespun as well. The Company of the Indies held a monopoly on the importation of fabrics to Louisiana and forbade local manufactures. Thus, more than 4,000 miles from home, the habitants would seem to have presented a rather smart appearance. It was a culture where that mattered. The Protestant ideal of modest dress and possessions masking solid financial assets held no sway in French Catholic Illinois. It was a society of orders and people tried to put on the best display they could (and often could not) afford to show their place in the scheme of things.

As the census figures indicate, Illinois depended upon slavery. Canada had slaves, but these constituted only about 5 percent of the population. In Illinois, the total came to nearly 40 percent. Slavery as practiced in Illinois had its roots in the French West Indies. Over time, however, it became something rather different: different, in fact, from anywhere else in the New World. To begin, the settlers themselves had little experience with it and were guided by a comprehensive set of regulations known as the Code Noir. In 1685, Louis XIV had established the Code for his West Indian possessions. The document was a strange combination of savage repression, prudery, piety, and pity. Under it, slaves who rebelled or assaulted a White were to be executed. Yet, they must also be baptized and raised Catholic. Bondsmen could not be forced to work on Sundays, feast days, or other holidays nor could they be forced to marry against their will. Slave marriages could not be broken up by sale or inheritance, and the issue might not be sold until puberty. Legitimate children of bondsmen and freedwomen were to be considered free. The Code also punished concubinage with heavy fines, and demanded that the woman and issue be confiscated if the relationship was adulterous, but ordered the offending man to marry his mistress and legitimize his children if he were single. Slaves might also go to court to protest ill treatment.

Many of the more humane features of the Code stand in sharp relief to those of the southern English colonies. In Illinois, however, Louis's slave laws underwent a further transformation. The simple fact that Africans cost a great deal of money tended to define their terms of servitude more than edicts from Paris or New Orleans. In 1726, one family of four was valued at 4,000 livres, more than a simple voyageur might earn in a lifetime. An adult male could command as much as 1,500. As a result, most families might own one or two slaves and their children but rarely more. Only the miner Renault and the Jesuits held considerable numbers of slaves and even these had only 22 each. In such a world, Blacks simply cost too much to mistreat. The French executed only one slave in Illinois. In 1725, a court convicted Pierre Perico of stealing stores from Fort de Chartre no less than eight times before he was finally caught.

According to the Code, a slave who assaulted a White had to be put to death. In Illinois things were not so simple. In 1730, the court tried a slave, Jean, for striking a habitant, the Sieur Bastien, who demanded that he hang. Slaves could testify in Illinois, and Jean stoutly maintained that the Frenchman had started the altercation and had actually hurt himself falling against a door. The court dismissed the death penalty, had the man flogged, and ordered him to kneel in public and apologize. Persons who abused rented slaves often found themselves dragged into court by their owners and made to pay compensation. This was particularly true of bondsmen the Jesuits put out for hire.

Under the English notion of social contract, "all men are created equal." In American slavery, this effectively became "all men who are not equal are not men." France, however, remained a society of orders where each rank enjoyed certain specific rights. In the Code Noir, this assumption meant that a freed slave became a free subject: "We grant to freed slaves the same rights, privileges, and immunities that are enjoyed by freeborn persons . . . and that this freedom gives them . . . the same happiness that natural liberty has on our other subjects."[3] Freed Blacks and Mulattoes could pursue ambitions denied American ex-slaves and rise in the trades and the militia. Finally, the frontier environment exerted a profound influence upon Illinois slavery. Slaves lived closely with their masters: working in the fields together and birthing each others' children, who would play with each other until each assumed their appointed role. When danger threatened, they took up arms together against the common enemy, as they did in the Fox and Chickasaw Wars. These circumstances made it difficult for the French to deny the humanity of the Blacks and produced perhaps the most benign bondage in the New World.

Relations between Whites and Indians were unusual as well. As elsewhere in the upper country, the French who arrived in Illinois were overwhelmingly young, single men. The casual liaisons which had characterized relations between White men and Indian women at the first Fort Saint Louis began to change in the 1690s at Pimitoui. In 1692, three of Tonti's men, Michel Accault, Louis Paquier de Launay, and Jean Coulon La Violette, all took Indian wives in church-sanctioned marriages. This began a pattern which would remain right down to the end of the French regime. Though color-blind, these unions had much in common with any other European marriage of the time, having as much to do with power and property as romance. With the return of Count Frontenac's favor and his own distinguished role in the Iroquois War, Tonti could feel secure in his possession of Illinois. It would seem that he told his men to formalize their relationships with local women to disarm criticism from the Jesuits.

Accault, for his part, went one step further, setting his sights on Maria Aramipinchic8e [sic], the Christian daughter of powerful Illiniwek chief Rouensa. Her father approved, seeing it as a way to strengthen his ties with the French. The only fly in the commercial ointment was that the blushing bride, a recent Catholic convert, did not want to marry him. She had already decided to offer her virginity to God and dedicate her life to spreading the Christian message. Accault, Rouensa, and Tonti were furious and blamed the Jesuits. Her priest, seeing himself badly outnumbered, tried to temporize. In the end, however, Maria solved the problem satisfactorily for all concerned. Accault had a reputation as the worst libertine in the Illinois country and his bride-to-be finally agreed to the union to convert *him* to the one true church.

Eventually, the settlement of the Gulf coast meant that a certain number of White women began to appear in the Illinois country, but well into the 1720s the majority of brides were Indian. The baptismal records of the Mission of the Immaculate Conception at Kaskaskia list fifty children born to mixed couples between 1695 and 1718. This pattern was not just true for the voyageurs. In 1718, a new commandant, the Sieur de Boisbriant, arrived in the colony. He brought with him Nicholas Michel Chassin as his *Garde de Magasin,* or quartermaster for the new post of Fort de Chartre. After four years' service, he received title to 17 arpents of land downriver from the post. With lands and position, Chassin had become a man of some stature and now cast about for a wife. In a letter to France he wrote:

> You see, Sir, that the only thing I now lack in order to make a strong establishment in Louisiana is a certain article of furniture that one often repents of having got and which I shall do without like the others until the company sends us some girls who have at least some appearance of virtue. If by chance there should be some girl with whom you are acquainted who would be willing to make this journey for love of me, I should be very much obliged to her and I should certainly do my best to give her evidence of my gratitude for it.[4]

Nothing came of his queries, and he married Agnes Philippe, the daughter of Maria Accault and her second husband Michel Philippe. This pattern of amiable miscegenation had distinct boundaries, however. Marriages between White men and Indian women were commonplace. Unions of White women and

Indian men did not happen. Among Métis families, however, the children might marry either Red or White spouses. This pattern apparently had no legal basis, but represented an ironclad social more.

Personal friendships, as well as marriages, also grew between the peoples of Illinois. In 1736, Pierre Orré, "La Rose," tried to desert from the garrison of Fort de Chartre, and Pierre d'Artaguette, the commandant, ordered him shot. This open-and-shut case, common among eighteenth-century soldiers, proved more complicated here. The Kaskaskias went to D'Artaguette begging for Orré's release. The execution now took on diplomatic implications and, as a matter of some delicacy, the commandant referred the case to the King. The peculiar terms of the enmeshment of Red and White in the Illinois country allowed a level of intimacy, cooperation, and reciprocal obligation unheard of in the English colonies. However there were still tensions.

In October 1731, Governor Périer had burnt three Chickasaw in retaliation for their raids along the Mississippi, placing the Illiniwek in an extremely awkward position. The incident enraged the Chickasaw and nations allied to the French had to decide whether to support or distance themselves from such a directly provocative act. The Illiniwek "took fire" over the incident and made it clear that they wished to remain neutral in what they saw as a French quarrel. Noting this, the governor wrote that "if [the Illinois] did not wish to take sides against us with the Chickasaw, it was not disposed to take our part against them."[5]

There were other problems as well. The growing White population created pressure for farmland. Slipshod French farming tended to make this worse. The habitants preferred to exhaust fields which might have held their fertility with better management and then seek out new lands. The Kaskaskias resented French encroachment and felt cheated out of payments for lands they had given up and for mineral rights on the Missouri side of the Mississippi River. The French, for their part, resented the packs of Indian dogs which roamed through the settlements and the Indian cattle which trampled French fields. The habitants' livestock often returned the favor, trampling Indian crops. By 1733, things had reached such a pass that the French feared an outright rebellion or defection to the Chickasaw. To defuse the situation, the governor recommended that the Illiniwek be encouraged to leave: "This proximity often causes dangerous disputes. He will do what he can to induce them to [go]."[6] The Illiniwek had long feared this. In 1726, Chief Chicago had gone to Paris with a delegation to request assistance against the Fox. He added a plea that the King not allow the settlers to push his people from their villages. In 1735, these "disputes" resulted in the murder of an Illiniwek chief, Duhalies de fer. The culprit was never caught and the Illiniwek resented what they considered French indifference. Together, these troubles set in motion one of the great tragedies of the upper country.

By the early 1730s, the Illinois settlements were relatively secure. The population had grown to the point where the colony could field its own troops and the Illiniwek could be relied upon to help defend it as well. After Governor Beauharnois's murderous assault on the Fox, there was no longer much danger from that quarter. The colony's only weakness lay in its tenuous, 1,000-mile supply line to New Orleans. The village of Kaskaskia lay about 390 feet above sea level and the Mississippi flowed free and unobstructed to New Orleans and the Gulf of Mexico. On an air line the Illinois colony lay only some 600 miles from New Orleans, but the lower Mississippi swept south through a series of bends and oxbows which nearly doubled the distance.

The first French had arrived in Illinois in birchbark canoes. The country, however, had no birch forests and so the Canadians quickly adopted the dugout craft of the Illiniwek. These pirogues of poplar, cedar, or cypress ranged from fifteen to 50 feet long with a beam of 2 to 4 feet and could carry as many as 30 men. Most tended to be about 25 feet in length with a cargo capacity of about three-quarters of a ton. Cheap, easy to build, and far more durable than bark canoes, they were well suited to the rivers of the Mississippi Valley. Voyageurs wishing to make the journey to the fur markets of Montreal, however, had to obtain bark canoes from Michilimackinac, Wisconsin, or Detroit, as even a relatively small pirogue could weigh as much as 2,000 pounds. The upper Illinois, Des Plaines, and Kankakee were far too shallow for these much of the year, and they could not be portaged. In addition to the pirogues, the Illinois French used bateaux. Descended from medieval French river craft, they too were sturdy and simple to build, but heavy. Double-ended and flat-bottomed, they could carry astonishing amounts of cargo. A

40-foot bateau with a beam of nine feet and sides four feet high could handle 12 tons. The largest known to have worked the Illinois country could carry 64 men or 25 tons. The largest craft of the Canadian fur trade, the *Canot de maitre,* might carry two.

Pirogues and bateaux bound for New Orleans usually set out between February and April to take advantage of the spring floods. Standing out into the middle of the Mississippi where the current was strongest, they would go booming south at speeds over five miles an hour. The trip usually required only two or three weeks. Such a journey in Canada would require the better part of two months. The return trip was quite a different matter, however. In the days before the U.S. Corps of Engineers leveed and channelized the Mississippi, boatmen could usually find slack water along the bank. Working their way upstream, they would alternately row, track, or sail their craft along. The shallows offered relief from the current, but also contained shoals and sandbars which required the crews to lighten the boats and manhandle them over. Malarial mosquitoes, steaming heat, and humidity took their toll, as did dysentery. Working close to shore also carried with it the danger of surprise attack by Indians. In a day which extended from dawn to dusk, the boatmen considered themselves lucky to make fifteen to eighteen miles. It took three or four months of such labor to complete a passage to the Illinois country.

In the aftermath of the massacre at Fort Rosalie in 1729, the vulnerability of the Mississippi route became a serious issue, as Natchez and Chickasaw raids against shipping threatened the survival of the Illinois villages. If the French could not take their lead, meat, and crops to market in New Orleans, the colony would fail. Worse, if Illinois could not provision New Orleans, Louisiana would fail. Moreover, the English seemed to be lurking behind all this. By 1733, the problem had become critical, as Governor Bienville wrote: "The English have made infinite progress on their minds; the Chickasaw entirely belong to them, a part of the Choctaws is wavering, the nations on the upper parts of the river of the Alabamas are inclining more in their direction than ours, and the Illinois [Illiniwek] by the rebellion which they made last year [1732] and by the groundless quarrels that they sought with us leave no ground to do but that they were instigated by the English. Such is the general state of the

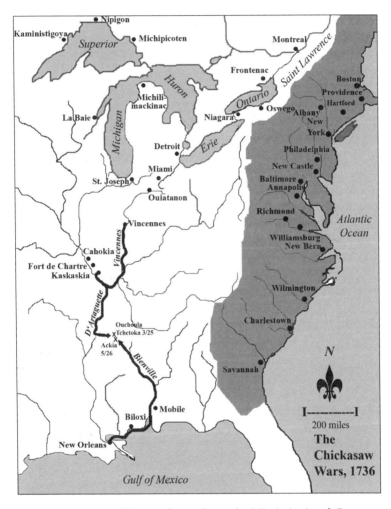

The movement of Illinois forces down the Mississippi and Governor Bienville's advance up the Tombigbee River during the French war against the Chickasaw Indians, 1736.

colony."[7] The danger did not seem to threaten only Louisiana. Governor Bienville had also received word that their influence had spread north into the Wabash country: "Sieur Vincennes... states that the Indians established on the Wabash are no more quiet than the Illinois; that he is in no position to prevent them from dealing with the English."[8] With the outcome of the Fox Wars still in doubt, it now appeared that *all* communication with the outside world was in danger.

The Chickasaw, moreover, were growing bolder. That summer of 1733, they struck on the Wabash, killing six voyageurs and two Miamis. In the fall of 1734, they inflicted a more serious blow. To provide protection for travelers, two royal convoys ascended the Mississippi each year. These might carry as many as 200 French troops, traders, and Black boatmen. Relatively secure from attack, the 1734 convoy nevertheless came to grief. Stopping at the Arkansas Post, one officer had left behind 1,700 livres of powder meant for the Illinois country as part of an illicit trading venture. D'Artaguette ordered a bateau with an officer and ten soldiers to retrieve it. The party descended the river and recovered the powder, but on the return trip 240 Natchez and Chickasaw surprised them as they rested near the bank. The attackers killed 8 soldiers and captured the others. The loss of so much ammunition, the governor wrote, "was the most distressing event that could happen to the colony."[9]

Clearly, the situation required action and Bienville ordered a massive two-pronged assault on the Chickasaw for March of 1736. One prong would ascend the Tombigbee River from Mobile to attack them from the east, while the other would descend the Mississippi from Kaskaskia to the Prudhomme Bluffs (present-day Memphis), march overland, and assault them from the northwest. A good plan, it countered the Indian tactic of withdrawing before a superior force until its supplies failed, which had stymied Denonville in 1687 and humiliated De Lignery forty years later. A converging offensive, however, required close coordination. If this failed, the defenders could deal with each column separately.

Bienville stripped the garrisons from Natchez, Balize, and Natchitoches, formed companies of voyageurs, unmarried men, the militia of New Orleans, and 45 slaves under free Black officers—perhaps 500 men—and departed for Mobile to begin the expedition. He waited all winter for a ship carrying mortars to bombard the Chickasaw towns. It finally arrived in February, but without the guns. With his timetable now seriously out of joint, the governor sent word to Illinois that Governor D'Artaguette should delay his departure until the end of April. From here, things only became worse. Headwinds and a shortage of boats delayed the transfer of the last troops to Mobile until March 22 and the last provisions until March 28, and the expedition did not begin the ascent of the Tombigbee until April 1.

Ascending the river, the spring current and torrential rains slowed Bienville's progress. The Choctaws who had agreed to support the expedition finally arrived, but Bienville lost several days reassuring them of his warlike intentions. Not until the end of May did the governor's force reach Ackia, the first of the Chickasaw towns. Here Bienville had a shock: "We distinguished there some Englishmen who were making great efforts to prepare the Chickasaws to withstand our attack. In spite of the irregularities of this conduct, at our arrival they had in one of the three villages raised an English flag to make themselves recognized."[10]

Nevertheless, Bienville ordered an assault on the morning of May 26. Advancing, a French storming party composed of grenadiers, militia, and a company of Swiss infantry encountered such a heavy fire that the attackers had to take cover among some cabins, hopelessly pinned down and suffering heavy losses. The Chickasaw had plenty of ammunition, between the stores the English had brought and the powder stolen from the French along the Mississippi. The wounded Chevalier de Noyan, leading the assault, sent an urgent message to Bienville: "If [he] did not have the retreat sounded or did not send reinforcements soon, the rest of the officers would soon meet the fate of the first; as for himself he did not wish to be carried off for fear that the few men who remained might seize the opportunity to leave helter-skelter."[11] Having lost 60 or 70 men and with the rest near panic, Bienville had no choice but to recall the attack. The order disgusted his Choctaw allies. They had successfully halted a large Chickasaw force marching to relieve the town and had lost 22 of their own men to no apparent purpose.

Bienville now faced a difficult decision. Without cannon or mortars, he could do little against the Chickasaw defenses, which were unlike anything he had seen before in the west. The English had taught their allies how to build fieldworks: "Having surrounded their cabins with several rows of large piles, they dig holes in the ground inside in order to hide themselves up to their shoulders and they fire through loopholes that they make almost flush with the ground." Their lodges presented a problem as well. Practically redoubts compared to the bark houses common in the north, "the covering of these cabins is a wall of earth and wood proof against burning arrows and grenades so that nothing but bombs can harm them."[12] Even if the French could break into the compound, they would face a murderous cross fire from what amounted to fortified bunkers. In the face of all this, Bienville had little choice but to withdraw the way he had come.

The expedition had failed miserably, but there was worse. On the return trip, an Indian arrived at Bienville's camp with shattering news. D'Artaguette had landed at the Prudhomme Bluffs on March 4, per the original instructions, with a force of 30 soldiers, 100 voyageurs and militia, and a party of Kaskaskia, Michigamea, and Mission Iroquois from the Saint Lawrence. A few days later, the Sieur de Vincennes arrived from the Wabash, bringing his strength to 400 men. As ordered, D'Artaguette sent scouts to find Bienville's force and receive the governor's orders. These returned to report that they could find no sign of the main body. The next day, couriers arrived with the letters Bienville had sent in February ordering him not to set out until April. Calling a council of war, the Illinois commander decided he would advance, as he lacked provisions for a two-month wait for the governor. Scouts had also reported the existence of an outlying Chickasaw village of no more than 30 cabins, which seemed like an easy target. Known as Ougoula Tchetoka, it might also have provisions which would allow the French to remain in the country long enough to effect the linkup with Bienville.

Moving quickly, D'Artaguette reached the town on Palm Sunday, March 26, unobserved, or so he thought. Leaving 30 men with his baggage, he advanced. As the attack opened, however, a force of 500 Chickasaw hidden behind a nearby hill swept down upon him. The forces were actually nearly even, but the Illiniwek and Vincennes's Miami gave way almost immediately and streamed to the rear. With the bulk of his little army gone, D'Artaguette and his French along with the 40-odd Mission

Illinois and the Chickasaw Wars 129

Iroquois and 28 Arkansas now fought a desperate rearguard action to protect his ammunition and stores. Despite a valiant fight, the Chickasaw overwhelmed them and captured D'Artaguette and more than 20 others along with the baggage. The victors now pursued the fleeing survivors, killing another 40 men and wounding a number more. Finally night and a violent rainstorm forced them to break it off.

The battle had been a debacle and, like any other disaster, produced its share of both rogues and heroes. A sixteen-year-old soldier, the Sieur Voisin, claimed to have rallied some of the fleeing troops and used them to carry off the wounded. They marched nearly 100 miles without food, fighting Chickasaw the while, yet refused to abandon their injured comrades. Impressed, Bienville made inquiries into the young man's story, could find no one who could remember seeing any of his remarkable deeds, and finally dismissed it as "pure fable."[13] No one questioned the conduct of the Canadian Indians, however. D'Artaguette's Mission Iroquois, veterans of every French war since Denonville's time, had covered themselves with glory, giving ground stubbornly and slowing the victorious Chickasaw. In his report, Bienville frankly admitted that "everybody agrees that except for the firmness of the Iroquois and the Arkansas not a single Frenchman would have returned from this unhappy campaign."[14]

The conduct of the French captives would also earn them a place in Louisiana legend. D'Artaguette suffered gunshot wounds to the hand, leg, and abdomen, and the Chickasaw took the Sieur de Vincennes trying to help him from the field. Someone had offered the Jesuit Father Senat a horse to escape, but the priest refused to abandon the wounded and was taken as well. That night, the Chickasaw killed 20 of their prisoners, including D'Artaguette, Senat, and Vincennes. As the priest burned, he called to the others "to do honor to their religion and their nation by their courage and patience."[15] According to another witness, "our Frenchman sang, in the manner of the Indians who judge the valor of a warrior only by The strength or weakness of the sounds of his voice at the moment when they are having him killed."[16] Vincennes in particular played the man right to the end, by which time even his tormenters had complimented his courage. The ghastly spectacle moved the Carolina traders to rescue a few of the captives, and persuaded the Chickasaw to ransom a man named Drouet de Richardville. James Oglethorpe, the famous humanitarian governor of Georgia, paid it and gave him a passport to return to Canada. He also freed Sergeant Louis Gamot. For reasons known best to himself, Gamot never went home and settled in Charlestown, remaining there until at least 1750.

The great question of the campaign was why had the Illiniwek bolted when the Chickasaw appeared in strength coming over the hill? These reinforcements might have checked the assault on the village, but the situation had not been hopeless. Though hardly the greatest warriors of the upper country, the Illiniwek had fought stoutly enough against the Iroquois and the Fox. Why then did they abandon D'Artaguette? The warnings Bienville had received in 1733 about English influence and Illiniwek resentment against the French settlers probably had something to do with it. According to another French officer, the real reason was the murder of Duhalies de fer the year before. The Illiniwek, he said, had fled the field in retaliation for what they saw as D'Artaguette's indifference to the incident. The merging of the fur trade and settlement frontiers had cost the French dearly.

Whatever its cause, the victory emboldened the Chickasaw. According to one survivor of the D'Artaguette debacle, they had gained "possession of powder to the amount of 450 pounds, 1200 pounds of bullets, 30 jugs of brandy, 11 horses, and all the provisions and clothes which individual soldiers, or Frenchmen of the militia had."[17] That July, 400 Chickasaw, Natchez, and Cherokee, newly equipped with French ammunition, stores, and clothing, came north to settle on the Ohio 200 miles above its mouth. A number of English traders accompanied them. Clearly, Bienville thought, they intended to sway the Ohio nations from their allegiance. Shortly after they arrived, the Chickasaw attacked a canoe with six voyageurs on its way to Illinois, killing four of them. The other two escaped to the French settlements, where they raised the alarm. The Miami, Kickapoo, and Mascoutin all quickly sent raiders against the intruders. The Mission Iroquois, on their way home from the D'Artaguette expedition, passed through Detroit and related the story of the disaster. Some 200 Huron and Ottawa swore vengeance and set out south as well. These uncoordinated attacks, however, produced very little. Bienville quickly decided that only a second, even larger,

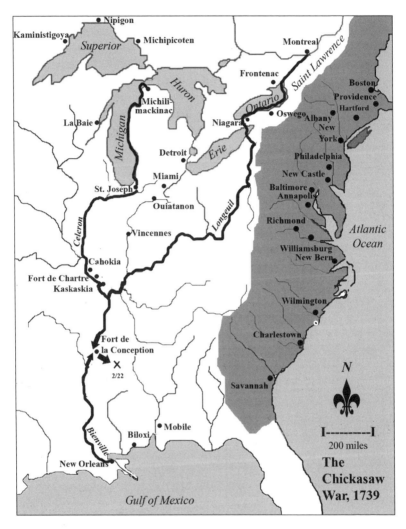

In 1739, later in the Chickasaw Wars, French contingents from Montreal, Michilimackinac, Illinois, and New Orleans converged at what is now Memphis, then proceeded inland. Although the French committed larger forces than earlier, and adopted a more complex strategy, they still failed.

invasion could stop the Chickasaw and it must happen soon: "We think his Majesty will wish a second campaign to be made without which the reputation of our arms would be destroyed among the Indian nations from which we should not obtain the same assistance after too long a delay."[18]

In fact, this second expedition took three years to organize and became the most elaborate operation in the history of New France. The governor left nothing to chance this time. He planned for a force of 800 men to advance north from Louisiana, supported by a second expedition from Michilimackinac, a third from Illinois, and a fourth from Montreal. They would assemble at the Prudhomme Bluffs and then march inland against the Chickasaw. He also requested brass cannon, 50 grenade mortars and grenadiers to work them, 500 grenades, 400 fire arrows and a dozen steel crossbows to launch them, 50 rifled muskets for snipers, a dozen *cuirassier,* or breastplates, to impress his allied Indians, and miners to handle siege operations.

Despite the careful planning and 800,000 livres for men, provisions, and equipment, Bienville's second expedition failed. The three columns successfully rendezvoused at the Prudhomme Bluffs, but much too late in the year. The governor only left New Orleans on September 12 and did not arrive until November. A fever had broken out before the expedition departed, forcing him to send back boatloads of sick soldiers even before they reached the rendezvous. Oxen and horses sent south from Illinois to pull carts and cannon either strayed, died en route, or arrived too weak to be of any service; and then it began to rain. With the roads they planned to use for the advance impassable for artillery, Bienville could do little except camp on the Mississippi and wait for better weather which never came. The disgusted Canadian Indians soon "deserted in squads"[19] and only the flooded countryside prevented them from decamping en masse. In December, the governor sent back most of his artillery, as he had no way to use it. In January, he sent back the rest along with 100 sick soldiers.

By the middle of February, disaster loomed and Bienville called a council of war. He began by laying out the situation: Half of the livestock had died of the heat over the course of the preceding summer. The rest had arrived in December, but so broken down as to be useless. The governor proposed that by sending home all

Illinois and the Chickasaw Wars 133

but 800 French and 400 Indians with one cannon and a mortar, it might still be possible to advance. His officers gallantly responded with a unanimous vote, 10–0, *against* the proposal. The campaign had finally come to an end. However, the governor had sent Pierre-Joseph Céloron de Blainville, commanding the French and Indians from Michilimackinac, with 180 Canadian voyageurs, and 400 Mission Iroquois, and Choctaw to try to recover some French and Black captives on February 6. Approaching their forts on the 22nd, Céloron saw the Chickasaw march out under flags of truce. The Choctaw, however, wanted no part of a peace and fired into them. The Chickasaw fled back into their village and raised three English flags. Céloron then ordered an attack which lasted some three hours but accomplished nothing and for the next three days he had to content himself with sniping at the palisades and slaughtering livestock. Finally both sides agreed to a truce and began to negotiate a peace.

On March 31, 1740, Bienville and the Chickasaw concluded the Treaty of Fort Assumption, but neither side put much stock in it. The governor encouraged the Choctaw to continue their war against the Chickasaw to obstruct English trade. They needed little encouragement, as "the entire nation seems very much irritated and breathes nothing but vengeance."[20] The northern Indians, too, seethed at the outcome. The Mission Iroquois killed and scalped five Chickasaw and took three captives as they departed for the long trip back to Montreal. The Chickasaw, too, remained unrepentant. In 1740, a war party accompanied by an English trader overwhelmed six French pirogues paddling up the Wabash, killing and scalping 16 and carrying off 14 more. By the spring of 1742, they were conspiring with the Illiniwek, resuming their raids toward the Wabash, and English traders were again on the Ohio distributing lavish gifts to lure away the French allied nations. That year, Beauharnois dispatched more than 600 Indians against them, but with little result. The Chickasaw would remain a threat to the southern frontier of the upper country well into the 1740s.

Exhausted by his campaigning and distraught over his failures, Le Moyne de Bienville requested a replacement shortly after he returned to New Orleans. In March 1742, he wrote that "a sort of fatality [has been] set for sometime upon wrecking most of my best-planned projects."[21] The last of the Le Moyne brothers—d'Iberville, Saint Helene, and Maricourt, who had won renown in Hudson's Bay, Schenectady, and the Beauport shore below Quebec—the old man had sadly discovered that the western country could be the graveyard of reputations as well as their birthplace.

SIX

A Country More Worthy of His Majesty's Attention, 1736–1754

FRANCE'S IMPERIAL VENTURE in the Great Lakes reached its zenith between 1736 and 1754. The fur trade would extend more than 2,000 miles into the interior, settlements grew, and the French experimented with resources more substantial than furs. The settling of the Illinois country, Detroit, and the villages along the Wabash 1,000 miles from the sea was a considerable achievement. Though more tenuous, the far-flung outposts of the northwest extending nearly 1,000 miles from Lake Superior to the Canadian prairies were remarkable as well. The English frontier, by contrast, had advanced scarcely 100 miles since Jamestown.

However, time was running out. By 1740, the Anglo-American colonies had grown to nearly 900,000 people, 1.5 million by 1755. Their exports paled before those of Britain's Caribbean plantations, but nevertheless amounted to some £814,000. Canada, by contrast, had grown to only 43,000 by 1739 and 55,000 by midcentury. Other than fur, it had no export of any consequence and this produced only some 1 million livres (£50,000) annually. Deducting the cost of garrisoning troops, providing presents for the Indians, and administration, Canada made no profit at all.

Equally serious, France's Indian allies were disappearing. In 1736, an officer at Michilimackinac made a rough census of the Great Lakes. Based upon the word of the voyageurs, he estimated a total of 5,400 warriors, broken down as shown in table 6.1. Assuming military-age men represented a fourth of the

TABLE 6.1. *Census of the Great Lakes Nations, 1736*

Nation	Warriors
Ottawa	570
Ojibwa	440
Miami	210
Illiniwek	600
Huron	600 (Huron and Tobacco Huron)
Sauk	150
Potawatomi	300
Kickapoo	80
Menominee	160
Winnebago	230
Mascoutin	60
Sioux	2,000
Total	5,400

population, this makes for around 21,600 people. Some historians, however, have used ratios of 1 in 5 or 6, which produce figures of 27,000 and 32,000. The Iroquois had perhaps 6,000 or a little more. Taken together, then, the Indian population of the upper country stood at between 27,000 and 38,000, barely 15–20 percent of the population a century earlier.[1]

The greatest losses had occurred in the seventeenth century. However, the decline continued. The Fox Wars alone killed several thousand people. The Chickasaw Wars and other, smaller conflicts had taken a toll as well. Still, disease remained the principal killer. Between 1704 and 1706, smallpox struck the Illiniwek and the Ottawa. In 1714 an epidemic, possibly measles, swept the Illinois country, killing 200. In 1715, it struck among the Ouiatanon carrying off 15 to 20 people a day. A war party of 200 setting out against the Fox had quickly shrunk to 20 or 30. In 1721, an epidemic ravaged the Sauk and a decade later, a batch of bad or possibly poisoned liquor killed more than 300 Miami, Ouiatanon, and Piankeshaw. Smallpox swept the Iroquois in 1732 and spread to the Mission Indians around Montreal and then the western nations, ravaging Detroit in 1734. It returned in 1752, killing nearly 80 Potawatomi and Ottawa before it subsided. That same year, it became general throughout the region.[2]

The effect of all this was profound. The once-mighty Iroquois saw a steady erosion of their territory and influence. As they became increasingly vulnerable, their neutrality eventually degenerated into British clientage. In 1720, the Seneca gave New York permission to build a post on the Niagara River. The French managed to stop this, but two years later, the Iroquois were forced to cede their lands east of the Blue Ridge to the English. In 1727, they permitted them a fort at Oswego on Lake Ontario. The Anglo-Americans could now deal directly with French-allied nations coming south to trade. In 1744, at the Treaty of Lancaster, the Iroquois ceded their claim to western Virginia. The English, however, interpreted the agreement as including the entire Ohio Valley. This the Iroquois vehemently denied, but could do little about it.

The Iroquois's ties to London preserved the appearance of power and prestige, but at a terrible price. In a council near Montreal in 1754, New France's Mission Iroquois, asked: "Brethren, Are you ignorant of the difference between Our Father and the English? Go see the forts our father has erected, and you will see that the land beneath his walls is still hunting ground, having fixed himself in those places we frequent, only to supply our wants; whilst the English, on the contrary, no sooner get possession of a country than the game is forced to leave it; the trees fall down before them, the earth becomes bare, and we find among them hardly wherewithal to shelter us when night falls."[3] The Iroquois certainly knew this, but under the relentless pressure of the Americans they had little choice. Had they allied with the French, it would only have provided the Americans with a pretext to move against them more swiftly. Fort Oswego and the Treaty of Lancaster allowed the colony of New York essentially to dispense with the Five Nations. Oswego could now do business directly with the Canadian Indians and did so, luring away thousands of pelts which otherwise would have gone to Montreal. In 1744 alone, this illicit commerce amounted to over 600 bales.[4] Equally serious, the treaty, as interpreted by the Americans, gave them the right to trade and settle in the Ohio Valley. These facts could only mean a collision with New France; it was now just a matter of time.

To meet this threat, New France had some 40,000 people by

1736, a nearly threefold increase since 1700. French presence in the lakes had grown considerably as well. By 1739, Pierre Gaultier de Varennes, Sieur de La Vérendrye, had established trading posts from Lake Superior to the Saskatchewan River and the French had rebuilt Fort Beauharnois on the upper Mississippi. From 1740 to the mid-1750s, except during King George's War from 1743 to 1748, 80 to 100 canoes hauling two tons apiece and manned by 600–800 voyageurs set out from Montreal each spring for the upper country. They returned each fall with more than 5,000 bales of furs. The Montreal men, called *Mangeurs du lard,* or "pork-eaters," from their rations of leached corn and hog fat, would make the run to Detroit and Michilimackinac. Others would push on for the western shores of Lakes Michigan and Superior, where they would meet the *hivernants,* or "winterers," coming down from the upper Mississippi or the Saskatchewan and the two would exchange cargoes: goods from Montreal would continue westward to the far posts and the furs would begin the 1,000-mile journey back to Montreal.

The fur trade was essentially a commerce in luxuries, and the profits obtained were smaller than it might seem. By the 1750s, the Canadians had pushed west to Saskatchewan, more than 2,000 miles from Montreal. The distance to the Illinois country was nearly 1,500. A cargo canoe cost some 500 livres in 1755. Wages for six men for the journey at 250 livres per man would run another 1,500. Provisions and equipment for the journey just to the Great Lakes cost 230. Thus, the expense of moving two tons of merchandise to the upper country would run some 2,300 livres. At a shipping cost of 1 livre value for every 2 livres weight, transportation absorbed much of the profit. Shipping costs across the Atlantic were more like 10 livres per ton, about 1 percent of the cost of canoe transport.[5] Time, moreover, was money. The merchant outfitting a voyage borrowed the funds at interest to purchase merchandise and outfit the canoe. On a passage to Lake Winnipeg and beyond, he might have to wait two or even three years to see a return. Under ordinary circumstances, a voyage to the Great Lakes and back would require a year. The interest on the loan would then have to reflect these long turnaround times. Finally, despite their considerable prowess, the canoe men frequently lost canoes to rapids, storms, or robberies. One mistake on the downbound run could cost a year's profits. In the end, the returns of a voyage to the west might come to as little as 10 to 15 percent.[6]

Nevertheless, the number of French in the upper country grew to perhaps 3,000 by midcentury. By the early 1730s, the threat from the Carolinas and Albany had made Detroit the most important post on the lakes. It also provisioned both the army and the voyageurs. In 1714, the post produced 800 minots (roughly a bushel) of corn a year. The next year, a crop failure wrecked De Lignery's expedition against the Foxes. Clearly, Detroit now mattered.

Cadillac's original post, a stockaded enclosure of about an acre with walls some 15 feet high, contained a warehouse, a church, officer's quarters, a forge, and the homes of the garrison and the voyageurs who had accompanied them to Detroit, about 100 men all told. Most would have been small *poteaux en terre* houses less than 20 feet on a side. By 1706, a brewer had arrived and Cadillac ran a windmill to grind the habitants' corn. By 1708, the population had declined to 63. A quarter century later it remained small and Governor Beauharnois recommended measures to promote the growth of the town. He wanted a larger garrison "to whom lands might be conceded, whose value they might improve. And they would Afterward Become good settlers."[7] He furthermore requested convicts, in particular salt smugglers, to set up as farmers. Nothing much came of the proposal. The British, meanwhile, sent nearly 50,000 convicts to America in the first half of the century.

The French town, however, constituted only part of the community. Villages of Ottawa, Potawatomi, and Huron stood close by and the four interacted daily. According to a 1718 report: "The Hurons live perhaps an eighth of a league [from the fort]; they are an exceedingly industrious nation. They hardly dance at all and work continually raising a very large amount of Indian corn, peas, beans and sometimes French wheat. . . . Their soil is very good; Indian corn grows from ten to twelve foot high; and their fields are kept very neat so that one cannot find a single Weed in them, although they Are quite extensive."[8] The care they took with their fields extended to the town. Surrounded by a strong double palisade, "They build their cabins all of bark and make them very substantial, high and rounded like arbors, and very long. . . . In Their Cabins, they have a sort of chamber in which they sleep, and which is closed. [These] are very neat."[9] The Ottawa village resembled that of the Huron, but neither so tidy nor well made. The Potawatomi town consisted of reed huts.

Though perhaps less industrious, the Potawatomi were great lacrosse players. Their game resembled that played by the Illiniwek and they shared that nation's passion for wagers: "They play for large sums and often the prize Amounts to more than 800 livres. They set their goals up and begin their game midway in between; one party drives the ball one way and the other in the opposite direction, and those who can drive It to the goal are the winners. All this is very diverting and interesting to behold."[10] The Potawatomi women took a measureless pride in their dancing. Dressed in white linen chemises and trade jewelry, they would adorn their faces with vermilion and dance all night accompanied by singers, drums, and gourd rattles.

Detroit was a strange place in the early to middle decades of the eighteenth century, full of intrigue and illicit trafficking. By 1730, Detroit, Ouiatanon, and the Miami fort exported 1,000 bales of pelts annually. At the same time, however, the same Huron who kept such tidy fields and villages also smuggled furs to Oswego and Albany. Other tensions lay just beneath the surface as well. The Huron had always resented their dependence on the French and chafed under their commercial restrictions. Their neighbors to the south, the Miami openly trafficked with the English, and the Detroit peoples availed themselves of this connection as well. In time, there would be a reckoning.

By 1735, Detroit had grown to 40 families, with a garrison of 17 and a militia of 80 men. Its farms produced 1,300–1,400 minots of wheat. That year the governor granted an additional 16 farms and pressed for a garrison of 30 soldiers.[11] The next year his intendant requested 60, "some [of whom] will settle on the Spot every year and become good habitants." Together with the local voyageurs, they would "constitute a good militia force capable of overawing the savages and opposing the Enterprises the English might someday attempt against the post."[12] The Minister of Marine objected, citing the British example, to which the intendant tartly replied: "It is true that there are but few regular troops in new England, but insubordination and Independence reign there, an evil to be foreseen and Avoided in the

[French] colonies where the population is beginning to be numerous and has been allowed to live with a little too much liberty."[13]

By the 1750s, the town had grown to some 200 year-round residents and nearly 500 habitants had taken up farms along the river. Each year Detroit exported between 800 and 1,000 bales of pelts and produced 2,500 minots of wheat along with large crops of corn, rye, and hay with yields of 20 to 1. The habitants also possessed some 200 cows, 500 sheep, 150 horses, and 250 pigs. The Indian villages nearby were home to nearly 2,600 Indians: 800 Huron, 1,100 Ottawa, and 700 Potawatomi.

Detroit's collective passion for gambling and sport remained. There were the traditional lacrosse matches, but a new contest had appeared as well. Each spring, the four towns along the river would hold their famous footraces, "as celebrated as horse races in England."[14] With 500 to 1,500 spectators, the contestants would run a course laid out from the Potawatomi village to Fort Ponchartrain and return, a distance of nearly a mile and a half. The French and Indians would wager large sums: bales of pelts against bales of trade goods. By consensus, the best runner was a Canadian, one Campeau. His successes reached a point where he was thrown out of the races, as he spoiled the betting.

Illinois had grown as well. By the early 1750s, it was home to 1,366 French, Blacks, and Indian slaves. Another 800 Tamaroa, Cahokia, Peoria, Michigamea, and Kaskaskia lived nearby. Primarily a farming settlement, Illinois produced only 100 bales of pelts a year: beaver, wildcat, fox, otter, and deer hides. To the north, Pimitoui produced nearly 250 bales of pelts annually. An Illiniwek village and a small French town grew up nearby there as well. During the early 1750s, the Louisiana authorities ordered a new stone fort to replace the moldering Fort de Chartre. Largely completed by 1754, it seemed an imposing structure, nearly 500 feet on a side with bastions at each corner. Within stood a magazine, bakehouse, officers' quarters, a storehouse, and barracks for the garrison. However, appearances could be deceiving. It was built, one British officer would write "only as a defense against the Indians, the walls being but two feet two inches thick."[15] To ease the difficulty constructing and supplying such a large post, it was built on low ground rather than on the bluffs to the east, making it extremely vulnerable to flooding. It would largely collapse in the spring high water of 1770.

Near the southeast corner of Lake Michigan stood Fort Saint Joseph, protecting the 5-mile Saint Joseph and Kankakee Portage. In the early 1750s, it consisted of a small stockade and a village of 55 French and Métis families and produced 400 bales of furs annually. Farther southeast, three French posts guarded the Maumee-Wabash route. The most considerable, Vincennes, remained a military and fur trade post until 1740. After that date, it began a transition to a farming community supplying foodstuffs to New Orleans. During the 1750s the commandant, Saint Ange, granted a number of farms around the post and, by 1757, Louis Antoine de Bougainville could report that: "The post of Vincennes is a pretty village dependent upon New Orleans which sends there the commandant. It has three horse mills, and about seventy-five habitants who till the soil and harvest grain."[16] A small fur trade remained, producing perhaps 80 bales of pelts annually. In 1762, Thomas Hutchins described the village: "They raise Indian Corn, Wheat; and Tobacco of an extraordinary good quality; superior, it is said, to that produced in *Virginia*." Like the Virginians, Canadians set a considerable store by horses: "They have a fine breed of horses (brought originally by the *Indians* from the *Spanish* settlements on the western side of the River *Missisippi*) and large stocks of Swine, and Black Cattle." To make things complete there were wild grapes, "which the inhabitants in the Autumn, make a sufficient quantity (for their own consumption) of *well-tasted Red-Wine.*"[17]

By the 1750s, Fort Ouiatanon had become a substantial post as well: "the finest palisaded fort in the upper country, consisting of a stockade and a double row of [10] houses."[18] It also boasted a chapel, a forge, and traders' shops. Beyond the walls, stood perhaps 90 French, Indian, and Métis dwellings. The trade of the post was considerable, amounting to some 400–450 bales annually. Less impressed, the Englishman Hutchins described it a few years later as "a small stockaded fort on the western side of the *Wabash*, in which about a dozen families reside. The neighboring Indians are the *Kickapoos, Musquitons, Pyankishaws,* and a principle part of the *Ouiatanons.* . . . The annual amount of Skins and Furrs, obtained at *Ouiatanon* is about 8000."[19]

A Country More Worthy of His Majesty's Attention 143

The final post guarding the southeastern frontier, Fort Miami, was generally acknowledged a wretched place. A Jesuit who visited in 1749 left the following description: "The fort of the Miamis was in a very bad condition when we reached it; most of the palisades were decayed and fallen into ruin. Within there were eight houses,—or, to speak more correctly, eight miserable huts.... The French there numbered 22; all of them, even to the commandant, had the fever."[20] Nevertheless it produced between 250 and 300 bales of pelts annually.

Guarding the eastern portal of the upper country stood Fort Frontenac. Essentially a square 300 feet on a side with bastions at each corner and built of stone, it was perhaps the most imposing post west of Montreal. As with Fort de Chartre, however, appearances could deceive. As late as 1750, it had embrasures for cannon, but no guns. Worse, as one French officer wrote, "The fort has a simple revetment of masonry, with poor foundations of small stones badly set, and the lime is bad; one could easily damage it with a sledge or a pick. The wall is about three to three and a half feet thick at the bottom and two at the top. The walls are between twenty and twenty-five feet high, and there are no moats."[21] Worse, the post also stood on low ground near the bay dominated by two nearby hillocks "contrary to all the rules of fortification."[22] However, during the long peace between 1713 and 1744, it had become less a fort than a warehouse and boatyard for the three vessels the King maintained on Lake Ontario. In 1749, it employed more than 36 civilian employees: interpreters, carpenters, surgeons, carters, boatwrights, sawyers, bakers, a blacksmith, a cowherd, and Marie Anne Lacomb, the laundress.

Guarding the portage between Lakes Ontario and Erie stood Fort Niagara. In 1725, Governor Vaudreuil obtained permission from the Seneca for a trading house. The definition of "house," however, was quickly stretched to considerable lengths. A new building was begun having the appearance of a substantial dwelling, but in reality a fortress. Overhanging dormers provided firing positions which swept the ground in front and rear. Its thick stone walls could withstand musketfire and the second floor could handle the recoil of artillery fired out the windows. It housed a garrison of 60 officers and men, and could withstand a siege with storerooms, a bakery, a magazine, and an internal well. By this bit of chicanery, the Frenchman had closed Albany's door to Lake Erie, the Maumee River, and Detroit. By the 1750s it produced 200–250 bales annually. In 1749, the Jesuit Father Bonnecamp described it as "a square made of palisades, faced on the outside with oak timbers, which bind and strengthen the whole work. A large stone barrack forms the curtain-wall, which overlooks the lake. . . . It will soon be necessary to remove it elsewhere, because the bank, being continually undermined by the waves . . . is gradually caving in, and the water gains noticeably on the fort."[23]

Michilimackinac, La Baie des Puans, and the posts of Lake Superior and the far west remained much smaller. The largest, Michilimackinac, served as headquarters for the northern forts and its commandant controlled the affairs of all of the northwest, but with poor soil and a short growing season it never attracted habitants. Despite this, the village grew. Six hundred miles removed from the epidemics which swept the Saint Lawrence with the arrival of the ships each summer and too far north for the malaria and fevers which ravaged the Illinois country, it proved a remarkably healthy place for Europeans. Having built within yards of the beach, the inhabitants did not have to rely upon wells contaminated by animal waste and privies as did so many colonial farmers. Strong winds off the lake kept back the mosquitoes as well. It was cold in winter, but in the 1730s wood remained abundant and the villagers drove back the frost with roaring fires. The army fuel ration specified some five cords per man per year, and the villagers must have consumed about as much. In this regard, they probably fared better than their counterparts in France. Though always a shameless promoter, Cadillac probably had had it right when he wrote, "It is always healthy at Michilimackinac."[24]

Marchand de Lignery's original post, a stockade of upright logs about 150 feet square, was entirely rebuilt during the late 1730s. By 1730, Michilimackinac and its dependent posts produced some 2,000 bales of furs annually and the old fort was just too small to house and store the people and goods engaged in the trade. The compound, now nearly 300 feet on a side, enclosed a church, priest's quarters, forge, powder magazine, and

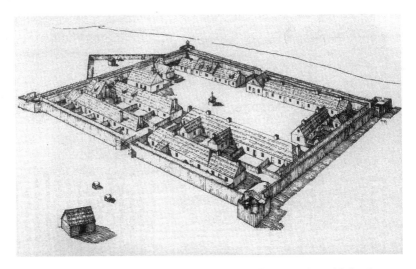

"Artist's Reconstruction of Michilimackinac from 1749 Lotbinière's Map." Courtesy of Mackinac State Historic Parks.

row houses divided into more than 40 separate dwellings, shops, and storerooms, all "very badly built," as a French officer would observe a few years later.[25]

Only a handful of Frenchmen actually settled at Michilimackinac, but they reproduced at an awe-inspiring rate. The blacksmith, Joseph Amiot, married a Sauk woman and raised eight children. The largest clan, the Chevaliers, would have eighteen. The oldest family, the Villeneuve-Langlades, had seven, as did the trader Pierre Parent. In 1738 a voyageur, the Sieur Hamelin, arrived after some years in the backcountry with an Indian wife and four children. In a four-day marathon, he had all five baptized and his marriage legitimized by the Jesuits. Over the next few years, the couple went on to have several more. The army kept a small garrison and a carpenter at the fort and many of these married local Indian women or village Métis and raised families as well.

Most of the traders had one or two Indian slaves as servants and these also married and produced families. Their owners, too, took occasional liberties. The church register of the Parish of Ste. Anne de Michilimackinac frequently refers to what the priests called "natural children." Sometimes, no father would be mentioned; others, a passing voyageur might be named; in yet others, the priest would enter that the slave "declines to name the father." In a few instances, the entry was less discreet: "June 22, 1743, I solemnly baptized in the church of this mission, marie joseph, natural daughter of Thomas Blondeau and of a female Savage, aged about five years, whom both he and demoiselle marie joseph de Celles, his present lawful wife, residing at this post undertake to educate."[26]

Unlike the Illinois country, Michilimackinac had very few Africans. In 1738, the missionary recorded the birth of a Black child, Augustin, to a slave of the Sieur Marin d'Urtibize. In 1743, a slave couple belonging to a soldier wintering over on his way to Illinois baptized another. The next year a Black named Charles, aged twenty, and a servant of the commandant, requested baptism, as he did not know if he had ever received it. Charles is the only Black for whom there is evidence of residence at the fort.

Given the prolific families, as many as 100 soldiers, French, and Métis might have lived at Michilimackinac in the 1740s. Along with the Ottawa town nearby, the total population came to perhaps 1,000 people. In summer, this number periodically swelled as voyageurs stopped in to trade or deliver supplies, obtain provisions and tobacco, and slake thirsts whetted on the long voyage from Montreal. They partook of less innocent pursuits as well. Baptismal records often spoke of the father of an illegitimate child as being "a voyageur now in the west."

For traders not engaged in voyages to the interior or Montreal, daily life had much the same leisurely character which Henri Joutel had described at Fort Saint Louis a half century earlier. The traders did little farming or gardening at the post, one visitor sniffed, as "it would cost them too much effort to procure these good things for themselves. They prefer strolling around the fort's parade ground, from morn till night, with a pipe in their mouth and a tobacco pouch on their left arm, rather than take the least pain to make themselves more comfortable." The aristocratic observer thought them presumptuous, as most had been born farmers, but they had not fought Foxes, Mascoutins, Sauks, and Chickasaws nor paddled and portaged thousands of miles of lakes and rivers to resume the status of their birth. In any case, it was hardly necessary. The nearby Ottawa did a considerable trade in foodstuffs and the French need only go "to the edge of the lake, as if going to market, to get their supplies of corn and fish when the Indians bring some."[27]

The traders' wives conducted themselves similarly. They dressed as well as they could, and the merchants' inventories list china, dancing shoes, and black watered silk along with the usual trade guns, blankets, and a particularly nasty war club, the "Headbreaker." "The women are no more laborious than the men. They put on lady-like airs and to keep up appearances they spend time every day going from house to house for a cup of coffee or chocolate."[28] Despite these snide observations, the traders of the post did a considerable business, shipping 600–700 bales of pelts annually.

The volume of trade attracted a new sort of merchant, different from the old Métis families. One of these was René Bourassa. Born at La Prairie on the Saint Lawrence in 1688, he followed his father into the fur trade. During the 1720s he traded into Wisconsin and may have had a hand in a smuggling venture to New England. During the 1730s, he had gone west with La Vérendrye. In 1736, the Sioux captured him and he barely escaped with his life. Fleeing to Michilimackinac, he resupplied, returned to Minnesota, and traded the winter at the mouth of the Vermillion River. Falling out with La Vérendrye, Bourassa settled at Michilimackinac, trading with the Indians and equipping war parties departing for the Chickasaw country. During the 1740s he brought his family up from the Saint Lawrence. Perhaps the richest trader in the village, he owned a number of slaves and sent his daughter Charlotte off to school at Quebec. Unlike most of the old families, he had no special ties to the Indians. They seemed, in fact, to have disliked him. Enterprising, brave enough, he nevertheless stood apart from the old model of the fur trader. He never entered the Indian world, but sought only his fortune there.

Michilimackinac was generally quiet. Occasionally, however, things could turn ugly. In June 1737, the commandant the Sieur de Verchères reported that 30 coureurs de bois, armed with "swords, guns, and pistols wherewith to fight those who might oppose their passage" had camped nearby with a large party of Indians.[29] With his garrison outnumbered more than three to one, De Verchères could not arrest them. Eventually, however, they moved on without incident. In 1742, Beauharnois complained to a delegation of Ottawas that their young men had taken to pilfering from the fields and gardens around the fort and killing and wounding livestock. He sternly ordered his guests to speak to them about the matter. This incident must have been unusual to warrant the governor's attention. Normally people went about their business, with the peace broken only by the clang of the blacksmith's hammer, noisy herds of children—Red, White, and those in between—and the bawdy songs of the passing voyageurs.

The La Fourche Ottawa, some 800 Indians, kept the post supplied with corn, fish, and game, and fought in the Fox and Chickasaw Wars. Michilimackinac was, in fact, untenable without them and they knew it. In 1742, they flexed their muscle in a seemingly mundane incident which became a transatlantic crisis. Claiming their farm plots had become exhausted, they informed Governor Beauharnois that they intended to move to more fertile lands in southern Michigan. The situation was common enough, but in this case the fate of Michilimackinac hung in the balance. The governor also suspected they intended to take advantage of the illicit trade out of Detroit to move their pelts to New York. Referring the matter to Paris, Beauharnois encouraged them to move across the Straits to the Pine River, about 25 miles away. The land there was good and they could still supply the fort. The Ottawa equivocated and proposed a compromise site: L'Arbre croche, 40 miles south, if the French would help clear new fields. Much relieved, Beauharnois agreed and ordered the garrison to provide the men. The spectacle of Whites clearing fields for Indian settlers could only happen in the upper country. The French regime in the Great Lakes was imperialist, without question, and often bloodily so. Yet both Red and White found themselves so interdependent that it was difficult to say just who ruled whom.

North and west of Michilimackinac lay Forts Chequamegon, Kaministigoya, Nipigon, Michipicoten, the posts of the upper Mississippi, and those of western Ontario and eastern Manitoba. Chequamegon, the most substantial of these, boasted a mill, wharf, and farm fields. The rest tended to be smaller. Fort Beauharnois on the upper Mississippi measured only 100 feet on a side. Nearby Fort Duquesne measured 80 by 120. Fort Saint Charles on Lake of the Woods was 100 by 60. In 1727, the missionary Father Guignas left a description of the building of Fort Beauharnois. His party erected in four days a 12-foot-high log palisade 100 feet square with bastions on two corners. Within, they raised four buildings 25–38 feet long and 16 feet wide. Local Indians quickly arrived and there were soon 95 lodges outside the walls. The fort had a blacksmith to repair tools, weapons, and firearms, and game, corn, and wild rice might be bartered for European goods. With these exchanges of services, both sides benefited. Living close to a post also obviated the need to travel distances to trade, not an unimportant consideration in hunter-gather societies.

The ramshackle posts frequently came to grief, particularly by fire. Stonework was expensive and often impossible at the trading posts, and chimneys tended to be of logs plastered with mud or clay. As this flaked off from the heat, they often caught fire. The combination of brandy and inveterate smokers like the Canadians posed a danger as well. Fort Duquesne on the upper Mississippi was partially destroyed by fire. The trading post at Sault Sainte Marie burned, and Chequamegon did so more than once. The spring after its founding, Fort Beauharnois had to be abandoned for a month due to a flood which put it three feet under water. That summer, the Sioux burned it to the ground. In the end, none of this mattered very much. Posts might burn, flood, or fall down of their own accord, but it was the trade itself and the men who made it work which counted.

By 1750, the French tended a line of posts extending to the lower Saskatchewan River. Jacques Le Gardeur Saint Pierre in 1750 left an account which conveys the immensity of the country. Departing Montreal on June 5, he arrived at Michilimackinac on July 12 after a journey of some 600 miles. Resting his crews for nearly three weeks, he set out on August 6 for Fort Saint Pierre on Rainy Lake, a distance of nearly 800 miles, arriving September 29. "I must note that this route is the most difficult," he wrote, "and that considerable experience is necessary to know its paths; however difficult I may have imagined them, I could only be amazed by them. There are thirty-eight portages: the first is four leagues [9.7 miles], and the least of all the others is a quarter league [0.6 miles]."[30] Of the remaining 700 miles to Fort Jonquière on the Saskatchewan, he observed, "The route that remained for me was not in the slightest more pleasant. I was assured that it was infinitely worse and moreover very hazardous. Indeed, I had the opportunity to learn from personal experience that every moment one is in danger of losing not only one's provisions and belongings, but even one's very life."[31] In 1752, he would make the trip from Lake Superior to Lake Winnipeg in 66 days. Not a pretty place, its name means "dirty water" in Ojibwa. Some 280 miles long north to south and 40 miles across at its widest point, Lake Winnipeg contained treacherous shoals that waited a few inches under the surface to gut the passing canoes. Fierce prairie winds swept the shallow lake into a maelstrom of steep, closely spaced waves in as little as half an hour. The route up the lake, moreover, required a series of long traverses, two well over 10 miles wide. It was and remains the most dangerous lake in Canada.

Then there was the climate. Buffered by the Great Lakes, Michilimackinac had average temperatures which today range from 78 degrees in summer to about 6 degrees in winter. Manitoba, by contrast, has an average temperature spread of 80 degrees in July to −11 in January. This translated to extremes of 100 degrees above to 40 below. In summer the voyageurs worked drenched in sweat and swarmed by clouds of mosquitoes so thick that they drove the moose insane. In winter, they would venture from the posts for trading or provisioning expeditions known as *drouine.* Shod with snowshoes, or *racquettes,* they covered immense distances each day at a rolling jog. In the early nineteenth century, one voyageur at Michilimackinac walked 100 miles in 24 hours on a bet. A man unaccustomed to snowshoes, however, could break down before he went 20. The bindings required special care or they could rub the flesh of a man's foot to pieces within hours. More common was the *mal de racquette,* a form of acute tendonitis. According to Alexander Henry, one of the first English traders in the country, the Indians and *Hommes du nord* had a sovereign cure for the condition: "The remedy prescribed in the country is that of laying a piece of lighted touchwood and leaving it there till the flesh is burned to the nerve. Though I had seen it frequently attended with success in others, I did not think to make it upon myself."[32] Winter travel required other skills as well, not the least of which was how to survive the bitter nights sleeping on the ground. The men would stamp down a depression in the snow and build a fire. They would then girdle trees and wrap themselves and their blankets in the bark as a ground cloth, windbreak, and covering against the falling snow.

They also had to learn to manage their temperamental flintlock weapons in all sorts of weather. In the rain, men would seal the frizzen pan with a gasket of animal grease and then cover the lock assembly with a sleeve of deer hide. This usually assured a reliable shot, but in the north the equation was not so simple. As the temperature fell, the grease sealing the frizzen could freeze and cause the weapon to misfire or not fire at all. Knowing the freezing point of various fats then became an important consideration in setting out on a hunt. Anglo-American farmers, by this point, largely hunted for sport and could pick their weather. The Hommes du nord could not and became expert in handling their weapons in all sorts of conditions.

Finally, there were the people they had to contend with. Three or four months' journey from Montreal, the French were rather thin on the ground west of Lake Superior. They never encountered foes on a par with the Fox or Chickasaw, but the 1,000-mile route from the Grand Portage to Fort Jonquière passed through a number of hostile nations and the French had to steer a delicate course between them. West of Lake Superior, the Sioux and Ojibwas warred over the wild rice marshes which replaced the maize fields farther south. Even though both were nominally French allies, traders had to tread carefully. Farther west, Assiniboins, Crees, and Monsonis sporadically fought both Sioux and Ojibwas. Most of the French posts stood on lands belonging to the latter, but the routes to these forts passed through the territories of the former.

It was ultimately an impossible situation. In 1734, the French equipped a Cree and Assiniboin expedition against the Sioux of the Prairies, and Jean-Baptiste Gaultier, Sieur de La Vérendrye (the son of Pierre, mentioned earlier in the chapter), accompanied them as an advisor. Once under way, the warriors informed the Frenchman that they actually intended to attack the Sioux of the upper Mississippi River, allied to the French. La Vérendrye departed immediately, but the damage was already done. Two years later, he set out from Fort Saint Charles with 19 men for Michilimackinac to purchase supplies. A few miles out, a party of Sioux set upon them, killed the lot, and carried off their heads as trophies. So far from home, the French who found their remains could only gather up the corpses and bury them under the fort's chapel. The Crees, Assiniboins, and Monsonis wanted to avenge the dead (and drag the French into their war), but the traders could neither support nor afford such a conflict and could only try to conciliate both factions. That same week, the trader René Bourassa nearly perished at the hands of the Sioux.

Despite heat, hardships, cold, and carnage, the Canadians clung tenaciously to these posts. In 1735, the upper Mississippi and the lands west of Lake Superior produced 100,000 livres weight of beaver, more than half the pelts gathered in the colony. By the 1750s, they produced nearly 1,000 bales annually, but the traders still played a dangerous game in obtaining them. In February 1752, Le Gardeur Saint Pierre and 5 men at Fort Jonquière found themselves confronted by 200 armed Assiniboin, erstwhile allies, who had come calling. As the Indians began helping themselves to French goods, Saint Pierre coolly tried to shoo them out of the fort, chiding them for their lack of manners. The situation now turned ugly as the Indians seized the guardhouse and all of the post's weapons. Despite translation problems, the Assiniboin made it clear they intended to kill everyone in the place and plunder it. With the French outnumbered 40 to 1 and unarmed, the outcome left little to the imagination. Saint Pierre, however, seized a firebrand from his hearth and ran to the fort's magazine hotly pursued by the intruders. Kicking open the door, he stove in the top of a powder keg and calmly offered to blow the fort and everyone in it to glory. Impressed, the Indians fled. Saint Pierre concludes the story saying, "I very quickly got rid of my firebrand, and had nothing more urgent to do than to go close my fort's gate."[33]

They were an extraordinary people, the Canadians of the upper country: tough, cocky, and capable. They had no counterpart in France and as such appeared a menace to good order. They were, however, indispensable. Writing in the 1720s, Father Charlevoix observed: "I know not whether I ought to reckon among the defects of our Canadians the good opinion they entertain of themselves. It is at least certain that it inspires them with a confidence, which leads them to undertake and execute what would appear impossible to many others. It must, however, be confessed that they have many excellent qualities. . . . Their agility and address are unequalled; the most expert Indians are not better marksmen, or manage their canoes in the most dangerous rapids."[34]

They accepted authority only when it seemed merited, but as the priest observed: "When they are well conducted, there is nothing which they will not accomplish, whether by land or sea, but in order to do this, they must entertain a great opinion of their commander. The late M. d'Iberville ... could have led them to the end of the world."[35] It was a most peculiar empire, this upper country, built upon the manufacture of men's hats and held together by a class of men who seemed to threaten everything the Bourbons stood for.

In the late 1730s, however, Beauharnois hoped it might become something more. In October 1736, he wrote to Paris that: "If the affair of the copper mines should have as advantageous results as We have Reason to Hope, this country will become more and more worthy of his Majesty's attention and of the jealousy of its neighbors."[36] The "affair of the copper mines" was an enterprise launched by the Sieur de La Ronde, commandant of Fort Chequamegon. The French had known of the existence of Lake Superior copper since the 1660s. A strategic material, it was essential in the casting of bronze artillery. As Sweden, closely tied to Protestant Holland and England, produced most of Europe's supply, the French had long sought their own.

La Ronde took command at Chequamegon in 1727. Hearing stories of great floating islands of copper, he obtained samples, and sent them off to France for assaying. Between the breadth of the Atlantic and the depth of Bourbon bureaucracy, it took him six years to obtain the requisite permissions to organize a mining company. In 1734, La Ronde received a grant for Chequamegon for a period of years to defray his start-up costs. In exchange, he agreed to hire miners and laborers to extract the ore and to build ships to move it to the Saint Lawrence.

At Pointe aux Pins, west of Sault Sainte Marie, La Ronde built a sprit-rigged sloop of 25 tons burden. Scouting the south shore of Lake Superior, he came upon very promising samples near the Ontonagon River. One, a mass of nearly pure copper, weighed 10,000 livres. In 1737, La Ronde brought in two German miners, and all seemed ready for the first great copper strike in North America. The two found four likely mines and the delighted La

Ronde hired a dozen voyageurs to bring in tools, set up shelters, and begin the mining. From here, however, everything went wrong. They found pieces, probably dropped by the glaciers, but no real vein. Much of what they did find proved *too* good and the mining amounted to trying to bash solid metal out of the ground. Worse, the Sioux and Ojibwa went to war, wrecking the trade of Chequamegon, which supported the cost of the mine. In 1740, La Ronde went down to Quebec to arrange more financing. Returning to Michilimackinac he died, exhausted and nearly bankrupt, at age seventy. Beauharnois's dreams of a country "more worthy of His Majesty's attention" died with him. Bad luck may have played a role, but a Jesuit following La Ronde's misadventures saw something else at work: "An inexhaustible mine of copper has been discovered on the shores of Lake Superior, 700 leagues from here; but the profits will never be great, owing to the immense expense of transporting the copper."[37]

In the seventeenth century, the French laid claim to an immense portion of the continent. In the eighteenth, they learned that it was one thing to claim a continent and quite another to hold and exploit one. Military strategies which appeared elegant upon a map foundered against the inexorable laws of time and distance. They had destroyed poor old La Ronde as well. In the end, the French were learning that the west was just too far away.

By the end of the 1740s the long peace between Britain and France was coming to an end. There would be war in America, but to what purpose? Louisiana and the Saint Lawrence Valley produced nothing France needed. The fur trade garnered wealth of a sort but hardly enough to justify retaining the colony, and La Ronde's misfortune had demonstrated the futility of extracting anything of substance from the upper country. What then was the value of New France? In the end, Paris would come to an extraordinary conclusion. The colony's value lay in neither farms, nor furs, nor mines, but rather in the upper country itself: its Indians, coureurs, voyageurs, and Métis traders. One governor described these resources: "The first is the great number of Indian alliances that the French keep with the Indian Nations.... The second reason for our superiority over the English is, the number of French-Canadians who are accustomed to live in the woods like the Indians, and become therebye not only qualified to lead them to fight the English, but to wage war even against these same Indians when necessary."[38] History had come full circle from the days of Colbert. Neither his industries nor his farmers mattered now. Rather, the very people he had sought to stamp out had become Canada's greatest asset. Tragically, this assumption presupposed that the colony's only importance lay in the making of war. In the next decade, old France would expect value for all she had invested in the New World.

SEVEN

"A Few Acres of Snow," 1740–1754

IN 1738, AN IRATE British sea captain, Robert Jenkins, stormed into the House of Commons waving his pickled ear and demanding revenge on the Spaniards who had removed it in Havana some years earlier. Britain declared war and the two countries set about each other in Florida, Panama, and the Caribbean. This "War of Jenkins' Ear" had no direct effect on the Great Lakes, but it rapidly became part of a larger conflict which would rage for nearly two decades and reshape the history of the world.

By 1739, Britain and France had recovered from the War of the Spanish Succession and again eyed each other warily. Since 1710, French colonial trade had risen from 25 to 140 million livres annually, with a total overseas trade of 300 million: a potent challenge to Britain's commercial power. The following year, an opportunity arose for a new test of strength. The Habsburg Emperor Charles VI died without a male heir and Europe split over the accession of his daughter Maria Theresa. Britain supported her, while France sided with claimants from Bavaria and Saxony. Initially a war of diplomatic maneuver, it finally exploded into open conflict in 1743. The French army did very well, defeating the Dutch and English at Fontenoy in 1745 and Lafelt in 1747, and capturing Bergen op Zoop and Maastricht in 1747–1748. In 1745, a French-backed rebellion in Scotland had nearly captured London. In New France, the Canadians resumed their border raids against New England with results similar to those in 1690 and 1704. All in all, Britain had a hard time of it.

At sea, however, things were different. Here, the Royal Navy methodically drove French shipping from the Atlantic. Privateers based at the fortress of Louisbourg on Cape Breton Island retaliated against New England's fishing fleet. In response, a Massachusetts expedition supported by the Royal Navy captured the port in 1745. Britain now effectively blockaded Canada. The next year, France dispatched 73 ships and nearly 13,000 soldiers and sailors under Admiral Jean-Baptiste, De Roye de La Rochefoucauld, Duc d'Anville, to recover Louisbourg and lay waste to the coast of New England. They never got there. Alternately becalmed or beset by gales, the fleet took nearly three months to make the crossing and arrived too battered to be of any service. Moreover, 2,500 men had succumbed to disease. The commander died of apoplexy (stroke) shortly after dropping anchor and his second in command attempted suicide a few days later. Under the circumstances, their successor decided to return to France. Nevertheless, for all intents and purposes, the war resulted in an indecisive draw.

It had, however, a profound effect on the upper country. The wars against the Fox and Chickasaw had cost a great deal of money. Bienville's campaign of 1739 alone had run some 800,000 livres.[1] In the delicate diplomatic climate which followed the end of the Fox Wars, furthermore, the western post commanders increasingly relied on presents to keep the peace. With war looming, the King desperately needed to reduce the colonial budget. In March 1743, under pressure from Paris, Governor Beauharnois leased all the western forts except Michilimackinac and Detroit directly to the highest bidder rather than awarding them to the army officers charged with their care. From the start, it proved a bad idea which rapidly became a worse one. Saddled with the price of the lease and the cost of maintaining the forts and supplying the Indians, the merchants had to raise prices. After the declaration of war the following year, British depredations on French shipping drove them higher still, and the fall of Louisbourg in 1745 effectively closed the Saint Lawrence River for the duration of the conflict.

By 1747, neither the merchants of Montreal nor the governor had any merchandise for the western posts. The Indians had come to depend upon European goods and these shortages posed a serious threat. Resentments which had festered for decades now exploded. The Ojibwa killed three voyageurs near Saginaw, another at Bois Blanc Island near Michilimackinac, and attacked two canoes in the narrows between La Cloche and Manitoulin Islands. They captured one and killed all eight men aboard, but the second escaped and reached Michilimackinac. Voyageurs on Lake Superior were robbed and beaten as well. Emboldened by their success, the Ojibwa then moved on Michilimackinac. Warned by the victims of the La Cloche attack, the French at the Straits were ready for them and the Indians withdrew after burning a few outbuildings.

In the south, the situation was worse. The Miami killed five voyageurs coming from Fort Ouiatanon and plundered their canoe. At Detroit, the Huron chief Nicholas formed a coalition of Huron, Potawatomi, and Miami and planned to surprise the fort. A Christian convert, however, told missionary Father La Richardie of the plot and the commandant secured the town. A supply convoy had just arrived, and the commandant pressed the men into service on the walls. Nevertheless, Detroit would remain effectively under siege until the end of the summer. Nicholas then spread the rumor that it had actually fallen and this was enough to force the surrender of the Miami post on the Maumee River. His agents then sent word to the Illiniwek to join them in ousting the French and opening a road to Oswego.

Just at that moment, the Illinois country was fertile ground for rebellion. The failure of Bienville's great expedition in 1740 had enraged the Illiniwek. They had wanted no part of the war in the first place and the governor's disaster had laid them open to reprisals. In 1741 the Chickasaw did, in fact, come north and attack one of their villages south of Kaskaskia. Gauging their anger, the missionaries feared an attack at any time. In 1742, an Illiniwek had gone to the English at Oswego, where he received a warm welcome and the advice, "The Frenchman is a dog who devours you. He has only bad merchandise and he sells it too dearly."[2] The French prevented a large-scale Indian trading expedition the next year only by spreading rumors of a fictitious epidemic in the English colonies. Sensing the unrest, the Chickasaw sent agents to the Illiniwek offering to bring Carolina traders to the Illinois country. Two chiefs, Iron Collar and Cat Face, went over to the Chickasaw and the latter bragged he would fight for them if they would give him the powder and lead.

In 1742, Benoist de Saint Clair, commandant of Fort de Chartre, fearing all this would trigger an open revolt, wrote to Detroit, Saint Joseph, Ouiatanon, and the Miami fort requesting that any war parties marching against the Chickasaw be sent though the Illinois country as a show of force. Governor Beauharnois shared Benoist's concern, and feared that the rebellion might spread north. By the end of the year, however, the crisis seemed to have passed. The entente between the Illiniwek and Chickasaw had apparently broken down and the latter again struck along the Mississippi. Under the circumstances, the Illiniwek could not afford an open rupture with the French.

By 1747 all this had changed. Concerted attacks by Louisiana's allies and parties of Canadian Indians had broken the power of the Chickasaw. In the general unrest, the Illiniwek were now free to act. In August, the Chevalier de Bertet wrote Governor Pierre François Rigaud de Vaudreuil of "an almost universal conspiracy on the part of the Illinois" against the French.[3] Bertet ordered the habitants to move from their scattered villages to one defensible position, rounded up the chiefs he suspected of duplicity, and sent them to New Orleans along with the wampum belts they had received from the English. Feigning ignorance, Vaudreuil met with them and made a considerable show of rewarding their loyalty. The arrival of the fall convoy with supplies and additional men finally put an end to the business. A large supply convoy from Montreal got through to Detroit and Michilimackinac and the immediate crisis in the north passed as well.

Nicholas's failure to capture Detroit and De Bertet's success in cowing the Illiniwek effectively doomed the rebellion. Had Detroit fallen and the French been run out of Illinois, France's empire in the upper country would have collapsed. Louisiana would have been in trouble as well. Without the grain and foodstuffs coming down the river to New Orleans, the Gulf settlements would have had very little to eat. All in all, it had been a near-run thing. The failure of the Illiniwek to rise had been a particularly important part of this. The Chevalier de Bertet received high marks for his handling of the crisis, but other factors had actually shaped their decision. Perhaps the most Europeanized of the western nations, the Illiniwek had abandoned the hoe in favor of the plow and cattle had replaced their reliance on hunting. They had large fields and settled towns, and many had become Christians. Had the French with their blacksmiths and merchants abandoned the country, this new way of life would have ended. Moreover, the French had always coveted their lands. Had the Illiniwek lost, the habitants would have been free to take everything they had. One last issue had probably affected their decision as well. In 1746, the Shawnee had come north into Illinois, settling along the Lower Ohio and the Wabash. The Illiniwek wanted them out and by the winter of 1747–1748 had begun a ruthless campaign to drive them from the country. To alienate the French on the eve of such a war would have made no sense at all. Sifting through the reports that spring, Vaudreuil concluded that "I do not think there is anything to fear on that side. The Illinois today have more reason than ever to court us."[4]

As Vaudreuil wrote this, England and France began negotiations which concluded in the Peace of Aix La Chapelle that October. The agreement restored Louisbourg to France, ships could again reach Quebec, and the price of goods at the western posts quickly fell by almost 50 percent. Most of the rebellious nations came in to make peace and the French had little option but to accept their contrition with as good grace as possible. The Miami, however, remained defiant. Instead of making up with the French, they allied themselves with the traders of the Ohio Land Company. Formed in 1747 by a group of Virginia planters and London merchants, it obtained a grant of 200,000 acres at the confluence of the Monongahela and Allegheny Rivers. In exchange, the company agreed to bring in 100 families and build a fort. Though primarily a land speculating concern, it also engaged in trade to the extent that it could sway Indian opinion to its side. The leader of this venture, the Irish Protestant George Croghan, had arrived in western Pennsylvania in 1741. Quickly learning Iroquois and Delaware, he set himself up in the Indian trade. At the behest of the Ohio company he had sent men west into the Miami country and established a headquarters at the village of Pickawillany. The headman of the village, Chief Memeskia—"La Demoiselle" to the French and "Old Britain" to the British—had signed a treaty with the Americans at Lancaster, Pennsylvania, in July 1748, allowing them to trade in Ohio. With Croghan's men established at his village, he invited the other Miami, as well as Kickapoo, Illiniwek, and Potawatomi to trade.

In the midst of all this, the King recalled Governor Beauharnois. At seventy-six, he was considered too old to effectively command the colony. Rumor had it that he had become senile as well. The old man left behind him an equivocal record. The Fox Wars had succeeded in preserving French power in the west, but at a terrible cost to France's prestige. The failures against the Chickasaw had left the Carolina traders active along Canada's southwestern frontier and jeopardized the Maumee-Wabash canoe route, its principal line of communication to Louisiana. The 1747 rebellion had nearly destroyed the western alliance system and created a general sense it was no longer viable. Beauharnois, however, deserved better. The troubles with the Foxes had inevitably resulted from the expansion of the fur trade. He had probably erred in relying on force rather than diplomacy, but it is not clear that negotiation could have resolved any of the underlying issues. The Chickasaw Wars, too, had not been his fault. It was really Louisiana's problem and the idea that Canada could have much effect on its outcome a pipe dream. Canada's troubles in the War of the Austrian Succession had resulted primarily from France's parsimonious colonial policy. Beauharnois had seen the colony's weaknesses and had sought to remedy them. However, his requests for funds, troops, and supplies had fallen upon deaf ears. France did not want to hear such things and made it clear that his successor should do something, just as it had been incumbent on Beauharnois to act in the matter of the Foxes. The departure of the old man, cautious, pragmatic, and keenly aware of the weaknesses of his colony, would prove disastrous.

The British captured Beauharnois's original replacement, the Marquis de La Jonquière, on his way to Quebec and in his stead the King sent another naval officer, Roland-Michel Barrin, Marquis de La Galissonière. A true Enlightenment man, he arrived with little knowledge of the country, but a considerable determination to find out. He studied reports, sent out fact-finding missions, and set out to restore the embattled colony. Bombarding Paris with requests for troops, munitions, and money, he sent settlers to Detroit and the Illinois country and sought to reform the leasing system for the western posts, which he saw as the effective cause of the Indian revolt the previous year. Nothing much came of all this. The Crown had no money for Canada, and so his requests for troops and supplies came to little. In his fiscally embarrassed situation, the new governor could afford to send only forty-five settlers to Detroit and sixty soldiers and a few colonists to the Illinois country: hardly enough to make a difference. The leasing of the western posts remained as well. He also sought to promote manufacturing, but ran up against mercantilist regulations which limited this in favor of French-made goods.

Despite his energy and regard for the Canadians, La Galissonière requested a replacement almost immediately. He had never wanted a posting in Canada and had accepted his appointment only out of duty. He left in September 1749. The next year, however, he set down in a memoir the importance of Canada and why it should be defended. He began by observing that the King's honor required that he not abandon the Canadians, who had come so far and suffered so much to build the colony. The Indians as well, particularly the Christian converts, must be protected from the Protestants massing along their borders. The governor also observed that New France must eventually become an important place, given the fertility of the soil, the potential mining wealth, and so on.

Now, however, La Galissonière the military man got to the heart of his argument. Canada, he said, was "a barren frontier, such as the Alps are to Piedmont, as Luxembourg would be to France, and as it, perhaps, is to the Queen of Hungary." The colony had always imposed a financial burden on France and would probably continue to do so for a long time to come. Yet, for all of that, it constituted "the strongest barrier that can be opposed to the ambition of the English." France could never sustain a navy capable of challenging Britain. The moribund Spanish empire could not either. The explosive growth of the English colonies, now nearly a million and a half strong, posed a second problem. It seemed only a matter of time before the Americans, supported by the Royal Navy, would set out to seize the French and Spanish holdings in America, the West Indies, and eventually even Mexico. Canada offered the only hope of halting this disaster, "since the French Colonies, despite their destitute condition, have always waged war against the English of the Continent with some advantage, though the latter are, and always have been, more numerous." The crucial portion of the memoir read: "The utility of Canada is not confined to the preservation of the French Colonies, and to rendering the English apprehensive for theirs; that Colony is not less essential for the conservation of the Spanish possessions in America, especially of Mexico."⁵

This document became extremely influential. In fact, the Marquis became the King's de facto Canada expert. Describing him, one official wrote: "He had commanded in Canada. He had been in all our colonies; he had studied them and he knew them."⁶ Remarkable for its sense of moral obligation and geopolitical sweep, the memoir nevertheless rested upon a dangerous supposition. Essentially a "domino theory," it posited that if Ohio fell, then Illinois would succumb and then Louisiana. With Louisiana in British hands, Mexico would be next and with it the French Caribbean. Such a catastrophe would radically alter the balance of power in Europe. Like the United States in Viet Nam two centuries later, Canada found itself on a collision course with a determined enemy over a region which had no intrinsic value and which posed daunting problems of strategy, logistics, and diplomacy.

In 1749, La Galissonière had attempted to restore French prestige in the Ohio River Valley by a show of force. He dispatched Captain Céloron de Blainville with a party of 230 French and Indians on a tour of the country to try to bring the Miami back to their old allegiance. The governor had also ordered him to bury a series of lead plaques along the route to warn the Americans that the valley belonged to France. The expedition's chaplain, Father Bonnecamp, left an alarming account of the country they passed through:

> This Beautiful River—so little known to the French, and, unfortunately, too well known to the English—is, according to my estimate, 181 marine leagues from the mouth of the Yjadakoin to the entrance of rivière à la Roche.... Each village [they passed] ... has one or more traders, who have in their employ engagés for the transportation of peltries. Behold, then, the English already far within our territory; ... Their design is, without doubt, to establish themselves there; and, if efficacious measures be not taken as soon as possible to arrest their progress, we run very great risk of seeing ourselves quickly driven from the upper countries, and of being obliged to confine ourselves to the limits which it may please those gentlemen to prescribe to us.⁷

Nothing went right: the rivers were shallow and rocky, the going slow, the Indians equivocal, and the English traders contemptuous. Céloron, once described as "attentive, clear-sighted, and active; firm, but pliant when necessary; fertile in resources, and full of resolution,—a man, in fine, made to command," also had a tendency toward bluntness which endeared him to neither superiors nor subordinates. His report presented the situation with characteristic directness: "I do not know by what means they [the Miami] may be brought back. If force is employed, they will be notified and take to flight." Nor would trade goods help. "If we send to them for trade, our traders can never give our merchandise at English prices on account of the costs they are obliged to incur. . . . and if the French traders would speak the truth they would admit that their profits arise only from the trade that they carry on with the English by the exchange of peltries." In addition to shipping costs, the furs available in the country were of the wrong sort for the French market: "Wildcat, otter, and fisher are very cheap in England and with us very high, also in that vicinity these are the only peltries, and there is no beaver. This latter is sold to the English."[8] To confront this threat, the French had only Fort Miami. Bonnecamp had seen the place during the expedition and his assessment was not reassuring. Nevertheless, Céloron doubted that it would be possible to build a real post in the Ohio country given the distances involved and the competition the English could offer to French trade.

La Galissonière's replacement, Jacques Taffanel, Marquis de La Jonquière, nevertheless set out to quell the unrest in Ohio. In 1750, he ordered Céloron, now commanding at Detroit, to attack Pickawillany, seat of the pro-British Miami and one of Croghan's trading posts. Its headman, Memeskia, had snubbed Céloron's request for a council during the latter's visit two years earlier. Nothing came of the governor's order, and La Jonquière repeated it the next year. Céloron again declined, calling the plan too risky and claiming that, in any case, it would require a force of at least 1,800 men to assure success: an odd response from someone of his caliber. For a man who had led a winter march against the Chickasaw in 1739 and successfully conducted a 2,000-mile expedition through the very same country with a force of only 230 to demand six times that number to burn a village only 200 miles from Detroit makes no sense. It seems likely that he saw the Ohio country as a morass from which the French would never escape and sought to derail the disaster before it began. It also seems likely that his superiors took his response as just that. In 1753, the bellicose Marquis Duquesne became governor and put Céloron out to pasture as town-major of Montreal.

During the winter of 1751–1752, the crisis deepened. La Jonquière died, and the interim governor, the Canadian Charles Le Moyne, Baron de Longeuil, wrote in his spring dispatches that the western country seemed to be falling apart. Smallpox raged, but worst among nations traditionally loyal to the French. Crop failures at Detroit and in the Illinois country had paralyzed any military operations from that quarter and it seemed likely that many of the French there would have to return to the Saint Lawrence. Worst of all, the commandant at Fort Saint Joseph reported that "all of the nations appear to take sides against us."[9] Casual murders of French troops and traders took place all over the country. The commandant at the post of Vincennes responded even more bluntly. Writing to the commander of Fort Ouiatanon he implored him to "use all means to protect himself from the storm which is about to burst upon the French."[10]

That summer, however, the emergency seemingly evaporated in one crushing French stroke. On June 21, a young cadet named Charles Langlade led a force of militia and Ottawa down from Michilimackinac to storm Memeskia's village. With most of the Miami away hunting, the attackers swept in at dawn undetected, captured the women working in the fields, and quickly surrounded the English traders' cabins. Three gave up without a fight, but the other five barricaded themselves in their hut and put up such resistance that Langlade requested a parley. Offering to spare the village if the Miami gave up the traders, he received the surrender of the town. The Ottawa, however, their blood up, went on a rampage. They cut the heart out of one of the traders and ate it. Killing Memeskia, they made a feast of him as well. The attack, so swift and ghastly, left the Ohio nations stunned. Governor Duquesne described this silence in a letter to the Minister of Marine: "It is so rare, Monseigneur that a war with the savages can bring about a stable peace that I should not be surprised if, at the instigation of the English, the Miamis were to ask their allies for help. Nevertheless, I have had no news of it."[11] Over the course of the summer, the Ohio nations declared their allegiance and all seemed well.

By the old rules of the game, the French should have now followed up their victory by sending traders and presents into the region to cement the alliance. In Ohio, however, these no longer applied. A hundred packhorses led by 15 or 16 American traders could carry as many goods as 15 or 20 canoes manned by 100 voyageurs. Moreover, the distance and difficulty of the route from Montreal meant the canoes could make only one round-trip a year. Croghan's men working out of Harrisburg, Pennsylvania, could make two. Cheaper goods, lower overhead, and faster delivery times doomed the sort of economic competition which had contained the Hudson's Bay Company and kept the Great Lakes French. Equally important, the situation in Ohio carried a third dimension: Croghan. Even though the Indians had largely renounced their ties to the American traders, the Irishman had no intention of giving in without a fight. Langlade's raid had cost him three men and furs and goods worth £3,000. By early fall, his men had returned with arms, horses, and three cannon. Given all of this, it seemed the French had no option but to invade Ohio and occupy it.

Longeuil, however, wanted no part in such an undertaking. A veteran of the Chickasaw campaign of 1739, he knew only too well the difficulties the western country imposed on military operations. Despite pressure from Paris, he argued that the best policy was to "pacify the upper country" rather than launch adventures into Ohio.[12] He noted a second problem. In 1655, the Iroquois had driven the Erie nation from Ohio and claimed the region by right of conquest. To challenge that claim would drive them into the arms of the English, effectively ending their long neutrality. Finally, France's claim to the region seemed dubious at best. Paris held that they had title by right of discovery, based upon La Salle's explorations of the 1660s. Unfortunately, he never actually claimed to have found the Ohio River. Never one to hide his light under a bushel, he most assuredly would have announced the discovery if he had. Accordingly, Longeuil believed that "it was not just to drive them out" and proposed a campaign of *petite guerre* to terrorize the Miami rebels into obedience along with subsidizing traders to go into the country with goods.[13]

Longeuil spoke for the bulk of the Canadians in his opposition to overt action. The merchants of Montreal had no interest in an invasion of Ohio: the country had no value. The voyageurs, too, knew the rocky, shallow rivers to be overcome and the paucity of quality furs to be gained. The army also doubted the wisdom of such a move. The metropolitan French, however, saw things differently. Intendant François Bigot raged at Longeuil's inaction, declaring, "I had often and uselessly represented to them [Longeuil and his officers] . . . that the Ohio was the source of all of the disorders that reigned among the Indians; that the English traded as masters over a land which belonged to France, the possession of which was necessary to our communication with the Mississippi."[14] The arrival of the new governor Ange de Menneville, Marquis Duquesne, in July 1752 settled the dispute. Longeuil and the Canadians were now under the direction of another metropolitan. The delighted Bigot wrote: "Fortunately you have sent a general, for if the government had been another year in the hands of these gentlemen, the Canadian policy would have indeed prevailed and no one would have forgotten it."[15]

Duquesne had served in the French navy since the age of thirteen. Protestant until the revocation of the Edict of Nantes in 1685, his father had renounced the reformed religion. Nevertheless, advancement had been slow. He served on a vessel, the *Elephant,* which went aground below Quebec in 1726 and the incident tarnished the careers of all aboard. His family lacked the money to buy him promotion and his Protestant heritage haunted him. During the War of the Austrian Succession, however, he acquired a solid reputation and made the acquaintance of influential men, particularly La Galissonière. In 1751, the latter recommended him as a replacement for Governor La Jonquière and the King appointed him. After a number of meetings with La Galissonière, Duquesne received his instructions and set out for Canada. Given his background, his patron, and his instructions, there was little doubt as to his policy in the Ohio country.

The new governor quickly aroused the hatred of nearly everyone in the colony. He set out to whip the militia and regulars into shape and incurred the wrath of both. More seriously, he announced his intention to send an expedition into Ohio the following year and placed at its head Paul Marin de La Malgue. The Canadian military opposed the move, and the new governor's roughshod dismissal of their concerns infuriated them. Equally serious was the matter of Marin. The captain had won a name against the Foxes and in the War of the Austrian Succession, but had never commanded so large a force on so long an expedition. Duquesne had passed over the senior officers of the colony, Céloron and Longeuil, as a purposeful snub. The habitants had grievances as well. The harvests in 1751 and 1752 had been poor and Duquesne himself noted the "famine" which existed at the time of his arrival. The governor's practice of forcibly requisitioning provisions from the farms along the Saint Lawrence, something new in the colony, did not sit well with the independent-minded Canadians.

The expedition of 1753 lived up to Céloron and Longeuil's direst predictions. Marin set out for Ohio with a force of nearly 2,000 French Marines and militia. The long portages and shallow rivers the French had to negotiate on their way to the confluence of the Monongahela and the Allegheny crippled their progress. Horses sent to carry supplies over the portages arrived too exhausted to be of any service. The scarcity of provisions along the Saint Lawrence meant that the army had little to eat in the first place and the delays only made this worse. There were also accusations of sabotage. Horses dispatched to the Niagara Portage disappeared. Supplies sent at vast expense and toil often suffered the same fate. Provisions were either stolen or left to spoil. Before the expedition reached even the headwaters of the Allegheny, it had lost 400 men to malnutrition and disease, and less than half of those remaining were fit for duty. The governor ordered the bulk of the survivors back to Montreal at the end of the fall without having reached the Forks of the Ohio. The haggard, emaciated men returning from the campaign shocked everyone, and the Bishop of Quebec requested that the campaign be abandoned. Even Intendant Bigot turned on the governor. The Minister of Marine blamed Duquesne for the casualties and staggering expense of the project and asked how he could have picked Marin over more experienced men.

Marin himself did not live long enough to suffer any blame. Pushing himself as hard as he had his men, the old soldier had lost his health and probably his sanity. Bullying the Iroquois, driving his men beyond the breaking point, and feuding with his officers, he gradually lost touch with reality. When ordered to withdraw, he refused and requested that Fort Le Boeuf be

burned down on top of him as a funeral pyre. To everyone's relief he died a short time later. Tough, experienced, Le Gardeur Saint Pierre, newly returned from the far west, took command of the remaining troops at Forts Presque Ile and Le Boeuf with orders to hold on until spring when Duquesne would send reinforcements to descend the Allegheny to the confluence, where the French would construct the last of the forts.

That winter, Saint Pierre had an unusual visitor. Governor Robert Dinwiddie of Virginia sent a young militia officer to deliver an ultimatum to the French. Arriving at Fort Le Boeuf, he presented the message: "The lands upon the River Ohio, in the Western Parts of the colony of Virginia, are so notoriously known to be the Property of the Crown of Great Britain, that it is a Matter of equal Surprize and Concern to me, to hear that a Body of French Forces are erecting Fortresses, and making Settlements upon that River, within his Majesty's dominions." After politely inquiring if the reports of the French expedition were in fact true, the governor's missive got down to the point: "Sir, in Obedience to my Instructions, it becomes my duty to require your peaceable Departure; and that you would forebear prosecuting a Purpose so interruptive to the Harmony and good understanding, which his Majesty is desirous to continue and cultivate with the most Christian King."[16]

Saint Pierre replied equally politely that he lacked the authority to make such a move, but would forward the governor's letter to Quebec. He then loaded the English emissary's canoe with provisions and liquor and sent him on his way. The young man, George Washington, returned to Williamsburg with the French reply. Outraged, Dinwiddie then ordered him back to the Ohio with a force of 400 militia to build a post at the confluence of the Monongahela and the Allegheny.

By the time Washington arrived, however, the French had already seized the confluence and were constructing Fort Duquesne. Hearing this, the Virginians halted at the Great Meadows 50 miles to the south. Britain and France were still at peace at this moment, but it could not last long. Something like 2,000 armed French, Indians, and Americans were now camped within a few miles of each other. Official policies of peace meant little in the Ohio Valley just now and it would require only one miscalculation to ignite the whole country. And Washington now made it. On hearing of the Virginians' arrival, the commander of Fort Duquesne sent a party under Ensign Joseph Coulon de Villiers de Jumonville to warn him off. (Joseph was the son of the elder Coulon de Villiers, victor of the prairie siege of 1730 and killed by the Sauk in 1733.) Washington learned of their approach and, knowing nothing of their diplomatic mission, led 40 men and 13 Indians out to intercept them. On May 28, catching the unsuspecting Jumonville by surprise, the Virginians killed ten and captured 21 others.

Even by the standards of the time, the attack had been a small affair and might have been smoothed over. However, as the details of the incident came out, the French were in no mood for an accommodation. According to one Virginian, Jumonville had fallen wounded and one of Washington's Indian allies split his skull open with his hatchet and then scooped out the ensign's brains to wash the blood from his hands. The attackers had then left the French dead unburied, and someone had beheaded a corpse and placed the skull upon a stake. Anticipating retaliation, Washington began construction of a small stockade, which he named Fort Necessity. The enraged garrison of Fort Duquesne and their Indian allies, perhaps 700 men, under Jumonville's brother swept down upon the fort on July 3 and forced Washington to surrender. Both the French and Indians wanted vengeance, but as yet no war existed between England and France. Conscious of this, the French commander let the Americans go with the promise that they would not return for a full year.

By September, word of Fort Necessity had reached England. The normally pragmatic Duke of Newcastle wrote of the news: "Our Troops upon The Frontiers of Virginia . . . have been defeated by a superior number of French & oblig'd to retire. . . . The Insults, and Encroachments of the French have alarm'd the Inhabitants of Our Colonies to That Degree that many of Them have left Their Habitations, with Crops upon Their Lands. All North America will be lost, If These Practices are tolerated: and No War can be worse to This Colony."[17] Both sides had now succumbed to domino logic. The next year, Britain sent 2,200 British regulars under General Edward Braddock to America to drive the French from the Ohio Valley and the great war for empire began in earnest.

Neither side fully comprehended what they had blundered into. France's confidence in the élan of the Canadians proved misplaced. Britain's pride in its fleet and its disciplined troops would prove sounder, but only after seven years of bloody and catastrophically expensive warfare. Britain did indeed win Canada, but at the cost of her American colonies twenty years later. The Bourbons would have their revenge in the American Revolution, but at the cost of their heads in 1789. In the end, the philosophe Voltaire probably had the last word in his satire *Candide* of 1759: "'You are acquainted with England, then,' said Candide; 'are they as great fools there as in France?' 'They have a different kind of folly,' said Martin. 'You know that these two nations are at war about a few acres of snow in Canada, and that they have spent a great deal more upon this war than all Canada is worth. To tell you precisely whether there are more people who ought to be confined in a madhouse in one country than in the other, is more than my weak capacity is able to perform.'"[18]

Notes

ABBREVIATIONS

IHC: *Collections of the Illinois State Historical Library,* 34 vols. (Springfield: Illinois State Historical Library, 1903–1959)
JRAD: Reuben Gold Thwaites, ed., *The Jesuit Relations and Allied Documents,* 70 vols. (Cleveland: Burrows Brothers, 1898; reprint, New York: Pageant Books, 1959)
MPA: Dunbar Rowland and A. G. Sanders, eds., *Mississippi Provincial Archives: French Dominion,* 1729–1740 (Jackson: Mississippi Press of the Department of Archives and History, 1927)
NYCD: E. B. O'Callaghan, ed., *Documents Relative to the Colonial History of New York,* 15 vols. (Albany: Weed and Parsons, 1855–1883)
WHC: *Collections of the State Historical Society of Wisconsin,* 20 vols. (Madison: The Society, 1855–1915)

PREFACE

1. Fred Anderson, *The Crucible of War: The Seven Years War and the Fate of Empire in British North America, 1754–1766* (New York: Vintage Books, 2001), xvii.

PROLOGUE   The Fur Trade and New France to 1676

1. Claude Allouez, "Journal," in Louise Phelps Kellogg, ed., *Early Narratives of the Northwest* (New York: Barnes and Noble, 1967), 143–144.

2. Samuel de Champlain, *Voyages of Samuel de Champlain* (New York: Barnes and Noble, 1967), 131–132.

3. Ibid., 165.

4. Gilles Havard, *Empire et métissages* (Paris: Presses de l'Université Paris-Sorbonne, 2003), 118.

5. Helen Hornbeck Tanner, *Atlas of Great Lakes Indian History* (Norman: University of Oklahoma Press, 1987), 18–19; R. Cole Harris, *Atlas historique du Canada*, vol. 1 (Montreal: Les Presses de l'Université de Montréal, 1987), plate 12.

6. Havard, *Empire et métissages*, 118; Harris, *Atlas historique*, vol. 1, plate 17; George Irving Quimby, *Indian Life in the Upper Great Lakes, 11,000 B.C. to A.D. 1800* (Chicago: University of Chicago Press, 1974), 109.

7. Father Paul Le Jeune, in Allan Greer, ed. *The Jesuit Relations: Natives and Missionaries in Seventeenth-Century North America* (Boston: Bedford / St. Martin's Press, 2000), 27. This document may also be found in *JRAD*, 6:297–299.

8. Father Paul Le Jeune, in *JRAD*, 6:297.

9. Denys Delâge, *Le Pays renversé* (Montreal: Boreal Express, 1985), 134–135, 238.

10. Marc Lescarbot, *History of New France*, 3 vols. (Toronto: The Champlain Society, 1907–1914), 3:174.

11. Ibid., 3:213.

12. Father Vimont, "The Journey of Jean Nicolet," in Kellogg, ed., *Early Narratives of the Northwest*, 15–16.

13. Samuel Jackson, *The Autobiography of Chief Black Hawk* (Champaign: University of Illinois Press, 1990), 41–42.

14. François Le Mercier, in *JRAD*, 40:211.

15. Ibid., 50:237.

16. Jean-Baptiste Colbert to Jean Talon, April 5, 1666, in W. J. Eccles, *The Canadian Frontier* (Albuquerque: University of New Mexico Press, 1983), 104.

17. Ibid., 105.

18. Jean Talon, in *IHC*, 1:3.

19. Jean Talon to Louis XIV, October 10, 1670, in *NYCD*, 9:63–64.

20. Count de Frontenac to Colbert, November 2, 1672, in *NYCD*, 9:90.

21. Grace Lee Nute, *Caesars in the Wilderness* (New York: Arno Press, 1977), 61.

22. Pierre Radisson, "Third Voyage," in Kellogg, ed., *Early Narratives of the Northwest*, 35.

23. Ibid., 47.

24. Raudot "Memoir," in W. Vernon Kinietz, *The Indians of the Western Great Lakes* (Ann Arbor: University of Michigan Press, 2007), 367.

25. Baron La Hontan, in Eccles, *The Canadian Frontier*, 8.

26. Raudot "Memoir," in Kinietz, *The Indians of the Western Great Lakes*, 344–345.

27. La Potherie, "Adventures of Nicholas Perrot," in Kellogg, ed., *Early Narratives of the Northwest*, 90.

ONE Frontenac and La Salle, 1673–1682

1. W. J. Eccles, *Frontenac: The Courtier Governor* (Lincoln: University of Nebraska Press, 2003), 33.
2. Ibid., 87.
3. Ibid., 76.
4. Du Luth, "Memoir," in Louise Phelps Kellogg, ed., *Early Narratives of the Northwest* (New York: Barnes and Noble, 1967), 331.
5. Ibid., 332.
6. Pierre F. X. Charlevoix, *History and General Description of New France*, John Gilmary Shea, ed. and trans., 6 vols. (Chicago: Loyola University Press, 1962), 3:197.
7. M. Duchesneau, "Memoir on the Western Indians, 1681," in *NYCD*, 9:163.
8. Francis Parkman, *The Discovery of the Great West: La Salle* (New York: Rinehart & Company, 1960), 226.
9. "Memoir of the Sieur de La Salle Reporting to the Sieur de Seignelay the Discoveries made by Him under the order of his Majesty," in *IHC* 1:121–122.
10. Ibid., 1:119.
11. W. J. Eccles, *The Canadian Frontier* (Albuquerque: University of New Mexico Press, 1983), 110.
12. La Potherie, in Reuben Gold Thwaites, ed., *The French Regime in Wisconsin, 1634–1760*, vols. 16, 17, 18, in *WHC*, 16:100.
13. "The Memoir of Lamothe Cadillac," in Milo Milton Quaife, ed., *The Western Country in the 17th Century* (Chicago: The Lakeside Press, 1947), 16.
14. Ibid.
15. Letter of La Salle, 1682, in *WHC*, 16:107.
16. "La Salle on the Illinois Country," in *IHC*, 23:12–13.
17. La Salle to a Friend, October, 1682, at the Miami Indians Ethnohistory Archives, www.gbl.indiana.edu/archives/miamis3/M82-99_17a.html.
18. "Petition from M. de La Salle to the Governor of Quebec, 5th of October, 1682," at the Miami Indians Ethnohistory Archives, www.gbl.indiana.edu/archives/miamis3/M82-99_18a.html.
19. M. Duchesneau, "Memoir on the Western Indians, 1681," in *NYCD*, 9:160.
20. Ibid., 2:161.
21. Ibid., 2:162.
22. Ibid.
23. "Charter of Privileges Granted by William Penn esq. to the Inhabitants of Pennsylvania and Territories, October 28, 1701," at the Avalon Project at Yale Law School, www.yale.edu/lawweb/avalon/states/pa07.htm.

24. "James II, Instructions to Governor Thomas Dongan, 1682," at http://press-pubs.uchicago.edu/founders/documents/amendI_religions 8.html.

25. Thomas Dongan, in Bernard Bailyn, *The Peopling of British North America* (Madison: University of Wisconsin Press, 1985), 96.

TWO   The Great Turtle and the Rock, 1683–1687

1. *Canada: A People's History,* episode 3, DVD, directed by Serge Turbide and Claude Lortie (Toronto: CBC Television, 2000).

2. Baron Louis-Armand de La Hontan, *New Voyages to North America,* Reuben Gold Thwaites, ed., 2 vols. (Chicago: A. C. McClurg, 1905), 1:145–146.

3. Ibid., 1:146–147.

4. "The Memoir of Lamothe Cadillac," in Milo Milton Quaife, ed., *The Western Country in the 17th Century* (Chicago: The Lakeside Press, 1947), 9–10.

5. Ibid., 11.

6. La Hontan, *New Voyages to North America,* 1:148.

7. La Durantaye, "Account," in *IHC,* 23: 60–67.

8. Reverend Father Étienne de Carheil to Monsieur Louis Hector de Callières, at Michilimackinac August 30, 1702, in *JRAD,* 65:237.

9. M. de Denonville to the M. de Seignelay, Ville Marie, August 25, 1687, in *NYCD,* 9:343.

10. "Instructions of La Salle," Chicago, September 1, 1683, in *IHC,* 23:36–41.

11. La Salle, in Richard Hagen, *Progress Report of the Archeological Research at Starved Rock State Park La Salle County, Illinois* (Springfield: Division of Parks and Memorials, 1949), 79.

12. Ibid.

13. Henri Joutel, in ibid., 81.

14. Ibid.

15. Henri Tonti, in Carl O. Sauer, Gilbert H. Cady, and Henry C. Cowles, *Starved Rock State Park and Its Environs* (Chicago: University of Chicago Press, 1918), 55.

16. "Grant of La Salle to D'Autray, April 26, 1683," in *IHC,* 23:19–27.

17. "Grant of La Salle to Prudhomme, August 11, 1683," in *IHC,* 23:28–36.

18. "La Salle on the Illinois Country, 1680," in *IHC,* 23:7–8.

19. Ibid., 23:9.

20. "De Gannes Memoir," in *IHC,* 23:302–304.

21. Ibid., 23:321–323.

22. Ibid., 23:350–351.

23. Ibid., 23:328.

24. Henri Joutel, *A Journal of La Salle's Last Voyage* (New York: Corinth Books, 1962), 159.
25. "De Gannes Memoir," in *IHC,* 23:341–343.
26. Ibid., 23:343.
27. Ibid., 23:351–352.
28. Joutel, *A Journal of La Salle's Last Voyage,* 163.
29. "De Gannes Memoir," in *IHC,* 23:336.
30. Baugy to La Durantaye, March 24, 1684, in Pauline Dube, ed., *La Nouvelle France sous Joseph-Antoine Le Febvre de La Barre, 1682–1685* (Sillery: Les éditions du Septentrion, 1993), 132.
31. Denonville to Seignelay, Ville Marie, August 25, 1687, in *NYCD,* 9:343.
32. "De Gannes Memoir," in *IHC,* 23:338.
33. The King to La Barre, April 10, 1684, in *IHC,* 23:47–50.
34. "Proposition of the Onnondaga and Cayuga Indians, Albany, 2nd August, 1684," in *NYCD,* 3:417.
35. Louis XIV to Monsieur La Barre, March 10, 1685, in *NYCD,* 9:269.
36. Louis XIV to M. de Meulles, March 10, 1685, in *NYCD,* 9:269.
37. "Instructions of the King to Denonville, March 10, 1685," in *IHC,* 23:70.

THREE   War in the Wilderness, 1687–1701

1. "Memoir for the Marquis de Seignelay Regarding the dangers that threaten Canada, January, 1687," in *NYCD,* 9:319–322.
2. Ibid.
3. "Governor Dongan's Report on the State of the Province, including his Answers to certain Charges against him, 1687," in *NYCD,* 3:395.
4. "Information given by Adondaraheera Unedachseno Awitharon cheefe Sachims of the Sinnekes . . . , 2nd August, 1687," in Peter Christoph, ed., *The Dongan Papers, 1683–1688,* part 2 (Syracuse: Syracuse University Press, 1996), 72–73.
5. Pierre F. X. Charlevoix, *History and General Description of New France,* John Gilmary Shea, ed. and trans., 6 vols. (Chicago: Loyola University Press, 1962), 4:13.
6. Bacqueville de La Potherie, in Emma Helen Blair, ed., *The Indian Tribes of the Upper Mississippi Valley and the Region of the Great Lakes,* 2 vols. (Lincoln: University of Nebraska Press, 1996), 2:46–47.
7. Ibid., 2:50–51.
8. *Dictionary of Canadian Biography Online,* gen. ed. Ramsay Cook, www.biographi.ca/EN/index.html, s.v. "Sir William Phips."
9. Baron Louis-Armand de La Hontan, *New Voyages to North America,* Reuben Gold Thwaites, ed., 2 vols. (Chicago: A. C. McClurg, 1905), 1:247–248.

10. "Commission of Sir Edmund Andros for the Dominion of New England, April 7, 1688," at the Avalon Project at Yale Law School, www.yale.edu/lawweb/avalon/states/mass06.htm.

11. "Captain Duplessis' Plan for the Defense of Canada," in *NYCD*, 9:447.

12. "Narrative of the Military Operations in Canada, 1691–1692," in *NYCD*, 9:536, and Charlevoix, *History and General Description of New France*, 4:218–219.

13. "Narrative of the Most Remarkable Occurrences in Canada, 1692–1693," in *NYCD*, 9:562, and Charlevoix, *History and General Description of New France*, 4:237.

14. "Narrative of the Most Remarkable Occurrences in Canada, 1692–1693," in *NYCD*, 9:568–569.

15. Charlevoix, *History and General Description of New France*, 4:246.

16. "Memoir of the King to the Count de Frontenac and Sieur de Champigny, 8th May, 1694," in *NYCD*, 9:573; "Narrative of the Most Remarkable Occurrences in Canada, 1692–1693," in *NYCD*, 9:556.

17. "De Gannes Memoir," in *IHC*, 23:326–327.

18. "Narrative of the Most Remarkable Occurrences in Canada, 1692–1693," in *NYCD*, 9:569.

19. "Narrative of the Most Remarkable Occurrences in Canada, 1694–1695," in *NYCD*, 9:603.

20. "Narrative of the Most Remarkable Occurrences in Canada, 1695–1696," in *NYCD*, 9:648.

21. Reverend Father Lamberville to M. de La Barre, February 10, 1684, in *NYCD*, 9:227n.

22. "Narrative of the Most Remarkable Occurrences in Canada, 1697–1698," in *NYCD*, 9:681.

23. Claude-Charles Bacqueville de La Potherie, *Voyage de l'Amerique: contenant ce qui s'est passé de plus remarquable dans l'Amerique septentrionale depuis 1534 jusqu'à present* (Amsterdam: Henry des Bordes, 1723), 3:201–202, at Early Canadiana Online, www.canadiana.org/ECO/PageView?id=1cefbc38d18b30a&display=36897+0209.

24. Charlevoix, *History and General Description of New France*, 5:145–148.

25. "Ratification of the Peace concluded in the month of September last between the Colony of Canada and its Allies and the Iroquois . . . ," in *NYCD*, 9:722.

FOUR   The Foxes, 1701–1736

1. Baron Louis-Armand de La Hontan, *New Voyages to North America*, Reuben Gold Thwaites, ed., 2 vols. (Chicago: A. C. McClurg, 1905), 1:394.

2. Verner W. Crane, *The Southern Frontier* (New York: W. W. Norton, 1981), 110–113.

3. Tonti, "Memoir on La Salle's Discoveries," in Louise Phelps Kellogg, ed., *Early Narratives of the Northwest* (New York: Barnes and Noble, 1967), 297.

4. "The Voyage of Saint Cosme," in Kellogg, ed., *Early Narratives of the Northwest*, 351.

5. Father Allouez, 1670, in *WHC*, 16:70.

6. "News from the Ottawas, 1695," in *WHC*, 16:165.

7. Ibid., 16:161.

8. Louise Phelps Kellogg, "The Fox Indians during the French Regime," in *Proceedings of the State Historical Society of Wisconsin* (Madison: The Society, 1908), 157.

9. Carheil to Champigny, August 30, 1702, in *WHC*, 16:214–215.

10. Pierre F. X. Charlevoix, *History and General Description of New France*, John Gilmary Shea, ed. and trans., 6 vols. (Chicago: Loyola University Press, 1962), 5:185.

11. "Summary of the Inspection of the Posts of Detroit and Michilimackinac, November 14, 1708," in *WHC*, 16:254.

12. Ibid., 16:256.

13. Ibid.

14. Reverend Father Étienne de Carheil to Monsieur Louis Hector de Callières, at Michilimackinac August 30, 1702, in *JRAD*, 65:251–253.

15. Dubuisson to Vaudreuil, June 15, 1712, in *WHC*, 16:268.

16. Ibid., 16:272.

17. Ibid.

18. Ibid.

19. Yves Zoltvany, ed., *The French Tradition* (New York: Harper & Row, 1969), 129–130.

20. Ramezay to the French Minister, September 18, 1714, in *WHC*, 16:303.

21. "Proceedings of the Council of Marine, Jan. 6, 1717," in *WHC*, 16:345–346.

22. Perrot, "Memoir," in Emma Helen Blair, ed., *The Indian Tribes of the Upper Mississippi Valley and the Region of the Great Lakes*, 2 vols. (Lincoln: University of Nebraska Press, 1996), vol. 1, 260.

23. "Account of the Siege of Detroit, 1712," in Louise Phelps Kellogg, *The French Regime in Wisconsin and the Northwest* (New York: Peter Smith, 1968), 281.

24. Vaudreuil to the Council of Marine, October 14, 1716, in *WHC*, 16:342–343.

25. Kellogg, "The Fox Indians," 165.

26. Louvigny to the Count of Toulouse, October 1, 1717, in *WHC*, 16:348–349.

27. Vaudreuil to the Council of Marine, October 22, 1719, in *WHC*, 16:393.

28. Louvigny to the Council of Marine, October 19, 1720, in *WHC*, 16:390.

29. Du Tisné to the Company of the Indies, January 14, 1725, in *WHC*, 16:452.

30. Boulanger and Kereben to Du Tisné, January 10, 1725, in *WHC*, 16:456.

31. Beauharnois to the Minister of Marine, October 25, 1727, in Kellogg, "The Fox Indians," 171.

32. Hocquart to the Minister of Marine, January 15, 1731, in *WHC*, 17:129–130; Beauharnois to the Minister of Marine, November 2, 1730, in Kellogg, *The French Regime*, 324–327.

33. "Relation of the Journey of the Sieur de Noyelle, October, 1735," in *WHC*, 17:226.

34. Beauharnois to the Minister of Marine, October 17, 1736, in Kellogg, "The Fox Indians," 178.

35. Beauharnois to the Minister of Marine, October 16, 1737, in *WHC*, 17:275–276.

36. Ibid.

37. This idea of an Indian moral economy of war came from Denys Delage, "War and French Indian Alliance," *European Review of Native American Studies* 5, no. 1 (1991): 15–20.

38. Jean Baptiste le Moyne, Sieur de Bienville, "Memoir on Louisiana, 1726," at the Miami Indians Ethnohistory Archives, www.gbl.indiana.edu/archives/miamis7/M23-30_13a.html.

39. Kellogg, *The French Regime*, 340.

FIVE Illinois and the Chickasaw Wars, 1700–1740

1. Ramezay and Bégon to the Minister of Marine, November 7, 1715, in *WHC*, 16:331–332.

2. Raymond Phineas Stearns, "Joseph Kellog's Observations on Senex's Map of North America (1710)," *The Mississippi Valley Historical Review* 23 (December 1936): 353–354.

3. "Code Noir (The Black Code)," at http://chnm.gmu.edu/revolution/d/335/.

4. Natalie Maree Belting, *Kaskaskia under the French Regime* (Carbondale: Southern Illinois University Press, 2003), 19.

5. Bienville Report, August 25, 1733, in *MPA*, 200.

6. Ibid., 201.

7. Ibid., 193.

8. Ibid., 201.

9. Bienville to Maurepas, August 20, 1735, in *MPA*, 267.

10. Bienville to Maurepas, June 28, 1736, in *MPA*, 305.

11. Ibid., 306.

12. Ibid., 307.

13. Bienville to Maurepas, February 15, 1737, in *MPA,* 331.

14. Bienville to Maurepas, June 28, 1736, in *MPA,* 313.

15. Pierre F. X. Charlevoix, *History and General Description of New France,* John Gilmary Shea, ed. and trans., 6 vols. (Chicago: Loyola University Press, 1962), 6:121–122.

16. Crémont to the Minister, 1737, in Joseph Peyser, ed., *Letters from New France: The Upper Country, 1686–1783* (Champaign: University of Illinois Press, 1992), 160–161.

17. Parisien Anspessade, "Account of D'artaguiette's Defeat by the Chickasaws (April 1, 1736)," in Caroline and Eleanor Dunn, trans., "Indiana's First War," *Indiana Historical Society Publications* 8, no. 2 (1924): 129–133, at the Miami Indians Ethnohistory Archives, www.gbl.indiana.edu/archives/miamis8/M31–45_41a.html.

18. Bienville and Salmon to Maurepas, June 1736, in *MPA,* 315.

19. Salmon to Maurepas, January 29, 1740, in *MPA,* 419.

20. Louboey to Maurepas, May 10, 1740, in *MPA,* 463.

21. *Dictionary of Canadian Biography Online,* gen. ed. Ramsay Cook, www.biographi.ca/EN/index.html, s.v. "Lemoyne de Bienville."

six   A Country More Worthy of His Majesty's Attention, 1736–1754

1. These figures were compiled from "Enumeration of the Indian Tribes connected with the Government of Canada, 1736," in *NYCD,* 9:1052–1058, and Dean R. Snow, *The Iroquois* (Malden, Massachusetts: Blackwell Press, 1996), 110.

2. This discussion of disease was assembled from French reports in *WHC,* 16, 17, 18, passim.

3. Duquesne to M. de Machault, October 31, 1754, in W. J. Eccles, *The Canadian Frontier* (Albuquerque: University of New Mexico Press, 1983), 158.

4. Beauharnois to the Minister, October 9, 1744, in *WHC,* 17:443.

5. "Memoir of Bougainville, 1757," in *WHC,* 18:171.

6. Dale Miquelon, *New France, 1701–1744: A Supplement to Europe* (Toronto: McClelland and Stewart, 1987), 159.

7. Beauharnois to the French Minister of Marine, January 20, 1733, in *WHC,* 17:171.

8. "Memoir on the Savages of Canada . . . , 1718," in *WHC,* 16:368–369.

9. Ibid.

10. Ibid., 16:366–367.

11. Beauharnois and Hocquart to the French Minister of Marine, October 5, 1736, in *WHC,* 17:241–242.

12. Hocquart to the Minister of Marine, October 7, 1737, in *WHC,* 17:265.

13. Ibid., 17:265–266.

14. "Memoir of Bougainville, 1757," in *WHC*, 18:194.

15. Captain Philip Pittman, *The Present State of the European Settlements on the Mississippi* (Gainesville: University of Florida Press, 1973), 45.

16. "Memoir of Bougainville, 1757," in *WHC*, 18:176.

17. Thomas Hutchins, *A Topographical Description of Virginia, Pennsylvania, Maryland, and North Carolina by Thomas Hutchins, (1778)*, 26–30, at the Miami Indians Ethnohistory Archives, www.gbl.indiana.edu/archives/miamis21/M78_3a.html.

18. "History of Fort Ouiatenon," at www.tippecanoe.in.gov/egov/docs/1154005928875.htm.

19. Hutchins, *A Topographical Description*, 26–30.

20. Andrew Gallup, ed., *The Céloron Expedition to the Ohio Country, 1749: The Reports of Pierre-Joseph Céloron and Father Bonnecamps* (Bowie, Maryland: Heritage Books, 1997), 77.

21. "La Pause's Observations and Notes upon Fort Frontenac, 1756," in Richard Preston, *Royal Fort Frontenac* (Toronto: Champlain Society, 1958), 251.

22. Ibid., 250.

23. Bonnecamp, in Gallup, *The Céloron Expedition*, 67.

24. "The Memoir of Lamothe Cadillac," in Milo Milton Quaife, ed., *The Western Country in the 17th Century* (Chicago: The Lakeside Press, 1947), 15.

25. Marie Gérin-Lajoie, trans. and ed., "Fort Michilimackinac in 1749: Lotbinière's Plan and Description," *Mackinac History* 2, no. 5 (1976): 4.

26. "The Mackinac Register, 1695–1821," in *WHC*, 19:9.

27. Gérin-Lajoie, "Fort Michilimackinac in 1749," 9.

28. Ibid.

29. Beauharnois to the Minister of Marine, October 16, 1737, in *WHC*, 17:274–275.

30. Joseph L. Peyser, trans. and ed., *Jacques Legardeur de Saint Pierre: Officer, Gentleman, Entrepreneur* (Lansing: Michigan State University Press, 1996), 180.

31. Ibid.

32. Alexander Henry, *Travels and Adventures in the Canadas* (Chicago: The Lakeside Press, 1921), 68.

33. Peyser, *Jacques Legardeur de Saint Pierre*, 186–187.

34. Pierre F. X. Charlevoix, *Journal of a Voyage to North America*, ed. Louise Phelps Kellogg, 2 vols. (Chicago: The Caxton Club, 1923), 1:248.

35. Ibid.

36. Beauharnois and Hocquart to the French Minister of Marine, October 5, 1736, in *WHC*, 17:242.

37. Father Nau to Madame Aulneau, October 12, 1739, in *JRAD*, 69:39.

38. "Memoir of the Marquis de Galissonière, 1752," in *NYCD*, 10:223.

SEVEN   "A Few Acres of Snow," 1740–1754

1. William Eccles, *France in America* (New York: Harper & Row, 1972), 168.

2. Norman W. Caldwell, "The Chickasaw Threat to French Control of the Mississippi in the 1740's," *Chronicles of Oklahoma* 16, no. 4 (December 1938): 478, at http://digital.library.okstate.edu/Chronicles/vo16/vo16p465.html.

3. Vaudreuil to Maurepas, September 19, 1747, at the Miami Indians Ethnohistory Archives, www.gbl.indiana.edu/archives/miamis9/M46–48_15a.html.

4. Vaudreuil to Maurepas, May 24, 1748, at the Miami Indians Ethnohistory Archives, www.gbl.indiana.edu/archives/miamis9/M46–48_19a.html.

5. "Memoir of La Galissonière, 1751," in *IHC*, 27:5–22, passim.

6. "Memoir of Silhouette on the Inexpediency of Abandoning Canada, February, 1759," in *IHC*, 27:249.

7. Bonnecamp, in Andrew Gallup, ed., *The Céloron Expedition to the Ohio 1749: The Reports of Pierre-Joseph Céloron and Father Bonnecamps* (Bowie, Maryland: Heritage Books, 1997), 75–76.

8. "Journal of Celoron's Expedition down the Ohio," in *WHC*, 18:57.

9. M. de Longeuil to M. de Rouillé, April 21, 1752, in *NYCD*, 10:247.

10. Ibid.

11. Duquesne to the French Minister, October 25, 1752, in *WHC*, 18:129.

12. Bigot to the Minister, October 26, 1752, in *IHC*, 27:40.

13. Ibid., 27:41.

14. Ibid., 27:40.

15. Ibid., 27:41.

16. Robert Dinwiddie, Williamsburg, October 31, 1753, in Joseph L. Peyser, trans. and ed., *Jacques Legardeur de Saint Pierre: Officer, Gentleman, Entrepreneur* (Lansing: Michigan State University Press, 1996), 202.

17. Newcastle to Albemarle, September 25, 1754, in *IHC*, 27:50–51.

18. Voltaire, *Candide* (New York: Penguin Classics, n.d.), 110.

Bibliographic Essay

This discussion is not intended as a comprehensive bibliography. The works presented here were used in researching this book, and may serve as an introduction to the French experience in the Great Lakes region.

Document Collections

Reuben Gold Thwaites's *The Jesuit Relations and Allied Documents* (Cleveland: Burrows Brothers, 1898; reprint, New York: Pageant Books, 1959) is the starting point for any study of the upper country. Published annually between 1632 and 1678 as a fund-raising device, it provides a wealth of ethnographic and historical material on the Great Lakes. E. B. O'Callaghan's *Documents Relating to the Colonial History of New York*, 15 vols. (Albany: Weed and Parsons, 1855–1883) has numbers of state papers on Canada and the upper country. See particularly volumes 9 and 10. The collections also contain materials on the English governors and Anglo-French policy. Be careful, however, with the French papers, as the translations are sometimes faulty. Peter Christoph's *The Dongan Papers, 1683–1688* (Syracuse: Syracuse University Press, 1996) includes a number of valuable documents concerning that governor's dealings with both the French and Iroquois. Reuben Gold Thwaites's *The French Regime in Wisconsin, 1634–1760*, vols. 16, 17, 18, in the *Collections of the State Historical Society of Wisconsin* (Madison: The Society, 1902–1908) contain materials on the Fox Wars. Volumes 33 and 34 of *The Researches and Collections of the Michigan Pioneer and Historical Society* (Lansing: The Michigan Pioneer and Historical Society, 1904–1905) have useful documents on Cadillac and early Detroit. "The Ouiatanon Papers" in the *Indiana Historical Collections* contain materials on this important post. Richard Preston's *Royal Fort Frontenac* (Toronto: Champlain Society, 1958) has a great number of papers illustrating life there.

On the Illinois country, the *Collections of the Illinois State Historical Library,* 34 vols. (Springfield: Illinois State Historical Library, 1903–1959) has a number of volumes of valuable documents. Volume 1 has materials on La Salle. Volume 23, Calvin Pease's *The French Foundation, 1680–1693* has a wealth of correspondence and business documents on Fort Saint Louis I and II (des Illinois and de Pimitoui). Volume 29, Pease's *Illinois on the Eve of the Seven Year's War* contains valuable material on the diplomatic crisis of the 1750s. Volume 10, Clarence Alvord and Clarence Carter's *The Critical Period, 1763–1765,* has a wealth of papers on Illinois under the British regime. Dunbar Rowland and A. G. Sanders's *Mississippi Provincial Archives,* vol. 1, *French Dominion, 1729–1740* (Jackson: Press of the Department of Archives and History, 1927) contains important Louisiana papers. The documents on the Chickasaw Wars are particularly useful. Their *Mississippi Provincial Archives,* vol. 5, *French Dominion 1749–1763* (Baton Rouge: Louisiana State University Press, 1984) has material on the Illinois country in the 1750s. Pauline Dube's *La Nouvelle France sous Joseph-Antoine Le Febvre De La Barre, 1682–1685: letters, mémoirs, instructions et ordonnances* (Sillery: Les éditions du Septentrion, 1993) is an extremely useful collection of papers from the regime of that ill-fated governor. The correspondence of La Salle, the Chevalier de Baugy, Olivier Morel, Sieur de La Durantaye, and René Legardeur, Sieur de Beauvais, are of particular interest for Fort Saint Louis.

Travel Narratives and Accounts

Samuel de Champlain, *Voyages* (New York: Barnes and Noble, 1967) is a good short edition of the writings of this pivotal character. Louise Phelps Kellogg's *Early Narratives of the Northwest* (New York: Barnes and Noble, 1967) is a standard collection of early accounts by Radisson, Marquette, Perrot, Tonti, Du Luth, and others. The best edition of Pierre Radisson is Arthur T. Adams, ed., *The Explorations of Pierre Esprit Radisson* (Minneapolis: Ross and Haines, 1961). The book modernizes his atrocious English and Adams's editing and annotations help clarify many confusing aspects of his narrative. Emma Helen Blair's *The Indian Tribes of the Upper Mississippi Valley and the Region of the Great Lakes,* 2 vols. (Lincoln: University of Nebraska Press, 1996) is a reprint of a classic with good translations of the writings of the diplomat and trader Nicholas Perrot and the soldier Bacqueville de La Potherie.

In a class by itself is Baron Louis-Armand de La Hontan's *New Voyages to North America,* ed. Reuben Gold Thwaites, 2 vols. (Chicago: A. C. McClurg, 1905). As a historical source, it must be used with care. La Hontan explores fictitious rivers inhabited by equally fictitious peoples. His famous Huron "Adario" is less an Indian than a spokesman for La Hontan's opinions. On the other hand, he was fascinated by the country and his accounts of the people, both Red and White, he encountered and the events he witnessed make compelling reading.

W. A. Kenyon and J. R. Turnbull's *The Battle for the Bay* (Toronto: Macmillan of Canada, 1971) contains the memoir of the Chevalier de Troye, one of the great adventures of New France. His description of the canoe men and the hardships of the route to Hudson's Bay is a valuable portrait of seventeenth-century travel and war. Joseph Peyser's *Letters from New France: The Upper Country, 1686–1783* (Champaign: University of Illinois Press, 1992) contains many useful documents on the Great Lakes in the French regime. Milo Milton Quaife's *The Western Country in the 17th Century* (Chicago: The Lakeside Press, 1947) is another valuable source, containing the memoirs of Antoine Laumet, Sieur de Cadillac, and Pierre Liette. The first has a great deal of useful information about Michilimackinac in the 1690s. Liette served in Illinois for more than twenty years and his descriptions of both Forts Saint Louis des Illinois and de Pimitoui are indispensable. His observations of the Illinois nation are also among the most detailed and sympathetic portraits of American Indians that survive. Henri Joutel's *A Journal of La Salle's Last Voyage* (New York: Corinth Books, 1962) is an extraordinary document. Joutel was a man of surpassing courage and a remarkably objective observer of the country and its peoples. His account of Fort Saint Louis is among the best descriptions of that post. Louis-Henri, Chevalier de Baugy's *Journal d'une expedition contre les Iroquois en 1687: letters et pieces relatives au fort Saint-Louis des Illinois* (Paris: E. Laroux, 1883) has the best account of the siege of Fort Saint Louis in 1684. His narrative of Denonville's expedition is valuable as well. Finally, his description of the Atlantic passage to Canada and his canoe voyage to Michilimackinac and Illinois offer a fascinating picture of seventeenth-century life.

Pierre F. X. Charlevoix's *Journal of a Voyage to North America,* Louise Phelps Kellogg, ed., 2 vols. (Chicago: The Caxton Club, 1923) is an invaluable description of the upper country in the early eighteenth century. The priest had a clear sense that something unusual was happening in Canada. He saw its inhabitants as a new people, distinct from old France, and he makes a number of thoughtful observations about the phenomenon. *The Voyages of Father Emmanuel Crespel in Canada,* in John Gilmary Shea, ed., *Perils of the Ocean and Wilderness* (Boston: Patrick Donahoe, 1856) contains what is probably the best account of Marchand de Lignery's abortive 1728 expedition against the Fox nation. Joseph L. Peyser's *Jacques Legardeur de Saint Pierre: Officer, Gentleman, Entrepreneur* (Lansing: Michigan State University Press, 1996) is a fascinating collection of papers on the career of this important colonial officer. Peyser's *On the Eve of Conquest: The Chevalier de Raymond's Critique of New France, 1754* (East Lansing: Michigan State University Press, 1997) provides a useful and sometimes caustic discussion of the state of affairs in the upper country on the eve of the Seven Years War. Andrew Gallup's *The Céloron Expedition to the Ohio Country, 1749* (Bowie, Maryland: Heritage Books, 1997) contains the reports of Céloron de Blainville and Father Bonnecamp's account of his expedition. These are invaluable in understanding the Canadians' hostility to Governor Duquesne's western policy. Alexander Henry's *Travels and Adventures in the Canadas* (Chicago: The Lakeside Press, 1921) is another useful source on Michilimackinac and the upper country toward the end of the French regime. He was among the first Englishmen to arrive in the upper country after the conquest and he lived and traveled among the Canadians. Though often unreliable, he had a wonderful eye for the details of daily life. Captain Philip Pittman's *The Present State of the European Settlements on the Mississippi* (Gainesville: University of Florida Press, 1973) provides an interesting picture of French Illinois in the years just after the French and Indian War.

Secondary Sources

Reference

For portraits of the people who inhabited the upper country, Ramsay Cook's *Dictionary of Canadian Biography Online,* www.biographi.ca/EN/index.html, is an invaluable source of information on historical figures both great and small. R. Cole Harris and J. G. Matthews's *Historical Atlas of Canada* (Toronto: University of Toronto Press, n.d.) is a first-rate work with beautifully rendered maps and graphics researched by many of Canada's leading scholars. Helen Hornbeck Tanner's *Atlas of Great Lakes Indian History* (Norman: University of Oklahoma Press, 1987) has excellent maps of the Great Lakes and its peoples. The accompanying text is extremely useful as well. Eric Morse's *Fur Trade Canoe Routes of Canada: Then and Now,* 2nd ed. (Toronto: University of Toronto Press, 1979) is an essential reference for those working on the Canadian frontier. Over twenty-odd years, Morse paddled most of the routes of the fur trade, delved deeply into travel narratives, and produced an absorbing re-creation of the highways of the upper country. Among canoeists on both sides of the border, the work is revered simply as "Morse." Fred Hoxie's *Encyclopedia of North American Indians* (New York and Boston: Houghton Mifflin Company, 1996) is a comprehensive source written by a variety of specialists.

General Histories

Histories of Canada begin with Marc Lescarbot's *History of New France,* 3 vols. (Toronto: The Champlain Society, 1907–1914). Lescarbot came to the New World in 1606 and published his history in 1609. A valuable account of the earliest days of New France, it also contains some of the shrewdest assessments of the Indians ever written. Claude-Charles Bacqueville de La Potherie's *Voyage de l'Amerique: contenant ce qui s'est passé de plus remarquable dans l'Amerique septentrionale depuis 1534 jusqu'à present* (Amsterdam: Henry des Bordes, 1723) needs to be checked against other sources, but La Potherie was there and knew many of the principal characters. Pierre F. X. Charlevoix, *History and General Description of New France*, 6 vols. (Chicago: Loyola University Press, 1962), is an extraordinary work. Now more than 250 years old, it remains a lively, engaging story and very well written. Charlevoix's portrayal of the Indian nations was remarkable for his time. In his telling, they are neither savages nor forest philosophers, but rather rational people whose actions are governed by the same concerns as the Europeans. It is a very modern interpretation and one not used again for two centuries. Charlevoix also worked from primary papers and interviewed many of the principal characters. The standard of scholarship is remarkable for an eighteenth-century work. His nineteenth-century editor and translator, John Gilmary Shea, was a considerable historian in his own right and his footnotes and annotations allow access to the sources Charlevoix used to construct his narrative. Francis Parkman, *France and England in North America* (New York: Literary Classics of the United States Inc., 1983) has been relegated to the realm of literature rather than history, but remains a compelling and beautifully written narrative.

Modern Surveys

In print for nearly forty years, William J. Eccles's *The Canadian Frontier* (Albuquerque: University of New Mexico Press, 1983) remains the best concise introduction to New France and the west. His *France in America* (New York: Harper & Row, 1972) places the story in hemispheric context. *Canada under Louis XIV, 1663–1715* (Toronto: McClelland and Stewart, 1964) is a more detailed treatment of this important period. His "The Fur trade and Eighteenth Century Imperialism," *William and Mary Quarterly* (September 1983): 341–362, is a concise discussion of French policy in the upper country in the period 1700–1754. Dale Miquelon's *New France, 1701–1744: A Supplement to Europe* (Toronto: McClelland and Stewart, 1987) is the best survey of New France in the first half of the eighteenth century, and his chapter on the *Pays d'en haut* has a very good discussion of the economics, diplomacy, and events of the region. Richard White's *The Middle Ground: Indians, Empires, and Republics in the Great Lakes Region* (Cambridge: Cambridge University Press, 1991) has generated considerable controversy, but nevertheless contains a wealth of detail on the world of the Great Lakes.

Regional and Topical Studies

Louise Dechêne's *Habitants et marchands de Montréal au XVIIe siècle* (Montreal: Les Éditions du Boréal, 1988) has valuable material on the organization of the French fur trade. Stephen Saunders Webb's *1676: The End of American Independence* (New York, 1984; Cambridge, 1985) and *The*

Governors-General: The English Army and the Definition of the Empire, 1569–1681 (Chapel Hill: University of North Carolina Press, 1987) contain extremely useful discussions of the English military governors of New York and Anglo-Iroquoian diplomacy. Louise Phelps Kellogg's *The French Regime in Wisconsin and the Northwest* (New York: Peter Smith, 1968), originally published in 1928, remains a valuable narrative of the events of the upper Great Lakes. Her article "The Fox Indians during the French Regime" in *The Proceedings of the State Historical Society of Wisconsin* (Madison: The Society, 1908), 142–148, is also important as one of the earliest treatments of that important nation. Clarence Alvord's *The Illinois Country, 1673–1818* (Urbana: University of Illinois Press, 1987), originally published in 1918, remains a standard as well. David Armour's *Colonial Michilimackinac* (Lansing: Michilimackinac Park Commission, 2000) is a good introduction to this important fort by the historian who probably knows it best. Timothy Kent's *Fort Ponchartrain at Detroit* (Ossineke, Michigan: Silver Fox Enterprises, 2001) is an exhaustive study of the daily life and material culture of this important post. Gilles Havard's *Empire et métissages* (Paris: Presses de l'Université Paris-Sorbonne, 2003) is a very good account of the enmeshment of Red and White in the upper country. Verner W. Crane's *The Southern Frontier* (New York: W. W. Norton, 1981) provides a very good treatment of the collision of the French and English in the Ohio and Mississippi Valleys, as does W. Stitt Robinson's *The Southern Colonial Frontier* (Albuquerque: University of New Mexico Press, 1979).

Eric Hinderaker and Peter C. Mancall's *At the Edge of Empire: The Backcountry in British North America* (Baltimore: The Johns Hopkins University Press, 2003) is a broadly drawn synthesis of the Anglo-Indian frontier and a very useful look at the "other side of the hill." Natalie Maree Belting's *Kaskaskia under the French Regime* (Carbondale: Southern Illinois University Press, 2003) was a pioneering work and remains invaluable on the society and material culture of French Illinois. Charles Balesi's *The Time of the French in the Heart of North America, 1673–1818* (Chicago: Alliance Française, 1992) is a good modern treatment of the Illinois country. Carl Ekberg's *Colonial Ste. Genevieve: An Adventure on the Mississippi Frontier* (Tucson: The Patrice Press, 1996), though largely concerned with the British and Spanish periods of Illinois and Missouri history, still contains a wonderful description of the economic life and culture of the French settlements. His *French Roots in the Illinois Country: The Mississippi Frontier in Colonial Times* (Urbana and Chicago: University of Illinois Press, 1998) provides a detailed study of French land use patterns and material culture. Nehemiah Matson's *French and Indians of Illinois River* (Carbondale: Southern Illinois University Press, 2001) is a reprint of a middle nineteenth-century history of the Illinois River Valley. Matson, an entrepreneur and land speculator, is often wrong, but he interviewed many of the old families and some of his anecdotes are invaluable for getting a sense of the region. Jay Higginbotham's *Old Mobile: Fort Louis de la Louisiane, 1702–1711* (Mobile: Museum of the City of Mobile, 1977) has very interesting material on the connections between early Louisiana and Illinois. Donald H. Kent, *The French Invasion of Western Pennsylvania* (Harrisburg: Pennsylvania Historical and Museum Commission, 1999), is a short, carefully researched study of Duquesne's fateful adventure into the Ohio country.

For the environment which produced the voyageurs and coureurs de bois, see Marcel Trudel's *La Population du Canada en 1666: Recensement reconstitute* (Quebec: Les éditions du Septentrion, 1995) and R. Cole Harris's *The Seigneurial System in Early Canada: A Geographical Study* (Kingston and Montreal: McGill–Queen's University Press, 1988). See also Jack Verney's *The Good Regiment: The Carignan-Salières Regiment in Canada, 1665–1668* (Kingston and Montreal: McGill–Queen's University Press, 1991).

Indians

Denys Delage's, *Le Pays renversé* (Montreal: Boreal Express, 1985) provides an excellent discussion of the early collision of the French, Dutch, Huron, and Iroquois in the Saint Lawrence Valley and the eastern Great Lakes. The book is available in English as *Bitter Feast: Amerindians and Europeans in Northeastern North America, 1600–64* (Vancouver: University of British Columbia Press, 1993). Bruce Trigger's *Farmers of the North* (New York: Holt, Rinehart, and Winston, 1969) is a good introduction to the Huron nation. For a fuller treatment, see his *Children of Aataensic* (Montreal: McGill–Queen's University Press, 1976). Dean Snow's *The Iroquois* (Malden, Mass.: Blackwell Press, 1996) is a good introduction to that important people. Francis Jennings's *The Ambiguous Iroquois Empire* has a shrewd discussion of their complex diplomacy. George T. Hunt's *The Wars of the Iroquois* (Madison: University of Wisconsin Press, 1940) was a pathbreaking book when it first appeared and, though dated, is still a concise recounting of the "Beaver Wars." Anthony F. C. Wallace's *Death and Rebirth of the Seneca* (New York: Vintage, 1972) contains an important, interdisciplinary portrait of the worldview of the "Keepers of the Western Door." The early chapters of R. David Edmunds's *The Potawatomis: Keepers of the Fire* (Norman: University of Oklahoma Press, 1978) contain a treatment of these powerful French allies. Edmunds's *The Fox Wars: The Mesquakie Challenge to New France* (Norman: University of Oklahoma Press, 1993) is the best account of this complex conflict. The first half of Charles Cleland's *Rites of Conquest: The History and Culture of Michigan's Native Americans* (Ann Arbor: University of Michigan Press, 1992) provides a clear, readable account of the Ottawa, Ojibwa, and Potawatomi in the French period. Gilles Havard's *The Great Peace of 1701* (Montreal: McGill–Queen's University Press, 2001) offers a detailed study of the motives and maneuvers of the leaders, Red and White.

Biographies

Morris Bishop's *Champlain: The Life of Fortitude* (New York: Alfred Knopf, 1948) is a good introduction to the career of New France's founder. Father Joseph Donnelly's *Jacques Marquette, S.J., 1637–1675* (Chicago: Loyola University Press, 1968) is the best treatment of the explorer-missionary. Jean-Paul Morel de la Durantaye's *Olivier Morel de la Durantaye: officier et seigneur en Nouvelle-France* (Quebec: Les éditions du Septentrion, 1997) is a useful work on the life of this important colonial soldier. William Eccles's *Frontenac: The Courtier Governor* (Lincoln: University of Nebraska Press, 2003) was a landmark in Canadian historiography when it first appeared in 1957 and remains the best political biography of this pivotal figure. It is also a remarkable account of the events of the upper country. Grace Lee Nute, *Caesars in the Wilderness* (New York: Arno Press, 1977) is really the only biography of Pierre Radisson and Medart Chouart des Groseilliers. Lionel Groulx's *Roland Michel Barrin de La Galissonière* (Toronto: University of Toronto Press, 1970) has useful material on this important architect of French policy.

Index

Accault, Maria, 122
Accault, Michel, 29, 31, 40, 121, 122
African people. *See* slaves
Albanel, Charles, 16
alcohol: effect of on Indians, 20–21, 43; and European settlers, 16; sale to Indians, 27, 86
Algonquin Indians, 3, 9, 86
Allouez, Claude, 29, 41, 61, 93
American colonies, 17, 90–92; and Indian policy, 22–23; Iroquois seeking alliance with, 62–63; lands ceded to, 138; and William Penn, 44; population of, 89, 136; religious diversity in, 44–45; as threat to French, 138–39; at war with France, 73–74, 77–78
American Revolution, 173
Amiot, Joseph, 146
Andros, Edmund, 22–23, 47, 78–79
Annanhac, 49–50, 63
Arkansas Indians, 130
Assiniboin Indians, 28, 152, 153

Bacon, Nathaniel, 17, 23
Baugy, Henri, le Chevalier de, 52, 58–60, 61–62
Beauharnois, Charles de La Boische, Marquis de, 115, 118, 134, 154, 158, 160; as governor of Canada, 106–7, 148–49; and hostilities with the Fox, 106–7, 108, 109, 110, 124; recall of, 161–62
Beauharnois, Fort, 106, 108, 139, 149–50
beaver, trapping of, 6
beaver fur. *See* fur trade
Benoist de Saint Clair, 160
Berkeley, William, 17
Bertet, Chevalier de, 160
Bienville, Jean-Baptiste Le Moyne, Sieur de, 125–29, 130, 131–35
Bigot, François, 168, 169
birchbark canoes, 6
Bisaillon, 104
Black Hawk, 8–9
Black Kettle, 80–82, 83–84, 86
Boisbriant, Pierre Dugué, Sieur de, 116, 122
Boisrondet, François, Sieur de, 57
Bonnecamp, Joseph, 145, 164, 165
Bougainville, Louis Antoine de, 143
Bourassa, René, 148, 153
brandy. *See* alcohol
Broyeux, Jean de, 58
Broyeux, Marguerite de, 58

Caboto, Giovanni, 1
Cadillac, Antoine Laumet, Sieur de, 49, 77, 85, 86–87, 102, 145; in Detroit, 94–95, 140; as governor of Louisiana, 112–14; and hostilities with the Fox Indians, 93–94
Cahokia, 115
Cahokia Indians, 142
Callières, Hector de, 69, 80, 81, 86, 88, 89–90, 102
Calvinism, 23
Canada: attractions of, 17–18; British blockade of, 158; Colbert's plan for, 12–18; demographics of, 14; as French colony, 12, 136, 163–64; fur trade in, 2, 12, 16, 18; people of, 153–54; population of, 136; winter travel in, 151–52. *See also* French colonists; New France
canoes: birchbark, 6; challenges of travel by, 36–40, 125, 139–40; dugout, 124–25
Cap Tourmente, 13
Carheil, Étienne de, 51, 86, 94, 96
Casson, François Dollier de, 16
Cat Face, 159
Cayuga Indians, 9, 62
Céloron de Blainville, Pierre-Joseph, 134, 164–65, 169
Chambly, Fort, 71
Champlain, Samuel de, 2–5, 71; and alliances with Indians, 3, 9; and trade with Indians, 7
Charles II, 11, 15, 22, 23, 44, 47
Charles Town (Charleston, South Carolina), 90
Charlevoix, Pierre F. X., 29–30, 105–6, 153–54
Chartre, Fort de, 106, 142, 144
Chassin, Nicolas Michel, 122
Chépart, Sieur de, 114
Chequamegon, Fort, 149, 150, 154, 155
Cherokee Indians, 131
Chicago, Chief, 124
Chickasaw Indians, 91–92, 114, 115, 159; and hostilities with the French, 123–24, 127–35, 137, 160
Choctaw Indians, 92, 128, 134
Code Noir, 120–21
codfish, 1–2
Colbert, Jean-Baptiste, 21, 30, 42, 61–62; concerns of about expansion, 34–35, 36, 66; and fur exports, 27; and settlement of New France, 12–18
Company of the Farm, 27
Company of the Indies, 113, 117, 119
congés, 36
copper mining, 7, 154–55
coureurs de bois, 17, 18, 26, 28, 48, 63, 74, 116, 148
Courtemanche, Augustin Le Gardeur, Sieur de, 83, 84
Couture, Jean, 90, 91
Cree Indians, 5, 152, 153
Crevecoeur, Fort, 31, 32
Croghan, George, 161, 167
Cromwell, Oliver, 12
Crozat, Antoine, 113

D'Aigremont, François Clairambault, Sieur, 95
D'Anville, Jean-Baptiste, De Roye de La Rochefoucauld, Duc, 158
D'Artaguette, Pierre, 123, 127, 129–30, 131
D'Autray, Jacques Bourdon, Sieur, 54
Deganawida, 9
Denonville, Jacques-René de Brisay, Marquis de, 64, 66, 73, 77; and war with the Seneca, 68–71
Desjordy, François, 58
Detroit, 93–96, 99, 136; Indian neighbors of, 140–42
D'Iberville, Jacques Le Moyne, 67, 89, 92, 135, 154
Dinwiddie, Robert, 171
Disy, Michel, 53
Dongan, Thomas, 52, 67–68, 69–70, 79, 100; as governor of New York, 46–47; and the Iroquois, 62–63, 66, 73

D'Orleans, Duc, 113
Dover, Treaty of, 15
Doyon, Nicolas, 53, 54
Dubuisson, Renaud, 98–99, 102
Duchesneau, Jacques, 17, 42, 44
Dugay, 29, 31
Dugué, Michel-Sidra, 69
Duhalies de fer, 124, 131
Du Luth, Daniel Greysolon, Sieur, 40, 44, 51, 61–62, 63, 65, 68; as coureur de bois, 28–29; trading posts established by, 47
Duquesne, Ange de Menneville, Marquis, 166, 168–69, 171
Duquesne, Fort, 149, 150, 172
Duquet, Françoise, 48
D'Urtibize, Sieur Marin, 147

England, 12, 15; as ally of the Chickasaw, 131; and growing tensions with the French, 155–56, 157–58, 161–62, 163–66, 171–73; lands claimed by, 47; at war with France, 73–74, 77–78, 96–97. *See also* American colonies
Enjalran, Jean, 69
epidemics. *See* smallpox; yellow fever
Erie Indians, 5, 9, 167
Europe: power shifts in, 11–12; and trade with Indians, 2, 3, 7–8, 21. *See also* England; France

Filastreau, Jean, 54
firearms, 21–22, 152
fishing industry, 1–2
Five Nations. *See* Iroquois Indians
Fort Assumption, Treaty of, 134
forts: cost of maintaining, 158; role of, in French settlements, 51–52, 56. *See also* names of specific forts
Fox Indians, 47, 50, 51; and the Iroquois, 97; at war with the French, 92–111, 115, 124, 137, 162
France, 12; and growing tensions with the English, 155–56, 157–58, 161–62, 163–66, 171–73; at war with England, 73–74, 77–78, 96–97. *See also* Colbert, Jean-Baptiste; French colonists; Louis XIV, King; New France
French colonists: character of, 153–54; and English expansion, 101; and hostilities with the Chickasaw, 123–24, 127–35, 137; and hostilities with the Iroquois, 32, 60–61, 62–63, 68, 74–75, 79–87; problems with, 16; at war with the Fox Indians, 92–111, 115, 124, 137, 162. *See also coureurs de bois*; New France
Frontenac, Fort, 32, 34, 52, 84, 144; Seneca attack on, 71
Frontenac, Louis de Buade, Comte de: departure of, 42, 46; and Du Luth, 28; as governor of New France, 25–27, 58; and La Salle, 30; and return to Canada, 73; at war with the English, 77, 79; at war with the Iroquois, 80, 82–83, 85, 86, 87
fur trade, 1, 6–7, 136; in Canada, 2, 12, 16, 18, 27–28, 29, 86–87, 90, 100; impact of Iroquois on, 9–11; profits from, 139–40; in Russia, 2

Galinée, René Bréhant de, 16
gambling, 57, 142
Gamot, Louis, 131
Germany, 12
Great Lakes peoples. *See* Indians
Griffon (ship), 31
Groseilliers, Medart Chouart des, 22
Guignas (Jesuit priest), 150

Habsburg Empire, 12, 157
Hamelin, Sieur, 146
Hennepin, Louis, 29, 31, 40
Henri IV, King, 2, 3, 11
Henry, Alexander, 151
Henry VII, King, 1
Hiawatha, 9
Holland. *See* Netherlands

Howard, Lord, 62
Hudson's Bay Company, 22, 66–67, 101
Hughes, Price, 91
Hunault, André, 54
Huron, Lake, 37, 93
Huronia, 5, 7, 9
Huron Indians, 3, 5, 48, 69, 71, 104, 131, 159; in Detroit area, 140–41, 142; and intertribal tensions, 49–50; loyalty of, to the French, 75, 85–86, 88; and trade with Europeans, 7, 9–11, 67. *See also* Kondiaronk
Hutchins, Thomas, 143

Illiniwek Indians, 5, 11, 32, 41, 59, 83, 137, 159; and alliance with New France, 63–64, 65, 160–61; appearance of, 56; and Chickasaw Wars, 123–24, 129, 131; and hostilities with the Fox, 105, 106, 108; and intertribal tensions, 43, 49–50
Illinois, 54–56, 77, 136; agriculture in, 118–19; climate of, 54–55; expansion of, 142–43; family relationships in, 122–23; French settlement of, 112, 115–19, 142; and hostilities with the Chickasaw, 123–35; slavery in, 119–20. *See also* Saint Louis des Illinois, Fort
Indians: agriculture of, 5; as allies of the French, 136–37; effect of alcohol on, 20–21, 43; European trade with, 2, 3, 21; intertribal warfare among, 47, 49–50, 51, 59–60, 71–73, 85–86, 94–95, 99, 105–6, 152–53, 155; lands ceded by, 138; languages of, 5; losses suffered by, 137; population of, 137; religion of, 20. *See also names of specific Indian nations*
Iron Collar, 159
Iroquois Indians, 5, 44, 46, 50, 51, 137, 167; as allies of the French, 129–30; and the Fox Indians, 97; and hostilities with the French, 32, 60–61, 62–63, 68, 74–75, 79–87, 89–90; and hostilities with the Illiniwek, 41–42, 43, 63; and hostilities with the Shawnee, 59–60; land ceded by, 138; power of, 9–11; and treaty with Americans, 22–23

James, Duke of York, 47
James II, King, 44, 78
Jenkins, Robert, 157
Jesuits: and La Salle, 30, 40–41; missions established by, 41, 47, 61, 115–16
Jolliet, Adrien, 15–17, 30
Jolliet, Louis, 16
Jonquière, Fort, 150–51
Joutel, Henri, 53, 55, 56–57, 58

Kaministigoya, Fort, 47, 149
Kankakee River, 39
Kaskaskia, Fort, 101
Kaskaskia, Illinois, 117, 118–19, 124
Kaskaskia Indians, 32, 115–16, 142
Kellogg, Joseph, 116–17
Kichinabé, 85
Kickapoo Indians, 104, 105, 131
King William's War, 78, 87, 94
Kondiaronk, 71–73, 82–83, 85–86, 87–88

La Barre, Joseph Antoine Le Febvre de, 52, 58, 59, 65, 71; as governor of New France, 46, 47; and hostilities with the Iroquois, 62, 63; Louis XIV's displeasure with, 61–62, 64
La Cendre Chaude, 69
La Chine, 73, 74, 75
Lacomb, Marie Ann, 144
lacrosse, 57, 141
La Durantaye, Olivier Morel, Sieur de, 44, 47–48, 51, 58, 75–77; and Iroquois Wars, 50–52, 62, 63, 65, 68, 69, 73
La Forest, François Dauphin, 84

La Galissonière, Roland-Michel Barrin, Marquis de, 162–64, 168
La Hontan, Lom D'Arce, Baron, 48, 50, 70, 71, 78
La Jonquière, Jacques Taffanel, Marquis de, 162, 165, 166
Lamima, 97, 99
Lancaster, Treaty of, 138, 161
Langlade, Charles, 166
Lanoue, Sieur de, 83
La Richardie (Jesuit priest), 159
La Ronde, Louis Denys, Sieur de, 154–55
La Salle, Jean, 30
La Salle, René-Robert Cavalier, Sieur de, 25, 49, 61, 66, 91; assessment of, 29–30; explorations of, 30–36; at Fort Saint Louis, 52–54; and Jesuits, 30, 40–41
La Tourette, Claude Greysolon de, 51–52
La Tourette, Fort, 47
Launay, Louis Paquier de, 121
La Vérendrye, Pierre Gaultier de Varonnes, Sieur de, 139, 148, 152
La Violette, Jean Coulon, 121
Law, John, 113–14
Le Boeuf, Fort, 169–71
Leisler, Jacob, 79
Le Jeune, Paul, 7
Le Mercier, François, 12
Le Rocher, 39, 42, 58
Lescarbot, Marc, 7–8
Liette, Pierre, 55, 56, 57, 58, 61, 84
Lignery, Constant Le Marchand de, 100, 106–8, 140, 145
Longueil, Charles Le Moyne, Baron de, 166, 167–68, 169
Louis XIV, King, 11–12, 15, 25–26, 31, 42, 45, 90, 120; and establishment of New France, 14, 34; and La Salle, 61–62
Louisiana, 35, 41; Bienville as governor of, 125–29, 130, 131–35; French settlement of, 112, 113–14; population of, 112

Louvigny, Louis de La Porte de, 28, 74–75, 77, 82, 102, 103–4, 105, 106

Manthet, Nicolas D'aillesbout de, 73–74, 83, 84
Marest, Gabriel, 115–16
Maria Theresa, 157
Maricourt, Paul Le Moyne, 67, 135
Marin de La Malgue, Paul, 168–71
Marquette, Jacques, 16, 41, 48, 58
marriage: among Indians, 58; in New France, 14; between whites and Indians, 121–23, 146–47
Mascoutin Indians, 41, 98, 99, 104, 105, 131
Massachusetts, 17, 22
Memeskia, Chief, 161, 165, 166
Menominee Indians, 50, 98, 107
Metacomet, 22
Metacomet's War, 23
Métis families, 123
Miami, Fort, 101, 108, 144
Miami Indians, 34, 40–41, 83, 84–85, 94–95, 96, 129, 131, 137, 159
Michabous, 1
Michigamea Indians, 32, 142
Michigan, Lake, 34, 37
Michilimackinac, 29, 32, 34, 35, 47, 50–51, 67, 103; climate of, 55, 151; expansion of, 145–49; importance of, 48–49; Ojibwa attack on, 159; population of, 147
Michipicoten, Fort, 149
Mickinac, 85
missionaries: in conflict with traders, 25. *See also* Jesuits
Mississippi River: claimed by La Salle, 34–36; Indians as threat to travel on, 125. *See also* Illinois; Louisiana
Mohawk Indians, 9, 11, 69, 82, 87, 104, 110
Monsoni Indians, 152, 153
Montagnais Indians, 3, 9
Montmagny, Charles Huault, Chevalier de, 71

Montreal, 12, 74; as center of fur trade, 16, 26–27

Nafrechoux, Isaac, 29
Nairne, Thomas, 91
Na-Na-Ma-Kee, 8–9
Natchez Indians, 114–15, 127, 131
Necessity, Fort, 172
Netherlands (Holland), 12; French invasion of, 15
Newfoundland, 1
New France, 12; and alliance with Illiniwek, 63–64, 65, 160–61; expansion of, 92–93, 138–39, 150, 155; Frontenac as governor of, 25–27; La Barre as governor of, 46, 47; and ongoing tensions with the Iroquois, 89–90; and peace treaty with Indians (1701), 87–88; population of, 89, 138–39; threats to, 66–88; and Treaty of Utrecht, 100. *See also* Canada; Detroit; French colonists; Illinois; Louisiana
New Orleans, Louisiana, 114
New York, 15, 22; Dongan as governor of, 46–47
Nicholas (Huron chief), 159
Nicholson, Francis, 79
Nicolet, Jean, 8
Nipigon, Fort, 149
Nipissing Indians, 75
Noyan, Pierre-Benoit Payen, Chevalier de, 128
Noyelle, Nicolas Joseph de, 108, 109–10
Noyon, Jacques, 89

Oglethorpe, James, 131
Ojibwa Indians, 5, 11, 18, 47, 50, 105, 159; and intertribal hostilities, 51, 152, 155; myths of, 1
Oneida Indians, 9, 84
Onnaské, 85
Onondaga Indians, 9, 62, 80–82, 85
Orange, Fort, 9

Orré, Pierre, 123
Oswego, Fort, 138
Ottawa Indians, 5, 48, 49, 51, 67, 69, 87, 131, 137; in Detroit area, 140, 141, 142; and intertribal warfare, 85, 98; near Michilimackinac, 147–48, 149, 166; and relationship with the French, 42–43, 75, 94–95
Ottawa River, 80, 107
Ouachala, 105
Ouiatanon, Fort, 101, 108
Ouiatanon Indians, 137, 141

Pachot, Daniel, 104–5
Parent, Pierre, 146
Peace of Aix La Chapelle, 161
Pemoussa, 97, 99
Penn, William, 44
Pennsylvania, 44
Peoria Indians, 32, 106, 142
Pequot War, 23
Peré, Jean, 15
Perico, Pierre, 120
Périer, Étienne Boucher de, 115, 123
Perrot, Nicolas, 15–16, 84, 89; as trader and diplomat, 29, 51, 65, 74–75, 101–2, 104
Philippe, Agnes, 122
Philippe, Michel, 122
Phips, William, 77, 78, 79
Piankeshaw Indians, 137
Pilette, Richard, 64–65
Ponchartrain, Jerome Phelypeaux, Comte de, 113
portages, 37–39, 111. *See also* canoes
Potawatomi Indians, 5, 47, 50, 69, 137, 159; in the Detroit area, 140, 141, 142; and intertribal warfare, 85, 98, 104, 105
Presque Ile, Fort, 171
Prudhomme, Pierre, 53, 54

Quarante Sols, 88
Quebec, 2–3, 5, 7, 12, 26, 30

Radisson, Pierre, 17, 22
Regiment de Carignan-Salières, 11, 14, 47
religious freedom, 44–45
Renault, Philippe François, 117, 118
Richardville, Drouet de, 131
Rosalie, Fort, 114, 125
Rouensa, 122
Russia, fur trade in, 2
Ryswick, Treaty of, 87

Sac Indians, 98
Saguina, 98
Saint Ange, Sieur de, 108, 143
Saint Antoine, Fort, 51
Saint Charles, Fort, 149
Saint Cosme, Jean François de, 93
Saint Francis, Fort, 107–8, 109
Saint Helene, Jacques Le Moyne de, 67, 74, 77–78, 135
Saint Joseph, Fort, 85, 101, 108, 143
Saint Lawrence River, 15, 37, 158; dangers of, 13
Saint Louis de Pimitoui, Fort, 84, 115, 121, 142
Saint Louis des Illinois, Fort, 44, 52–54, 77, 121; attacks on, 62; French and Indian interaction at, 56–59; gambling at, 57
Saint Lusson, Simon-François Daumont, Sieur de, 16, 29
Saint Pierre, Fort, 150
Saint Pierre, Jacques Le Gardeur, 150, 153, 171
Sauk Indians, 8–9, 50, 107, 109, 110, 137
Schenectady, New York, 74
Seignelay, Marquis de, 66
Seminary of Foreign Missions, 115
Senat, Antoine, 130
Seneca Indians, 9, 67, 80; and assassination of Annanhac, 49–50; and hostilities with the French, 68–71, 83–84, 87; and treaty with the Huron, 85

Shawnee Indians, 59–60, 161
Sieur, Madame Le, 61
Simcoe County, Ontario, 5
Sioux Indians, 5, 28, 29, 50, 51, 105; and intertribal warfare, 47, 92–93, 152–53, 155
slaves: families of, 147; laws applied to, 119–22; in Louisiana, 114; population of, 117; trading in, 117
Sloughter, Henry, 79
smallpox, 83, 137
Society of Jesus. *See* Jesuits
Spain, 12. *See also* War of the Spanish Succession
Superior, Lake, 17, 37, 39
Susquehannock Indians, 5, 9

Talon, Jean, 14–15, 21, 26
Tamaroa Indians, 115, 142
Tataconière, 84
Third Anglo-Dutch War, 15
Thirty Years War, 12
Tisné, Claude Charles du, 106
tobacco, as commodity, 50–51
Tonti, Henri, 55–56, 82, 83, 84, 90, 91, 92, 121; and assassination of Annanhac, 49–50; at Fort Saint Louis, 52, 53, 54; and hostilities with Iroquois, 60, 65, 68; Indians' regard for, 59, 65; as La Salle's lieutenant, 31–32, 34, 42; and Richard Pilette, 64–65
traders: in American colonies, 91; in conflict with missionaries, 25; permits for, 36. *See also* fur trade
Trois Rivières, 12
Troyes, Pierre, Chevalier de, 67, 77

Utrecht, Treaty of, 97, 100

Vaudreuil, Philippe Rigaud de, 97, 100–101, 103–4, 105, 106, 144
Vaudreuil, Pierre François Rigaud de, 160
Verchères, Sieur de, 148

Villeneuve-Langlade family, 146
Villiers, Nicolas-Antoine Coulon de, 108, 109
Villiers de Jumonville, Joseph Coulon de, 172
Vincennes, Illinois, 143
Vincennes, Sieur de, 108, 127, 129, 130
Virginia, 17, 22–23
Voisin, Sieur, 130
Voltaire, 173

Walker, Sir Hovenden, 97
War of Jenkins' Ear, 157
War of the Spanish Succession, 97, 116, 157
Washington, George, 171–72
Welsh, Thomas, 91
Wilamak, 85
William of Orange, 79
Winnebago Indians, 5, 8, 107
Winnipeg, Lake, 151
Wisconsin nations, 50

Yamasee War of 1716–1717, 92
yellow fever, 92, 112